THE PROMISED LAND

Universalism and a Coming World State

During a journey through Jordan and Egypt a writer
reflects on his inner journey to unitive vision and
developing Universalism, on his seemingly Providential
life and works, and on his view of a Promised Land that
will bring all humankind together

JOHN HUNT PUBLISHING

First published by O-Books, 2023
O-Books is an imprint of John Hunt Publishing Ltd., 3 East St., Alresford,
Hampshire SO24 9EE, UK
office@jhpbooks.com
www.johnhuntpublishing.com
www.o-books.com

For distributor details and how to order please visit the 'Ordering' section on our website.

Text copyright: Nicholas Hagger 2022

ISBN: 978 1 78904 689 2
978 1 78904 690 8 (ebook)
Library of Congress Control Number: 2022917933

A CIP catalogue record for this book is available from the British Library.

Design: Stuart Davies

UK: Printed and bound by CPI Group (UK) Ltd, Croydon, CR0 4YY
Printed in North America by CPI GPS partners

THE PROMISED LAND

Universalism and a Coming World State

During a journey through Jordan and Egypt a writer
reflects on his inner journey to unitive vision and
developing Universalism, on his seemingly Providential
life and works, and on his view of a Promised Land that
will bring all humankind together

Nicholas Hagger

BOOKS

Winchester, UK
Washington, USA

Also by Nicholas Hagger

The Fire and the Stones
Selected Poems
The Universe and the Light
A White Radiance
A Mystic Way
Awakening to the Light
A Spade Fresh with Mud
Overlord, books 1–2
The Warlords
Overlord
A Smell of Leaves and Summer
Overlord, books 3–6
Overlord, books 7–9
Overlord, books 10–12
The Tragedy of Prince Tudor
The One and the Many
Wheeling Bats and a Harvest Moon
The Warm Glow of the Monastery Courtyard
The Syndicate
The Secret History of the West
The Light of Civilization
Classical Odes
Overlord, one-volume edition
Collected Poems 1958–2005
Collected Verse Plays
Collected Stories
The Secret Founding of America
The Last Tourist in Iran
The Rise and Fall of Civilizations
The New Philosophy of Universalism
The Libyan Revolution
Armageddon
The World Government

The Secret American Dream
A New Philosophy of Literature
A View of Epping Forest
My Double Life 1: This Dark Wood
My Double Life 2: A Rainbow over the Hills
Selected Stories: Follies and Vices of the Modern Elizabethan Age
Selected Poems: Quest for the One
No page number please
The Dream of Europa
The First Dazzling Chill of Winter
Life Cycle and Other New Poems 2006–2016
The Secret American Destiny
Peace for our Time
World State
World Constitution
King Charles the Wise
Visions of England
Fools' Paradise
Selected Letters
The Coronation of King Charles
Collected Prefaces
A Baroque Vision
The Essentials of Universalism
Fools' Gold
The Building of the Great Pyramid
The Fall of the West
The Algorithm of Creation

"Willy-nilly, I find myself cast in the role of the *Old Testament* prophet. I can see the future clearly, but, a product of the secularised, declining European civilisation..., I can do little on my own except write this book – this *'prolegomena'* to a vast work of several thousand pages – to warn the Western (European and American) world."

Nicholas Hagger,
The Fire and the Stones (1991), p.729

"Like the *Old Testament* prophet, the poet – the true poet – channels a sacred truth which is vital to the renewal, and survival, of the civilisation."

Nicholas Hagger,
letter to Sebastian Barker, 29 April 1991,
in Nicholas Hagger, *Selected Letters*, p.112

"A few months ago I brought out *The One and the Many* on a similar Universalist theme – again an almost lone voice crying the metaphysical vision in a wilderness of secular humanism."

Nicholas Hagger,
letter to John Cornwell, 5 October 1999,
in Nicholas Hagger, *Selected Letters*, p.264

"Dear Ones, I recently heard an interview over Air America that astounded me.... The man's name was Nicholas Hagger, and he is a *very* prolific author, historian, philosopher, and poet. Even though the interviewer was Thom Hartmann, a lefty, he did a *magnificent* job extracting the indisputable wisdom from this individual whom I would place in the upper ionosphere with Einstein, da Vinci, Augustine and possibly even Solomon and Moses."

David Clumpner of Washington DC, USA,
round-robin email dated 17 May 2007,
in Nicholas Hagger, *Selected Letters*, pp.417–418

"In this book I am going to try to sort out my thoughts on the subjects that have chiefly interested me during the course of my life. But such conclusions as I have come to have drifted about my mind like the wreckage of a foundered ship on a restless sea."

Somerset Maugham,
The Summing Up (1938), p.7

"The night-sea, foaming and flooding under me,
I cross it and pass over to the other side....
The sea of minutes, hours, days, weeks and months
I am crossing. Heroes of old England
Were carried out on a barge at night. May I
Achieve an understanding in this dying heart."

Nicholas Hagger, 'The Night-Sea Crossing', 1974

The front cover shows the view across the Dead Sea of the Promised Land from Mount Nebo; the stone map on its summit; and the six-petalled flower at the Roman theatre at Aspendos, Turkey, symbolising the *Pax Romana*, universal peace.

Acknowledgments

I am grateful to my wife Ann for accompanying me on my journey to Jordan, Egypt and Turkey during Covid's first wave. I am also grateful to my PA, Ingrid Kirk, who, despite coping with four other books in different stages of production and working from tapes and my emails without face-to-face contact during lockdowns, helped me to write this book between 29 August and 1 September 2020, and between 22 November 2020 and 30 March 2021, in just over four months. Without her assistance I could not have written this work.

Contents

Preface: The Promised Land of Moses, and Universalism's
Coming Democratic World State   xi

1   The Promised Land:
     Mount Nebo and the Kingdoms of the Earth   1
2   The Formative Years, 1960–1980:
     The Mystic Way and the Baroque Vision,
     The Forming of the Universalist Vision   21
3   The Wilderness Years, 1980–2020:
     The Unitive Vision, Shaping Universalism and
     its Structure   51
4   Universalism's Principles:
     Ten Commandments and the Muses   79
5   A Remarkable Life and its Pattern   101
6   Conclusions on a Providential Life and Works,
     and on European Civilisation   135
7   A View of the Promised Land:
     A World State and a Golden Age   163

Timeline   181
Appendices   199
     1   Visits   201
     2   Light   209
Index   221

Preface

The Promised Land of Moses, and Universalism's Coming Democratic World State

The Biblical Promised Land
'The Promised Land' goes back to God's promise of the land of Canaan to Abraham (*Genesis* 12.7; 15.18–21): "Unto thy seed will I give this land." Abraham had left Haran and travelled south to Shechem, midway between and towards the coast from Lake Galilee and the Dead Sea when God spoke to him.

God renewed his promise to Isaac (*Genesis* 26.3) and Jacob (*Genesis* 28.13), and finally to Moses (*Deuteronomy* 34.1–4), who

> went up from the plains of Moab unto the mountain of Nebo, to the top of Pisgah, that is over against Jericho. And the LORD shewed him all the land of Gilead, unto Dan, and all Naphtali, and the land of Ephraim, and Manasseh, and all the land of Judah, unto the utmost sea, and the south, and the plain of Jericho, the city of palm trees, unto Zoar. And the LORD said unto him, This is the land which I sware unto Abraham, and Isaac, and unto Jacob, saying, I will give it unto thy seed: I have caused thee to see it with thine eyes, but thou shalt not go over thither.

Moses saw the Promised Land from the top of Mount Nebo and died soon afterwards, before he could enter it, and was buried somewhere on Mount Nebo, the highest peak in the mountain range of Pisgah. And it was left to his "minister" Joshua to conquer Canaan and take the Hebrews into the Promised Land, which was described as including the territory from the Nile ("the river of Egypt") to the Euphrates (*Genesis* 15.18), from the Red Sea to the Mediterranean, "the sea of the Philistines" (*Exodus* 23.31).

My view from Mount Nebo and a coming World State
During a visit to Jordan in early March 2020 I stood on Mount Nebo where Moses stood, and looked down from 2,650 feet across the Dead

Sea and the Sea of Galilee towards the coast, the western half of this Promised Land. I saw what Moses saw, allowing for the fact that Jerusalem and Jericho were larger clusters of buildings than when Moses saw them. I saw Palestine (the land of the Philistines) in the distance and Israel, which had been in conflict with the Philistines since before the single combat between David the Israelite and Goliath the Philistine, and I saw across the Holy Land. But I was interested in more than the historical lands promised by God to Abraham and his descendants. What I saw was a symbol of the coming World State, which would one day be created by political Universalism.

It hit me while I was on Mount Nebo. There was quite a wind 2,650 feet above the Promised Land, but the symbolism came to me as a revelation and I stood scribbling the places I could see in my notebook and was struck by their resemblance to the nations of the earth. I stood for a long time completely lost to my surroundings, and when I came to I was alone, my fellow travellers had gone and the wind was blowing my hair.

There on Mount Nebo I was haunted by the parallels between my life and Moses' life. I was haunted by his 40 years in the wilderness, his receiving of the Ten Commandments on Mount Sinai, below which I had stood in 2005 before visiting St Catherine's monastery and looking at the place where according to tradition Moses saw the burning bush, now protected by a wall overhung by the bush's green leaves. I had developed ten principles of Universalism and ten Universalist commandments. I was haunted by the thought that he had been allowed to look at the Promised Land, "but thou shalt not go over thither". According to the *Bible* Moses died at the age of 120, but if generations and dates were calculated on a more realistic basis he would have died around 80, my own age. I saw through his eyes and his age, and I had the same feeling he must have had, that he could see the Promised Land but would not live long enough to enter it.

My Promised Land is the kingdoms of the earth unified under a democratic World State with a limited federal supranationalism that would give it sufficient authority to abolish war, enforce disarmament, impound nuclear weapons, combat famine, disease and poverty, solve the world's financial and environmental problems, including climate change – and solve the world's medical and health problems such as the menacing coronavirus that threatened to end my travels.

My travels and developing Universalism

I completed my tour of Jordan, got on my ship at Aqaba – and was told that she had been barred from docking in Israel because it was closing its borders due to coronavirus. I would not be allowed to enter Canaan just as Moses had not been allowed to enter it.

We visited Luxor and Cairo. The 95 on our ship were told we would be going to Alexandria, but a huge storm came up from the south of Egypt and the harbour of Alexandria closed for two days. We steamed through the Suez Canal and headed for south Turkey and saw Roman ruins. We were then barred from landing in Cyprus to catch our flight home. We eventually flew to Istanbul, and after a night there flew back to the UK.

During my travels in Jordan, Egypt and Turkey I saw links between my earlier visits to these countries and my developing Universalism. I had completed *A Baroque Vision*, which presents 100 selections from my poems, verse plays and masques taken from 50 poetic volumes to show how my early Baroque verse became Universalist; and had started *The Essentials of Universalism*, which showed the essential principles of Universalism. My tour of key places in Asia Minor and Egypt drew memories from previous visits in 1961, 1970 and 2005 to the fore, and in Cairo I again stood before the dead body of Ramesses II, which I last saw in 2005. There are good grounds for seeing him as the Pharaoh who opposed Moses. This hook-nosed brown man I stood before had met Moses.

My tour now seemed to reveal how my Universalism emerged in a way that would not have been clear had I been allowed to land in Israel and Cyprus. It was as though these had been pruned to leave me a clear insight into how my works led to the formation and revealing of all aspects of Universalism, and of the political Universalism which pointed to the Promised Land. The Lord did not stand beside me and show me the Promised Land as Moses was shown, but a pattern was fed to me through the order in which I wrote my works, and it was as if my Muse had guided me to write my works in the order in which they were written and had presided over the reception of my poems and ideas from the beyond.

Coronavirus

The disruption caused by coronavirus in itself cried out for a coming World State. Every day brought news of more and more deaths as fatalities in Italy overtook fatalities in China. We had hand gel on the ship and in our coaches, we had our temperatures checked with a hand-held 'gun' pointed at our temples or foreheads, and every Turkish port had a 'movie camera' on a tripod that detected high temperatures. Anyone with a temperature spike as they walked past such a camera would be detained and barred entry. A Roman theatre in south Turkey had a team of spacesuited men spraying the stone seats and columns after our visit. Turkey was keeping its ruins open but spraying them after tourists' visits.

There were unconfirmed rumours about coronavirus, Covid-19. We were asked to believe that it had surfaced in Wuhan, China but had no connection with the Institute of Virology there, where research into viruses took place as at the UK's Porton Down. There were suggestions it had been extracted from horseshoe bats or pangolins (or scaly anteaters). There were suggestions that researchers were seeking a bio-weapon in Wuhan, and also that coronavirus had leaked when a virologist had not scrubbed down thoroughly enough after working in the Institute of Virology. There were rumours that bats and pangolins used in research were legally required to be incinerated, but that some had been sold illegally to nearby restaurants for soup. A couple of dozen non-Chinese scientists had said that the virus was not genetically engineered and had simply transferred from wildlife to humans. Any mention of the Institute of Virology resulted in accusations of a "conspiracy theory", but the surfacing of the virus near the Institute of Virology in Wuhan seemed too coincidental for there to be no connection.

I was reminded of Spanish flu, which was said to originate in Kansas, USA (although that may have been a weaker and different strain of flu) or in north China before reaching Spain, and which killed 50 to 100 million between January 1918 and December 1920 after infecting 500 million people, about a quarter of the world's population. It was called Spanish flu because King Alfonso XIII was gravely ill with it, creating a false impression that Spain was especially hard hit. It was an H1N1 influenza virus like the swine flu epidemic of 2009. Again there were suggestions that the Spanish flu virus was linked to research into germ warfare in a laboratory to bring the First World War to an end, but nothing conclusive was ever proved. To this day it is a mystery as to how the pandemic of Spanish flu killed a huge number of 50 to 100 million people at the end of the First World War, more than died in battles during the whole war.

A World State will solve all problems

The Promised Land that I envisage will control and regulate virology more rigidly than at present and will make such pandemics a thing of the past. The coming World State has been longed for from Dante's medieval treatise on the need for a universal monarch in *Monarchia* (1309–1313); Kant's arguing in *Perpetual Peace* (1795) that an international state (*civitas gentium*) would "continue to grow until it embraced all the peoples of the earth"; and in my lifetime by Truman (who oversaw the founding of the UN after the Second World War and kept six lines from Tennyson's 'Locksley Hall' in his wallet), Einstein, Churchill, Eisenhower, Gandhi, Russell, J.F. Kennedy and Gorbachev. For some reason I seem to be the only Western writer who is going for a World State within this tradition, and it is entirely appropriate that at 80 I should find myself standing where Moses stood and seeing the Promised Land as the unified countries of the world as promised by a long line of thinkers since Dante and founded on the principles of Universalism that I have set out in the Prefaces to *World State* and *The Essentials of Universalism*, and in many of my 56 works (including this one).

21–22 March 2020

The Promised Land: Mount Nebo and the Kingdoms of the Earth

Jordan

Jordan has always been a magical country to me. It evokes the Roman Arabia I encountered while studying Classics at school, and also Lawrence of Arabia in the desert around Wadi Rum, not far from Aqaba. And it has Biblical lands. I wanted to travel to other cultures when I was at Oxford, and as soon as I finished, because there was a job going there, I went to nearby Iraq for a year, aged 21, to lecture at the University of Baghdad. As I walked through Baghdad's sandy main square, Bab Sherge, on my way home from my work each day I did not know it would become one of the most dangerous places on the earth.

Journey to Jordan in 1962: Qumran, Bethany, Jerusalem

At the end of the first semester, in January 1962, I journeyed on the desert bus from Baghdad to Amman, the capital of Jordan, across a wilderness of barren yellow, sometimes reddish, sand. I stayed in a primitive bed-and-breakfast house in Amman and wandered in the streets and got myself to some of the Biblical places on the West Bank that at that time could be visited from Jordan: to Jericho and the Dead Sea, and to Qumran in the Judaean Desert.

The bus driver stopped at Qumran near sandstone cliffs, and got out. We passengers followed. I walked to caves where the Dead Sea Scrolls had been found and peered at a group of Arabs bending as they carried a heavy jar. I was witnessing some of the scrolls being carried out. Scrolls had first been found there in 1951. Essenes, a peace-loving people, are reputed to have lived in the Qumran caves where the scrolls were stored, and, according to some, wrote them. According to others the scrolls came from the Jerusalem Temple.

I also visited Bethany, the town at the foot of the Mount of Olives where Lazarus lived with his sisters Mary and Martha, and where Jesus stayed during the Holy Week before his crucifixion. On a previous visit he had raised Lazarus from the dead four days after his burial. I visited Lazarus's tomb at El-Eizariya (which has been occupied by Israel since 1967), down 24 steps to an ante-chamber and then down more steps to his tomb. I was told that Jesus stood three rock steps down to raise Lazarus, but there was also a slit in the ante-chamber through which he could have called to Lazarus. In those days the house of Lazarus, Mary and Martha, reputed to be a 2,000-year-old house still standing, could be seen from the entrance of the tomb but its view has since been blocked by the 16th-century al-Uzair mosque.

I visited the River Jordan, and went to Jerusalem, regarded as the centre of the world in Crusader times, and I wondered what could unite the world today. I saw all the Biblical places and walked up the Via Dolorosa – I bought a silver Russian-Orthodox cross showing the crucifixion from a shop as I walked to Calvary, also known as Golgotha, the place of the skull, where Jesus was crucified. And I went to the Garden Tomb where the resurrection reputedly happened.

I went on to Damascus and Beirut, a would-be-writer sensing there were several dozen books ahead and visiting as many of the Middle-Eastern places as possible while living in Iraq, and wandering fearlessly in dangerous places with the immortality of youth which instinctively assumes it is inviolable and invulnerable.

I had wanted to go to Petra as one of the lecturers at the University of Baghdad, Turner, announced to the staff room, "I've just been to a wonderful place, Petra, 'the rose-red city half as old as time'. You must go." But it was well south of Amman, and the connections in those days were not good, and it was impossible to go there. I did not get to Petra during the next 58 years.

*

Journey to Jordan in 2020
Now I was making a journey to celebrate my 80th birthday nine months late. A cruise brochure had caught my eye in a newspaper in August 2018 while my wife Ann drove me back to Essex from Cornwall. It had a picture of Petra on the front and the journey was titled 'Passage through Antiquity'. It was billed to visit Jordan, Egypt,

Israel and Cyprus, with a pre-cruise extension in Jordan.

I was now a poet, man of letters, literary author, philosopher and historian, a writer on current affairs and foreseer of the future, and as I looked I realised that just before I was 80, after more than 50 published works within literature, history, philosophy and international politics and statecraft, and mysticism, religion and culture, I would be able to visit Jordan's Biblical places, including the Dead Sea and places connected with T.E. Lawrence, and at last Petra; revisit Luxor and Cairo; and then go into Israel and visit the Biblical places there. I reckoned it was the first time in my lifetime that it was possible to visit Jordan and Israel during the same voyage. I looked forward to revisiting a region that had many memories and much archaeological interest. The departure date was 28 February 2020.

We had heard of the new coronavirus during that January but it then did not seem something we should fear. Covid-19 featured more in the news in February as we made preparations to leave. We had paid our deposit in August 2018 and the balance in November 2019, and in our minds there was no question of not going. There were no restraints in England, no temperature checks, and distancing had not been mentioned. Looking back, I see how ill-prepared we were to be travelling through a pandemic without fully realising the gravity of the situation.

Amman

We flew from Heathrow. We landed in Amman in the evening with the orange moon on its back (how I had often seen it in Baghdad when I slept on the roof under the stars). We were driven to the Kempinski Hotel to begin our pre-cruise extension.

Next morning was free. After breakfast, which included honeycomb on toast, I arranged with the concierge to be collected by car, and Ann and I drove past the blue mosque up to the citadel. We got out and saw the Temple of Hercules and looked down to the Roman theatre below, from which a tunnel built by the Romans leads to the Citadel. We were above the seven hills of Amman – like Rome, and like Epping Forest's Loughton, Amman has seven hills – and we returned through the Old Town, near where I stayed in 1962.

Jerash, formerly Antioch

In the afternoon our tour party was driven north in a coach past the biggest Palestinian refugee camp in Jordan to Jerash by the River Orontes in the hills of Gilead. Once known as Antioch, Jerash was in Syria and then Arabia during Roman times, and in Syria during the Ottoman rule until the Sykes-Picot Agreement of 1916 dismembered the Ottoman Empire and carved up the Middle East.

Hadrian's Arch stood before the entrance to the site. It was built in honour of Hadrian's visit in 129AD, when he lived in Antioch for a year. I broke away to look at the architecture and noticed a small flower high up immediately above the arch (see picture on **p.4**). It had six petals that were pointed like star-flowered Solomon's seal, Star of Bethlehem and yellow stargrass, and as if a far memory was awakened, I knew that each petal represented a region of Hadrian's Empire and that it stood for the *Pax Romana* as beneath it was a shield and crossed spears. It signified peace – the people of Antioch had laid down their spears and shields and were welcoming the Emperor Hadrian into the walls of their city.

The *Pax Romana* was first mentioned by Seneca the Younger in 55AD. It really began with Augustus's principate in 27BC, after the battle of Actium of 31BC, and it lasted until Marcus Aurelius, c.180AD, for just over 200 years. Jerash was then in Syria.

Antioch had been founded around 300BC by Seleucus I Nicator, one of Alexander the Great's generals. It was the centre of the Seleucid Kingdom until Pompey conquered it in 63BC and the Romans made it the capital of their province of Syria and set up the Decapolis, or League of 10 Cities, in Gerasa (Antioch). It headed a regional administration of 16 provinces and was the main centre for Hellenistic Judaism, and was St Paul's headquarters in c.47–55AD. It was predominantly a Roman town, one of the best-preserved Roman cities in the world, known as "the Pompeii of the East". Julius Caesar visited in 47BC.

In 106AD the Emperor Trajan occupied the Nabataean kingdom of South Jordan, North Arabia and Sinai, and he annexed Syria and reorganised Antioch and four other cities of the Decapolis into the new Roman province of Arabia. In due course Antioch was ruled in

Hadrian's Arch, Jerash

Six-petalled flower high up on
Hadrian's Arch

Six-petalled flower on stone
tablet at the Roman theatre at
Aspendos, Turkey (see p.169
and front cover)

turn by the Arabs, Byzantines and Turks, who lost it during the First
World War.

It was a good mile and a half's walk from Hadrian's Arch to the
far end of the city. We walked along the colonnaded main street,
past the Temple of Artemis and several churches and a Cathedral. I
stood in the Roman theatre of 91AD, by the central stone that acted
as a megaphone or microphone and provided brilliant acoustics for
the actors. We walked to the oval plaza or Forum. As at Pompeii,
there were many shops, administrative buildings, drains and
manholes.

We returned to the coach and on the way back we stopped at the

Kan Zaman restaurant near the Hejaz Railway from Damascus to Medina. The railway was opened in 1908, and T.E. Lawrence ambushed Ottoman trains in 1917. The restaurant was in a 19th-century complex of stables, storehouses and residential quarters looking like a cross between a brick caravanserai and a fortress, and we ate humus and chargrilled steak cooked over a charcoal fire at high heat. I sat next to an Australian flying doctor who said that in his view when the Queen dies Australia will cease to have a UK monarch as Head of State.

Madaba

The next day we drove south in a coach to Madaba and visited the Church of the Apostles to see the Byzantine mosaics, which include Thalassa, a woman personifying the sea emerging from the waves c.578AD.

We went on to St George's Greek Orthodox church and looked at the 6th-century-AD Madaba map showing the Eastern-Byzantine world from Tyre and Sidon to the Egyptian delta, and from the Mediterranean to the Eastern Desert. Jerusalem, with its Church of the Holy Sepulchre, was central, but it also showed the Dead Sea

The 6th-century-AD mosaic map in Madaba, Jordan, showing part of the Eastern-Byzantine Empire

and the River Jordan and its neighbouring hills and towns, including Bethlehem and Jericho. It is the oldest surviving map of Palestine and the 6th-century Middle East.

We had lunch at 11am in the first-floor Al-Saraya in Haret Jdoudna village, which is in a courtyard shuttered from the main street and accessed by a doorway in the shutters.

Mount Nebo

At 12 we left in the coach under the impression that we were driving to the Dead Sea. Our itinerary said deliberately unspecifically (no doubt mindful of the possibility of bad weather): "Depart Madaba and drive towards Mount Nebo and visit the area. Continue your drive towards the Dead Sea."

We drove through the north part of the Jordan valley. The guide told us that Israel had attempted to take the Jordan valley and Mount Nebo (Jabal Nebu) at the battle of Karameh on 21 March 1968 but had been defeated. The guide then said, "Moses came to Mount Nebo. I need to tell you about the Exodus."

Moses, Yahweh and the burning bush

I had a *Bible* on my knees and, leafing through *Exodus* as she talked, I went over in my mind what I knew about Moses. The Egyptian Pharaoh of the day had treated the Israelites living in Egypt like slaves, "with hard bondage" (*Exodus* 1.14), and ordered that all newly-born male Hebrew children should be "cast into the river" to die. Moses had been born into the House of Levi, and was hidden for three months. Then his mother made an "ark of bulrushes [a chest of woven papyrus stalks], and daubed it with slime and with pitch [Nile mud]" and abandoned Moses in "the flags" (reeds, probably bulrushes) by the river's edge. The daughter of Pharaoh went down to the river to wash and saw the woven chest and took pity on the crying child. She sent him to be looked after by a Hebrew nurse, and eventually the child was returned to Pharaoh's daughter and became her adopted son. She called him Moses ('son of Moussa, son of water').

When Moses was a grown man he saw an Egyptian "smiting" a Hebrew and killed him and buried him in the sand. Pharaoh got to

7

hear of this and Moses fled to Midian, which was in the North-West Arabian Peninsula on the east coast of the Gulf of Aqaba, east of Eilat. Seven daughters of a priest preparing to carry water from troughs to their father's sheep were stopped by shepherds. Moses helped them, and was invited to their home. He was given one of the priest's daughters, Zipporah. He married her and had a son, Gershom, by her.

The Pharaoh died, and the Hebrews cried out, complaining of their bondage. Yahweh (God) heard. Yahweh had made a covenant with Abraham, Isaac and Jacob, and approached Moses when he was looking after his father-in-law Jethro's flock of sheep, which had wandered into the desert at Horeb (Mount Sinai), and spoke out of a burning bush which was not consumed by the fire.

St Catherine's monastery

I had visited the place where this was alleged to have happened. In 2005 I had visited Egypt for the first time since 1970 and from Sharm El Sheikh I had gone to St Catherine's monastery and had seen the burning bush in the monastery grounds, a green bramble, *Rubus sanctus*, which according to 4th-century monastic tradition is what Moses saw. (A tradition in Eastern Orthodoxy interprets the fire Moses saw as the inner Uncreated Fire or Light of the divine presence, experienced by all mystics and within all religions, which came into Moses near a bush.)

In 337 Helena, the wife of Constantine the Great, ordered the Chapel of the Burning Bush (also known as Saint Helena's Chapel) to be built where Moses saw the burning bush, and after a visit in 530 Emperor Justinian I enclosed it within the 6th-century St Catherine's monastery. St Catherine, daughter of the Roman Governor of Alexandria, had converted to Christianity, and she was tortured and beheaded in a public square in Alexandria on the orders of Emperor Maximinus. In the 6th-century Chapel festooned with hanging chandeliers, censers and icons I passed Catherine's wrist bone, which was allegedly found there in the 9th century and was now in a glass case.

The monastery was descended from 200 of Justinian's Roman soldiers, and the volcanic mountains behind it rose from the desert. We were 1,400 metres up, and Mount Horeb or Mount Sinai loomed above us in the sky 2,285 metres high in a mountain pass with mountains all round. I passed sitting camels on our way to the 6th-century fortified walls of the monastery.

St Catherine's monastery on Mount Sinai, beneath Willow Peak
(traditionally considered to be Mount Horeb)

I passed through the Chapel of the Transfiguration and into the Chapel of the Burning Bush. The burning bush used to stand inside it but was now outside, in earth behind a wall with trailing strands.

I went into the charnel-house and saw the 6th-century architect Stephanos, a robed skeleton in a glass case with piled bones of all the monks

The burning bush outside the Chapel

since then heaped together in an ossuary. There was a mound of 200–300 skulls. A Greek-Orthodox monk in a long black hat with a beard and spectacles told me in perfect

English as I paid to go in that one day his skull would join the skulls on show.

A land of milk and honey

Yahweh (God) told Moses from the burning bush that he would send him to Pharaoh to negotiate delivering the Hebrews from the Egyptians, and he promised to bring them to "a land flowing with milk and honey", "the place of the Canaanites, and the Hittites, and the Amorites, and the Perizzites, and the Hivites, and the Jebusites" (*Exodus* 3.8). Moses was to go to the new Pharaoh and arrange for the Israelites to leave Egypt and make a three-days' journey into the wilderness. Yahweh said that at first Pharaoh would not let him go, but he would "smite" Egypt, and then Pharaoh would let him go. Moses told Yahweh he was a stammerer: "I am not eloquent,... I am slow of speech, and of a slow tongue" (*Exodus* 4.10). Yahweh said he would be in Moses' mouth.

The Exodus

So Moses sought Jethro's permission to leave Sinai and return to Egypt. He set off on foot, leading an ass on which his wife and sons sat. Yahweh had asked Aaron, Moses' brother, to join him in the wilderness, to speak on the stammerer's behalf, and they gathered the elders of the Hebrew people and went to the new Pharaoh.

Moses and Aaron asked permission to leave Egypt ("Let my people go"). Pharaoh said, "Who is Yahweh that I should obey his voice?" He refused to let the Israelites go and ordered that their tasks should be harder, that they should find their own straw to make bricks and not be supplied with it, and their output must not diminish. They were harried and beaten for being behind with their work.

Exodus describes the ten plagues that followed: the river was filled with blood; there was a plague of frogs; then lice and flies; wild animals destroyed all in their path; a pestilence killed most of the domestic animals of the Egyptians; the Pharaoh, his servants, the Egyptians and their animals had painful boils; hail struck down all the crops and trees; and locusts devoured all crops and fruit.

And having reached the eighth plague I was taken back to my

days in Baghdad. Between lectures I would sometimes work in the small garden of the Centre for English Studies, where I was rigged up with a table and a chair so I could do some preparation and marking in the warm morning sun. Sometimes there was a plague of locusts. They were everywhere on the bushes in front of my table. They were enormous, over four inches long. Sometimes they tumbled off the shrubs onto my table and my marking like giant grasshoppers, and I would brush them off onto the ground. They were on me, one or two in my hair, several on my shoulders and arms, even on the back of my hand as I wrote, just as they would have been in the 13th century BC.

Pharaoh nearly relented. But there was no let-up in the plagues. There was thick darkness so Egyptians had to feel their way; and all first-born Egyptian sons and cattle died. And then Pharaoh relented and ordered the Hebrews to leave urgently with their flocks and herds.

The Ten Commandments and the wilderness

Now the Israelites journeyed to Succoth, about 600,000 on foot with their animals (*Exodus* 12.37–38), and camped on the edge of the wilderness of Etham. Pharaoh then turned against the Israelites and led chariots against them. The 'Red Sea' – probably an inland reed lake north of Succoth – parted in an east wind and let them through. Then the waters closed back over the pursuing chariots and horsemen. The Israelites went into the wilderness of Shur, and they journeyed through the wilderness to Elim and on to the wilderness of Sin on their way to Sinai. They were starving but Yahweh promised bread, which turned out to be coriander plants bearing their seed or "manna".

In the third month after the Exodus from Egypt, Moses climbed to the top of Mount Sinai. Yahweh told him to assemble the people but to keep them apart from the top. Tradition has it that Moses spent 40 days and 40 nights alone on the top of Mount Sinai (see picture on p.9). Yahweh then revealed the Ten Commandments to him.

Now began the wanderings of Moses and the Israelites in the wilderness. They would eat manna in the wilderness for 40 years (*Exodus* 16.35). They journeyed to the plain of Moab and passed Mount Hor and eventually reached Mount Nebo, at the top of Pisgah.

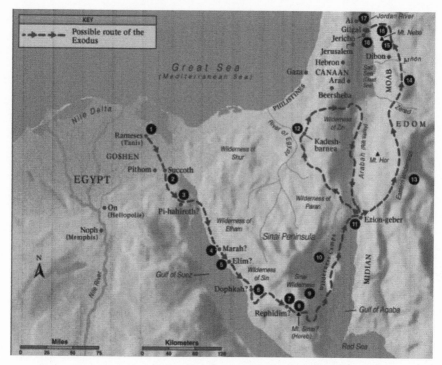

Map showing the route of the Exodus

Chronology: Moses and Ramesses II, c.1275–1235BC

I pondered the chronology of Moses' life. I knew the orthodox Biblical view of the Exodus from Egypt (in *1 Kings* 6.1) put it 480 years before Solomon rebuilt the Temple in Jerusalem in 960BC. This would put the Exodus at 1440BC and the Pharaoh who opposed Moses as Thutmose III. But Thutmose had his capital in Thebes, far to the south, and non-scholars are now agreed that the Exodus took place soon after Ramesses II became Pharaoh in 1279BC. The Exodus probably took place around 1275BC.

'Ramesses' means in ancient Egyptian 'Ra is the one who bore him'. Ramesses II believed in the sun-god Ra and despised Yahweh, the god of storm and the God of the Hebrews and Moses, and arrogantly asked, "Who is Yahweh?" (*Exodus* 5.2).

Moses received the Ten Commandments on Mount Sinai three months after the Exodus, in c.1275BC, and the Jewish and Christian traditions assume that the Israelites wandered in the wilderness for another 40 years (*Joshua* 5.6), and so Moses would have reached Mount Nebo around 1235BC.

I thought of the Trojan War. Some have dated the Trojan War to 1260–1180BC. Eratosthenes dated it to 1194–1184BC to coincide with the burning of Troy VII. Assuming that the Trojan War happened and began c.1260BC, Moses reached Mount Nebo about 40 years before the start of the Trojan War and was a contemporary of Agamemnon, who would have been over 40 when the Trojan War began. Ramesses II ruled for 67 years until his death in 1213BC, and he would have been alive at the same time as Achilles, Paris and Menelaos of the Trojan War as well as Agamemnon.

The exact route of the Exodus

I could see the Exodus as a whole. Assuming that Ramesses II was the Pharaoh, Moses led the Hebrews out of Egypt from Ramesses (Pi-Ramesses, the new capital built by Ramesses II at Qantir near the old site of Avarice) in the land of Goshen, past modern Ismailia and across the Reed Sea, a narrow freshwater lake of papyri in the north-eastern corner of Egypt, north of the Great Bitter Lake. An east wind made it easier for them to cross the Reed Sea or Lake Timsah, and when the east wind dropped the pursuing Egyptian army found themselves and their chariots in water and many drowned.

Map showing the Great Bitter Lake and Lake Timsah or Reed Sea

Moses led the Hebrews on to Succoth (see map on p.12) and well north of the Gulf of Suez to the wilderness of Shur. He turned south through the wilderness of Etham to Mount Sinai, where he had been

13

promised a land of milk and honey in the future during an earlier visit there, skirting the wilderness of Paran. Moses received the Ten Commandments in a thunder-and-lightning storm on Mount Sinai.

Moses and the Israelites wandered in the wilderness for 40 years, eating manna (*Exodus* 16.35). He spent 40 years in the vicinity of Mount Sinai and eventually headed for the land of milk and honey. He rounded Mount Hor and returned to Elath (modern Eilat, a few miles from Aqaba) and then turned north through Edom to Mount Nebo.

Moses' age

I turned to *Deuteronomy* (34.1–7) and read what happened next:

> And Moses went up from the plains of Moab unto the mountain of Nebo, to the top of Pisgah, that is over against Jericho. And the LORD shewed him all the land of Gilead, unto Dan, and all Naphtali, and the land of Ephraim, and Manasseh, and all the land of Judah, unto the utmost sea, and the south, and the plain of the valley of Jericho, the city of palm trees, unto Zoar. And the LORD said unto him, This is the land which I sware unto Abraham, unto Isaac, and unto Jacob, saying, I will give it unto thy seed: I have caused thee to see it with thine eyes, but thou shalt not go over thither.
>
> So Moses the servant of the LORD died there in the land of Moab, according to the word of the LORD. And he buried him in a valley in the land of Moab, over against Beth-peor: but no man knoweth of his sepulchre unto this day. And Moses was an hundred and twenty years old when he died.

Tradition (confirmed by the *Encyclopaedia Britannica*) holds that there were 12 generations from Moses to Solomon, and that Moses was 120 when he died. The Biblical view was that a generation was around 40 years – the 480 years from Moses to Solomon is now regarded as an editorial comment based on a generation's being 40 years – whereas modern scholars now see a Biblical generation as close to 25 years. Twelve generations would therefore be 300 years, from around 1275 to around 975BC, which fits in with the archaeological evidence, and Moses would be around 75 or more likely 80 rather than 120 (too old an age to be wandering in the wilderness and climbing Mount Nebo). Moses came to Mount Nebo around the age of 80, the same age that I was.

Mount Nebo

The coach had begun to climb. It passed a modern sculpture, and now the guide said, "We are going to see the view from the top of Mount Nebo." The coach climbed to the highest point of Mount Nebo, to 808 metres (2,651 feet) and parked near a church. Then the guide said casually, "Moses came here. He died on Mount Nebo. It's not known where he was buried."

Mount Nebo where (arrowed) Moses and Nicholas Hagger stood and were stunned by the view of the Promised Land

We got out. It was sunny and clear with a few streaky white clouds. A wind blew my hair. There were stragglers from a couple of groups returning to their coaches. We followed the guide to a wall, and I gasped.

View of the Promised Land

Below was a panoramic view with distant mountains (see front cover). A stone map on a square plaque had arrows pointing to the main locations. It indicated what was set out 2,651 feet beneath me. Though it was sunny and mostly clear there was a slight haze on the horizon, and the guide indicated: "Below on the left is the Dead Sea. Jerusalem is on the horizon, you can see the River Jordan and the Mount of Olives. Jericho is down there in front of you. Galilee is over on the right. All that down there is Canaan. This is where Moses stood shortly before he died, and saw the Promised Land."

Mount Nebo, Jordan, from a distance (above), from just beneath the summit (below left), and the view of the Dead Sea from its top (below right)

I was stunned. Following the stone map and looking down from a height of 2,651 feet across the Dead Sea on the left to Hebron, to Herodium (or Herodion), to Bethlehem and Qumran on the far edge of the Dead Sea, to distant Jerusalem and the Mount of Olives, Ramallah in Palestine, Jericho, Nablus and the Sea of Galilee, I felt a tremendous excitement and inspiration. I gazed and absorbed every detail. And I thought of Moses.

Here, from Mount Nebo Moses looked down on the Promised Land of milk and honey, the valley under the distant hills of Gilead, and he looked at Jerusalem and the Mount of Olives, and Jericho and Galilee, and of course the Dead Sea, below him to his left.

Vision of a unified earth and The Promised Land

I stood there, seeing what Moses saw, the Promised Land spread out below in sunshine and slight haze. I was in a trance, an ecstatic inspired daze, tense and clear-headed and completely at one with the moment, unaware of anyone else. I was reminded of when, on 3 May 1993 by the Arno in Pisa, I saw ten years' work ahead in two finished works for ten seconds: my epic poem *Overlord*, which I had discussed with Ezra Pound in 1970, and my *Classical Odes*. I saw their titles.

Now I realised I could be looking at the kingdoms of the earth, like Christ's view from the pinnacle of the temple alongside the Devil. It seemed absurd that the sweeping panoramic view below me should be divided up into separate nation-states – Jordan, Israel, Palestine, Lebanon – just as it seems absurd to a cosmonaut on the moon that the earth is not one unified ball but 193 separate and sometimes warring nation-states.

There, on Mount Nebo, I saw all the civilisations of the earth laid out beneath me, unified, one land basking in the sun. I saw the Paradise ahead, and realised that, like Moses who was close to the age of 80, I would never enter it. Moses' assistant Joshua fought for Canaan and the Promised Land after he died.

I was very moved and stayed on gazing from the top of Mount Nebo long after the other members of our group had turned to wander to the church and then back to our coach, including Ann, and I was completely alone. I saw all the kingdoms of the earth at peace within a World State, the Promised Land of Universalism. And as in Pisa in 1993 two works lodged in my mind.

One was a poem I scribbled down standing with the Promised Land beneath me, subsequently polished and called 'The Promised Land':

I stand where Moses stood and look across
The Dead Sea to Qumran and Jerusalem
And the River Jordan's valley green as moss,
And the oasis of Jericho, and Bethlehem
And the mountains from Hebron to Nablus, so fair,
Then I turn to where the hills of Amman throng,
And now a wind gets up and blows my hair
And I know that like Moses I have not long.
But just as Moses saw the Promised Land
And then died somewhere here on Mount Nebo,
So I too see a Promised Land entice
With a shimmering world peace beyond my right hand
And countries like these hills that are aglow
In a harmony that gleams a Paradise.

The other work was this work, which I saw completed and as a whole and knew what needed to be written. It included a book, *Conclusions*, I had to write. I had received it whole from the beyond, the inspiring source of a poet's creative power, from a source I called my Muses who fed me my works when I was in an absorbed state, my whole being alert and unified in a kind of superconsciousness that is way beyond normal everyday consciousness.

Mount Nebo and Moses

Moses died soon after seeing the Promised Land and according to Christian tradition was buried somewhere on Mount Nebo, perhaps on the mountainside not far from where I was standing. On the highest point of the mountain are the remains of a Byzantine church, first constructed in the 4th century to commemorate the place of Moses' death.

I now wandered back into this church and saw the Byzantine

mosaics of hunting scenes and exotic animals in the Diakonikon baptistery (c.530AD). The church was mentioned in an account of a pilgrimage by the Roman pilgrim, the lady Egeria, in 394AD, and six tombs have been found hollowed from the natural rock beneath the mosaic floor. According to the *Book of Maccabees* the Ark of the Covenant was hidden in a cave on Mount Nebo by the prophet Jeremiah (*2 Maccabees* 2.7).

Deuteronomy (34.6) says Moses was buried "in a valley in the land of Moab, over against [i.e. opposite] Beth-peor". Beth-baal-peor was to my right, down in the valley, I could see it, not far from the Ain Moussa (the springs of Moses). (Baal was the supreme god of the Canaanites.) There is a tomb near Jericho at Maqam El-Nabi Mousa – 11kms south of Jericho and 20kms east of Jerusalem – that is also reputed to be the tomb of Moses.

After standing where I stood Moses' Israelites made their way round Mount Nebo and turned left past Gilgal and proceeded to Jericho, to begin their conquest of Canaan under Joshua's leadership. The Israelites were perhaps overstated as being 600,000 in *Exodus* (12.37) and have sometimes been hugely overstated as being 2 million; there may by now have been around 15,000. But standing where Moses stood I knew that just as Yahweh told him he would not live to enter the Promised Land, so too, at the age of 80, I would "not go over thither". I could not expect to live to see the World State.

2

The Formative Years, 1960–1980: The Mystic Way and the Baroque Vision, The Forming of the Universalist Vision

The Dead Sea
From Mount Nebo we were driven to the edge of the Dead Sea and checked into the Mövenpick Resort and Spa with a view of the distant 'sea' from our window. The sea was 423 metres below sea level, the lowest point on earth, and it took a while for my ears to pop. We walked through lush vegetation beyond the swimming-pool and took a club car to the steps down to the Dead Sea. It looked grey and waves washed gently in towards the wall below, and a wooden landing-stage jutted out.

We walked back and sat in an open-air café and had chocolate-and-mango ice-creams by a 2,000-year-old olive tree and watched large fan-tailed ravens, Tristram's grackles and rock martins flit about, and green bee-eaters perch in the palms. We later supped in one of the restaurants.

The next morning we breakfasted in the open air under a bamboo trellis with sparrows flitting to and fro in the vines, and with a view of the bougainvillaea in the gardens. A wind was getting up and we went back to our room and put on our swimwear and took a club car through the hotel grounds down to the top of the steps, picking up towels on the way, and went down onto the beach. The red flag was flying.

Seeing I was over 80 an Arab lifeguard insisted on carrying my towel, took me by my right wrist and led me to a sun-lounger, put my towel on it, waited while I got ready to swim and then led me to the sloping wooden landing-stage.

The Dead Sea was now quite rough. I stepped down into the water, surprised by the waves whipped up by the wind, trod

Nicholas Hagger floating in the Dead Sea

awkwardly on uneven boulders, sat back and floated effortlessly. I turned over to try and swim on my front and was drenched by a wave that poured into my eyes and throat, so I turned back onto my back and floated. I did not realise I was drifting away from the land, and I felt my right ankle grabbed. My lifeguard had rescued me and propelled me back to the landing-stage. He helped me out and then helped Ann in while I walked back to my sun-lounger.

I had swum in the Dead Sea. As I dried myself, Ann was brought back by the lifeguard and swimming was banned for the rest of the morning as the waves were now too strong.

Bethany-beyond-the-Jordan: the baptism of Jesus by John the Baptist
After lunch we went by coach to Bethany, a few kilometres north of the Dead Sea. We passed Tel Mar Ilias, Elijah's Hill, a low rounded hill where Elijah allegedly ascended to Heaven on a chariot of fire, drawn by horses of fire (2 *Kings* 2.11). The coach stopped and I wandered away and pondered Elijah's ascension into Heaven.

For many years Bethany was in a military zone and inaccessible, but following the 1994 peace treaty between Jordan and Israel archaeologists returned and in a UNESCO heritage site known as Bethany-beyond-the-Jordan five Byzantine churches, a monastery and baptismal pools were being excavated. We stopped and made our way through tamarisk bushes to look at some of these sites. Then we walked on towards the River Jordan. Our path led us to the Greek Orthodox church of St John.

We came to dozens of steps that lead down to a wooden platform built out above the River Jordan, a narrow, muddy river below this landing-stage – although the previous week the river had been up to the top step. The other side of the narrow river was Israeli territory and had been since 1967, and we could see Israeli soldiers staring at us. Jordanian soldiers stared back from our side.

Our guide told us that this was the place where Jesus was baptised by John the Baptist (Al-Maghtas, the Place of 'Dipping', 'Immersion' or 'Baptism'). John was a mystic, perhaps an Essene – the Essenes lived in caves – and as he died around 32AD he may have known of the transfiguration of Jesus on Mount Tabor.

The wooden platform at Al-Maghtas, the Place of Baptism by the River Jordan, where Jesus was baptised by John the Baptist, viewed from Jordan (top three pictures) and from Israel (fourth picture); and the cave where John the Baptist lived on locusts and honey beneath Elijah's hill within walking distance nearby

John the Baptist lived on the east bank of the Jordan in a cave beneath Elijah's hill. Looking back from the top of the slope above the steps I could see the flood plain and distant hills, and John lived in one of several caves in the distance there, feeding on locusts and honey. His clothing was camel's hair and he had a leather girdle round his loins, and he preached in the wilderness of Judaea, saying:

> The voice of one crying in the wilderness,
> Prepare ye the way of the Lord,
> Make his paths straight.
> (*Matthew* 3.3)

John had walked to this spot above the steps. Jesus had come from the Israeli side, the west bank, with at least four apostles. According to our guide he crossed the Jordan by walking on a line of boats, holding on to a shoulder-high rope that was fastened on either side of the river and suspended. The boats rose and fell with the tide and were never submerged, as a bridge would have been. He met John the Baptist a hundred yards from the river, about where I was standing. He was baptised in the river by lying back and having his head dunked in the water (*Matthew* 3.13–17). John would not have got into the water. John's left hand held Jesus's head and his right hand would have scooped water onto his forehead.

John the Baptist's right hand

I thought back to my travels the previous year. I was in Kotor, Montenegro. We had an hour of free time before we returned to our ship, and I found out from a guidebook that there was a relic of John the Baptist in Cetinje monastery nearby. We walked there, and the monastery, originally a 15th-century Orthodox church, looked shut. I spoke to a gardener, who understood a little English, and said I was interested in John the Baptist. He was embraced by a friend who had just arrived, and his friend said in English that I must see the monk. He led me in and the monk, a middle-aged bearded man, established my religion and then said, "I will show you the relic."

He led me into a room with a large coffin and unlocked it and lifted the curved lid. It contained St Peter of Cetinje, a monk who became Metropolitan of Montenegro and the secular leader of the Montenegran Serbs and fought Napoleon's army. He had died in 1830 and had never decayed. His face looked old but his skin was intact.

Above his folded hands were two boxes with glass reveals. One contained a fragment that was alleged to be from the cross on which Jesus was crucified. The monk lifted the other box and I was looking at the swarthy right hand that was alleged to be John the Baptist's, the first and second fingers intact, two stubs for the other two fingers and no thumb. I was looking at the two fingers that had baptised Christ.

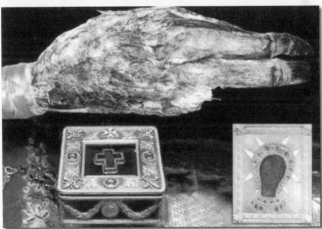

Two views of the two surviving fingers of John the Baptist's right hand which baptised Jesus, kept in Cetinje monastery in Kotor, Montenegro

John the Baptist had been beheaded in Machaerus Castle near Madaba in c.32AD, on Herod's orders, and his head had been served on a platter for Salome. The hand was apparently severed at the same time and kept as a relic. I was told that Crusaders found it, and it was taken to Russia. It was held by the Tsar's family until 1917. Then the Tsarina, alarmed at the threat of the revolutionary Bolsheviks, sent it to the monastery in Kotor for safe keeping, and after the murder of the Tsar's family including the Tsarina, it had remained in Kotor. That was its apparent provenance.

I bent and inspected the hand carefully. Its flesh was intact and I thought it belonged to a swarthy Middle-Eastern man, which is what John the Baptist was. I had seen the hand that baptised Christ, and now at Bethany-beyond-the-Jordan I had seen where it baptised Christ.

The essential experience of all religions: the Fire or Light, "the vision of God"

On the coach back to the Dead Sea I reflected that Bethany-beyond-the-Jordan (in other words, on the east bank when viewed from the west bank, hence 'beyond') was sacred to Jews, Christians and Muslims. There John the Baptist preached, Jesus met him and was baptised. There Christianity, a new religion, was born, and the *New Testament* began. Christianity was only one of many religions. I had found in my writings that all religions had the same essence, the same essential experience of the Fire or Light which mystics claim to be "the vision of God".

I had focused on the spiritual and divine experiences of human beings, which had first been revealed to me in the Zen temples of Japan, and the religions with which I had come into contact in my travels: Islam, Buddhism, Taoism and Hinduism. But my Universalist view of the importance of religions had really begun in my first visit to the Holy Land in January 1962, and Bethany-beyond-the-Jordan had supplemented what I saw in those early days.

Kerak Castle

The next day we were driven south to Kerak Castle, a Crusader castle on a hill. The Crusaders started building it in 1142. They built it on seven levels, with a precipitous drop at the back, and it was built to be a fortress for a garrison that could withstand a siege. I wandered through the top three levels, the bottom four not having been excavated.

There was a wide central passage with arched stone-walled halls on either side. These were used as living quarters and stables, and as shelters against missiles during sieges. I lingered in the Crusaders' kitchen and dining-room, and saw the dungeons on the fifth level (two from the top).

From 1176 to 1184 the Castle was under the rule of the cruel Crusader Reynald de Châtillon, a French adventurer who took part in the Second Crusade in 1147 and then settled in the Kingdom of Jerusalem. He plundered Muslim caravans and ships on the Red Sea for booty, and arguably provoked the fall of Jerusalem in 1187. He did, however, prevent Saladin from unifying the Muslim states near the Castle.

Saladin, the Muslim leader and conqueror of Jerusalem, besieged Kerak Castle in 1183 and again in 1184 before giving up. In late 1183 or early 1184 he fought the Crusaders in the Battle of Hattin, and captured and personally beheaded Reynald. In 1188 the Castle was besieged again and surrendered.

Kerak Castle, where Crusaders surrendered to Saladin in 1188

I stood at the place where prisoners were thrown over the precipice a long way down to the minute village below, and reflected on the Crusaders' brutality. They were ready to be killed so they could go to Heaven, and had no sympathy for their prisoners. They were in this respect like the fighters of Islamic State, who 800 years later were similarly ready to be killed to go to Paradise and were cruel to Christians and Yazidis. Its leader, Abu Bakr al-Baghdadi, had been a student at the University of Baghdad after I left.

As a historical Universalist, I was aware that the Islamic Arab civilisation, being younger, was 600 years behind the European civilisation and was undergoing the religious fanaticism that the European civilisation had been going through during the Crusades, the Tudor Reformation and the English Civil War. The radical Islamic groups had the same attitudes the Crusaders had: killing their enemies in the name of their religion, which guaranteed them an eventual place in Heaven. And the Muslim world was now experiencing a Reformation, with Shias challenging Sunnis.

Little Petra

After lunch at the Falcon Rock Hotel we were taken by coach to Little Petra, to a sandstone gorge with carved tombs from the 2nd century BC to

The Painted Biclinium (dining-room), Little Petra

the 2nd century AD. I climbed precarious steps to the high-up Painted Biclinium (dining-room), painted with vine leaves and flowers and cupids, Pan and Eros, and seemingly a head of Dionysus, the Greek god of wine and religious ecstasy: it is thought a Dionysian sect camped here. I nearly fell as I climbed back down the uneven steep rocky steps – there was no handrail and a drop of 30 feet – but I was struck by how the Graeco-Roman religion had found its way to the land of the Nabataeans, another instance of the spreading of religious ideas.

We walked more than a kilometre to the Neolithic village of Beidha: about 60 stone structures from c.7000–6500BC, the early ones circular and the later ones rectangular, with walls, staircases, hearths, grindstones, plastered floors and doorways from a time when nomadic hunters became settled farmers. I stood and looked back nine thousand years to evidence that humankind was then organising itself into farming and making a better living as farmers than as hunters roaming in search of animals to kill.

Circular early (above), and rectangular later (next page), stone houses in Beidha's neolithic village, 7000–6500BC

I was looking back to a source from which civilisations arose, and I thought of the Kurgans who had spread from the Russian steppes to Danubian Europe c.3500BC and built many of the megaliths c.2700BC, and seemed to have had a hand in building Stonehenge, before being replaced by a new wave of immigrants c.2300BC. Standing among these Neolithic stone houses I was back in a time before there were any major religions except for primitive worship of the sun.

*

Universalism and the oneness of the universe and humankind

Before I left for Jordan I had begun assembling *The Essentials of Universalism*, 75 selections from 25 of my prose works. The subtitle sums up Universalism as: "A philosophy of the unity of the universe and humankind, of interconnected disciplines and a World State."

A cosmonaut looking at our earth from the moon sees a blue ball with North Africa – the Sahara – a pale yellow, and from that distance and his perspective the earth looks a unity, and out among the stars the universe too appears to be a unity, One. Because the earth seems one entity with no signs of division,

A cosmonaut's view of the earth from the moon

to the cosmonauts it seems that humankind is a unity, and that all disciplines are fundamentally one discipline, and are interconnected, just as the bands of a rainbow are one rainbow. And it seems natural to look for the political union of humankind in a World State.

A longer and more informative version of my subtitle, which preceded the shorter version, was: "A revolutionary philosophy and world-view of the fundamental unity of the universe and humankind, and a movement to reconfigure all disciplines as interconnected wholes and bring in a World State."

The philosophy of Universalism *is* revolutionary in seeing the universe as One, as did some of the ancient Greek philosophers, with all the apparent contradictory phenomena being reconciled within its unity. I grasped this in Japan when sitting meditating in Zen temples and absorbing Taoism, and the two opposites of *yin* and *yang*, female and male, night and day and so many other pairs of opposites, which are united in the *Tao*.

Junzaburo Nishiwaki, Japanese poet

Junzaburo Nishiwaki, Japan's T.S. Eliot, was Professor Emeritus at one of my universities, Keio University, and I was taken to spend an evening with him at his house and later met him round the corner from Keio University in a *saké* (rice-wine) bar. There I asked him, "What is the essence of the wisdom of the East?" He wrote down on a business-reply card I had in the front of *Encounter*, a magazine my grandmother sent me every month: "+A + –A = 0, Great Nothing."

I immediately grasped that day and night, being and non-being, life and death, time and eternity and all pairs of opposites are reconciled in the underlying unity behind the universe which Chinese call the *Tao* and Westerners God. I grasped that all religions are essentially one, a unity, and was on the way to seeing the essence of religions as the

Business-reply card showing "+A + –A = 0, Great Nothing"

mystical experience of Reality, the Fire or Light at the centre of the universe.

Initially I had approached the oneness of the universe through literature, in Wordsworth's

Wisdom and Spirit of the universe!
Thou Soul that art the eternity of thought,
That givest to forms and images a breath
And everlasting motion...,

and Shelley's

The One remains, the many change and pass;
Heaven's light forever shines, Earth's shadows fly;
Life, like a dome of many-coloured glass,
Stains the white radiance of Eternity...,

and in the writings of Blake and the Metaphysical poets. But I had moved outside literature, and my 56 books are within seven disciplines – literature, mysticism, philosophy, history, religion, international politics and statecraft, and world culture – which are essentially one just as the rainbow is essentially a rainbow although it has seven bands. In my writings I have acted out the interconnectedness of the key disciplines.

My Universalism had grown over a decade of working abroad, and in Jordan I could see the links between my visits to different parts of the world as a young man. The visits were experiences, and they shaped me. "Go abroad, young man, and get some experience," I occasionally heard when I was an undergraduate. It's true; opening to experiences does shape our way of looking.

In Jordan, travelling in coaches to antique places, I looked back at my formative years, at the years that formed my literary and philosophical vision, that formed the vision that shaped my books.

Universalism in Greek and Roman history and literature
I could see that my Universalism grew out of my reading of Greek and Roman history and literature at school. I saw parallels between the might of the invading Persians and the heroic stand of the Greeks at Thermopylae, and the wartime Battle of Britain. I saw parallels between the Athenian Empire and the British Empire of my boyhood, and between the Peloponnesian War and the wars with Germany. I saw

parallels between the two Punic Wars between Rome and Carthage and the two 20th-century world wars. I saw the common essence of war that could be found in both Homer's *Iliad* and Virgil's *Aeneid*.

I had lovingly collected Greek and Roman coins, going up to Seaby's in London and spending my pocket money on Greek drachmae and copper Roman coins bearing the heads of the Emperors. These were in a rejects tin, where coins all had blemishes and were sold for 6d. (2.5p) rather than dozens or hundreds of pounds, which they would have fetched in pristine condition. I longed to have lived in Greece and Rome, and as soon as I could travel I toured the Roman ruins in Rome, Naples, Capri and Sicily in 1957 when I was still seventeen, and the Greek ruins of the Peloponnese and islands in 1958, when I was eighteen; and after doing the same in Spain in 1959, I revisited Greece in 1960. The Greek world matched my new love of the Romantic poets who drew on Greek and Roman mythology.

Greece and Italy taught me to look at dead civilisations and find parallels, and this came out later in my study of 'the decline of the West' for a year's lectures I was asked to give at my main university in Tokyo in 1966–1967, and my study of 25 civilisations in *The Fire and the Stones*, later updated as *The Rise and Fall of Civilizations*. I had already been alerted to the fundamental unity of history in the late 1950s and early 1960s, and was already a Universalist historian before my lectures in Japan.

Universalism in Iraq

In the 1960s in the UK most young men leaving university worked in an industrial city, generally London. I, living on the fringe of London, contacted the British Council and somehow headed for Baghdad with a new wife, instinctively knowing I had to get to know the desert surrounding Baghdad, a wilderness where the human condition could be simplified to a lone Arab standing against sand and sky, undistracted by city-living. Sleeping under the stars on our roof in baking heat with the half-moon on its back, I instinctively knew I should be on a Mystic Way.

The Middle East extended my knowledge of religion from Christianity into Islam. Living under Islam in Iraq and hearing the

Muslim muezzin crying the hour of prayer through a loudspeaker in a minaret at set times every day, calling all to stop work and pray, made me aware of the essence of religions. Living in Iraq also took me back to the early Mesopotamian civilisation. In Baghdad in late 1961 I crossed the River Tigris by bus or taxi every day, and drove to the River Euphrates from time to time.

Baghdad is on the Tigris at its closest to the Euphrates 25 miles to the west, and the land between is known as Mesopotamia ("between rivers"). I lived between the two ancient rivers and their monuments.

I went to Gourna (or Qurna), where the Tigris and the Euphrates meet and become the Shatt al-Arab until their combined flow discharges into the Persian Gulf. Gourna is on the site of the Garden of Eden, Paradise, and I saw the split trunk and leaves of a jujube tree (then alive but now recently dead), said to have been planted by Noah after the Flood on the exact spot where the Tree of the Knowledge of Good and Evil stood in the Garden of Eden, bearing forbidden fruit (*Genesis* 2.9). Tradition states that Abraham

A jujube tree said to be on the site of the Tree of the Knowledge of Good and Evil, where Eve ate the forbidden fruit, at Gourna, Iraq

prayed beneath its branches. Nearby was the tomb of the 5th-century-BC prophet Ezra.

I went to Babylon, which is on the Euphrates 50 miles south of Baghdad, and walked under the palm-trees. I found where the ziggurat stood, the stepped tower surmounted by a temple, the Tower of Babel where all the world's languages could be heard in a babble of foreign tongues, a World Centre during its heyday.

I was living under a nationalistic dictatorship, the dictatorship of Brigadier-General Kaseem, but in Iraq, and in the Holy Land I visited in 1962 as I have already described (see pp.1–2), I saw three religions –

Christianity, Islam and Judaism – co-existing in the vicinity of Biblical sites, a powerful image and reminder of religious Universalism.

I was slowly, imperceptibly, returning to the mysticism that had fascinated me in literature, in the works of the Metaphysical and Romantic poets. Every day, coming home from work at the University of Baghdad, I passed a building associated with Suhrawardi (1154–1191), founder of the Iranian school of Illuminationism based on the Light, the Divine and Inner Light of Illuminationist philosophy, who went to live in Iraq for a while. The ancient house he occupied was pointed out to me with pride by taxi-drivers and others as I drove past, and I made a note of his name and did not then realise I would come to admire his vision. It now looks as if I was being shown my way.

Universalism in Japan

I went to Japan with the British Council in 1963, and as an Invited Foreign Professor of English Literature at the age of 24 I was given free use of a bungalow in the Bunkyo-ku district overlooking Tokyo.

It was an immensely fertile time for me. The Representative of the British Council and technically my boss, who had me to lunch before I began lecturing, was E.W.F. Tomlin, a published metaphysical philosopher and friend of T.S. Eliot, who wrote Tomlin a hundred letters (see Tomlin's book *T.S. Eliot: A Friendship*). My discussions with Tomlin strengthened my philosophical Universalism.

I lectured on T.S. Eliot for a year at Tokyo University, and spent much of the time on Eliot's philosophical *Four Quartets*. After Eliot's death I contributed an essay 'In Defence of the Sequence of Images' to a book Tomlin edited, *T.S. Eliot: A Tribute from Japan*. Tomlin told me before he died that he had arranged for me to visit Eliot when I was back on leave in 1966, but Eliot's death in 1965 prevented this.

Through colleagues at my universities I meditated in Zen Buddhist temples and absorbed the wisdom of the East, strengthening my philosophical and mystical Universalism.

In Japan I discovered myself as a poet. I had poems published in Japanese literary magazines, including *Eigo Seinin, The Rising Generation*. Between 1963 and 1966 I wrote all the poems in *A Stone*

Torch-Basket and *The Early Education and Making of a Mystic*, and between 1965 and 1967 my most important poem 'The Silence', most of the poems in *The Wings and the Sword* and 'Old Man in a Circle'.

The turning-point was my Modernist poem 'The Silence', a poem about Freeman (my Everyman), his self-discovery and transformation, and his experience of the unity of the universe and (towards the end) of humankind. This poem coincided with the arrival at a nearby university of the novelist and short-story writer Frank Tuohy, who was older than me and quickly took me under his wing as a budding writer who could talk literature with him, and became my closest friend, and it cemented my literary Universalism.

All my poetic themes can be found in the works I wrote in 1965–1967. The seeds of all my later works, including my Universalism, can be found in these years. Within this period I spent 18 months writing 'The Silence'. While on leave in England I wrote 'Archangel', my poem on Communism which includes a vision of the World State, and 'Blighty' about the UK's decline. On 8 July 1966 I visited the Banqueting House in Whitehall where, in the 17th century, Ben Jonson's masques were performed, and where in 2019 I set *The Coronation of King Charles*. And on 15 July I wrote my first short story (the first of 1,400 short stories). On my way back to Japan I wrote 'An Epistle to an Admirer of Oliver Cromwell' and back in Japan 'An Inner Home', which anticipated my writings on Epping Forest, and 'Old Man in a Circle', my poem on European and Western decline. In these years I laid the foundations for, and extended the range of, my literary Universalism.

All my historical themes can be found in work I did in this period. I taught Prince Hitachi, Emperor Hirohito's younger son, for three-and-a-half years and taught him all world history, the history of the last 5,000 years. As I have intimated (see p.34), I was asked to teach a course titled 'The Decline of the West' to eight postgraduate students for a year, which included teaching Gibbon, Spengler and Toynbee, and – while covering all the main events of history with Prince Hitachi – I discovered in embryo a fourth way of understanding the 25 civilisations of history, which would become *The Fire and the Stones*, and which I reflected in my poem 'Old Man in a Circle', and I arrived at my historical Universalism.

All my political themes can be found in this same period. In March 1966 I went to China (with Tuohy) and was the first to discover the Chinese Cultural Revolution (see p.108), and I went to Russia twice, once on my way to London on leave and again on my way back to Japan. I put my experiences of Russian and Chinese Communism in 'Archangel', and indirectly called for a World State at the end of the poem by presenting a glimpse of a World State I had had in the Cathedral of the Archangel in the Kremlin. I was already a political Universalist.

As tutor to the Vice-Governor of the Bank of Japan I had to write the Governor's speeches in English, including his speech on the opening of the Asian Development Bank, which alerted me to the need for international co-operation and strengthened my political Universalism.

But it was my poem 'The Silence' which characterises my four years in Japan the most and it drew together all these mystical, literary, historical and political strands. It was central to my unconsciously-growing Universalism. While writing 'The Silence' I experienced an awakening, a centre-shift from my ego to my deeper self; purgation and the first glimmerings of illumination which connected me with Suhrawardi and put me on the path of mystical Universalism. I recorded these inner events in *My Double Life 1: This Dark Wood* on pp.185, 187–188:

Inner images

A further development began on 11 September 1965. I had worked on my essay all day and could not sleep. I closed my eyes and a succession of images rose: scrivenings in a foreign language – Arabic or Hebrew – in yellow and blue; a puddle and an orb of fire within it; corn stalks with many ears of corn; a whirlpool. Then it seemed I was going down a well, and saw the orb of the sky getting smaller as I descended. These images should be regarded as visions, a 'vision' being "something which is apparently seen otherwise than by ordinary sight; especially an appearance of a prophetic or mystical character, or having the nature of a revelation, supernaturally presented to the mind in sleep" (*Shorter Oxford English Dictionary*). Two days later on 13 September,

I had more images (or visions) behind closed eyes, also late at night. A series of gold heads went slowly by as if on a conveyor belt: some Egyptian, some Negroid, some Babylonian. Then there were exquisite diamonds in green and mauve which lasted 30 seconds.

When I got off to sleep I dreamt I was on the second floor of a Turkish Byzantine café. There was an earthquake and I rushed down the stairs and out into the courtyard through falling masonry to find everything in ruins, all foundations crumbled. Then I was in a morgue among many corpses, which suddenly sat up and came to life, jingling their bones. When I awoke I thought I had dreamt about a centre-shift. I thought I had opened to my imagination and the bubbling-up from the spring of my inspiring Muse which could even occur in sleep....

Light, Satori: *round white Light in soul, end of First Mystic Life*
The next morning, Monday 18 October, something extraordinary happened to me. I stayed at home, and my *Diaries* record: "All morning I have been filled with a round white light: I cannot see it, except occasionally when I glimpse it and am dazzled, but I know it is there. It is like a white sun. This is, I suppose, what Christians refer to as the soul – the centre of the self. And the mystical experience is given meaning by the relation between the centre and the sun, so that everything is one." I observed that it was not the universe that had changed, but my self and my perception of it "so that it now seems more harmonious".

I discovered myself as a mystic who was on the Mystic Way, and having glimpsed the Light behind closed eyelids like a dazzling white sun breaking through inner dark in October 1965 while undergoing my transforming centre-shift, I tried to understand what was happening to me. There was little help in the books I had access to in Japan, and I did not think of myself as a mystical or literary Universalist then. I grappled with what was happening to me in relative isolation – it was beyond Tuohy's experience and ability to help, although he suggested I should add 'Ancient-Mariner'-style marginal glosses to 'The Silence' to aid understanding of the inner experiences I was going through – and at the time I grasped that my post-centre-shift combination of spirit and sense was Baroque. I saw my combination of Romantic individualism (in the tradition of Wordsworth and Shelley) and Classical social alertness as Baroque, and from the beyond I received lines in Japan that I put into 'The Silence' when I revised it in 1973:

> I heard a cry from the old Professor's darkened room,
> "The Age of Analysis is dead!"
> Books lined with dust, a buzzing fly....
> > While, naked on the petalled lawn,
> A new Baroque age is born.

These lines were drafted in Japan, and the "buzzing fly" was in my Tokyo study the day I wrote them. The lines came as a whole from a very deep place. I was not sure what they meant. But looking back now I see that I was being told I should give up being an analytical Professor to be a writer conveying the spiritual-sensual Baroque vision in my works, and bring in a new Baroque Age. Before leaving for Jordan I had completed and sent off *A Baroque Vision*, 100 selections from 50 of my poetic works, which traces how Universalism grew out of my Baroque vision.

In 1967 I was offered a Chair as Professor in English Literature for life. I resigned the next day, knowing I had to be a writer of Baroque works, not a Professor who would give his life to analysis and not write such works. I knew I had to be true to my vision of the birth of a new Baroque Age in my writings. I walked away from a Chair for life and returned to the West.

But my development had not finished. While I returned to England in 1967 I visited eleven countries in the Far East and Middle East and experienced their religions and cultures. I visited Vietnam. The boom of guns on the edge of the city reached my hotel window in Saigon, and I went to Bien Hoa, where the last battle of the Vietnam War was fought, through Viet-Cong-held villages on an American bus for GIs. I visited Nepal and India and saw Hindu and Buddhist religions work with other religions. Besides being a mystical, literary, philosophical, historical and political Universalist in 1967, I was also a religious and cultural Universalist.

What I found in Japan has never left me. I saw my future self as my Shadow. The hot sun of Japan often accompanied me when I walked to work at my main university and returned, and I was always accompanied by my shadow. During my centre-shift in Tokyo I saw my ego as my Reflection, which I saw in shop-windows near Myogadani station opposite my university (behind one of which windows I had my hair cut), and I saw my Shadow as my future self, aged over 80, which had achieved wisdom, the over-80 self I believe I have now become. 'The Silence' begins:

> Walk, my shadow,
> Down these lanes of the mind.

Now I have become my Shadow and have (arguably) arrived at some wisdom, I look back on my young self then and marvel at how much I achieved in those four years, transforming and resetting my self to be a poet, a man of letters, a cultural historian, a philosopher and writer of current affairs conveying political Universalism. I prepared my self to write books on mystical and literary Universalism, philosophical and religious Universalism, historical and political Universalism, and last but not least cultural Universalism. All this self-remaking came out of my early experiences in Iraq, the Middle East and the Holy Land in 1961–1962. There I began a process which led to this outcome.

Universalism in Libya

From 1968 to 1970 I lectured in English Literature at the University of Libya in Tripoli. It was hot and near the Sahara Desert and I maintained my Universalist history by visiting the well-preserved Roman cities of Sabratha and Leptis Magna. I wrote articles on the Roman ruins of Libya for *The Daily News* (see Appendix of *The Libyan Revolution*).

I recall seeing on the way to Leptis a scarlet-robed Bedouin standing on a wilderness of red-brown earth, a tiny figure against a vast sky, and I was moved by the tininess of man against the vastness of the universe. A man standing in a vast desert between red earth and blue sky, to me this was how a solitary man lived: ground and sky and his lone questing self.

In *My Double Life 1: This Dark Wood* I have described how I was entrammelled in nationalism. My landlord had been a Colonel in the Libyan Army – Gaddafi had been his boot boy – and he put together a *coup* against King Idris with some of the current ministers. I was invited to their parties where they planned their *coup*, which was to take place on 5 September 1969. Gaddafi, then 28 and unknown, got wind of it and struck first on 1 September 1969. I was an eyewitness of his *coup*.

I had been approached on 30 May 1969 by British Intelligence to act in the British and Western interest. Gaddafi's dictatorship promoted Arab nationalism. I saw his nationalism at first hand. I had been asked to be involved in British nationalism. These two nationalisms took me away from my Universalism.

In *My Double Life 1: This Dark Wood* I have described how my work for British Intelligence under the Gaddafi regime in conditions of great danger, particularly in successfully arranging for a Czech to defect with Soviet nuclear knowledge to the UK instead of the US, broke up my marriage in December 1969. I lived in danger. When Col. Nasser visited Tripoli I was one of a handful of Westerners in a crowd that lined the streets and Nasser and Gaddafi, both standing, passed within a few feet of me in a Jeep.

A few days later, early in January 1970, Gaddafi came to the University of Libya. We all lined up to greet him, and my students surged forward to welcome him, threw their arms round him and kissed him, and he was thrown, in uniform, against my left shoulder. I raised my shoulder and knocked his dictator's hat to the ground.

I underwent a Dark Night of the Soul, the beginning of purgation, that took me further along the Mystic Way, and I retrieved my Universalist perspective when I visited Egypt during a vacation between the two semesters. I watched the dorsal-fin-like sails of boats on the Nile from my Cairo balcony and visited the Pyramids, Memphis, Saqqara, Luxor, Alexandria and El Alamein (where I located a SAM-3 missile transporter just delivered from Russia to Egypt). My dentist had been the brother of Howard Carter, the discoverer of Tutankhamun's tomb, and visiting the tombs in the Valley of Kings from Luxor I made sure I visited the tomb of Tutankhamun. Amid my grief I saw a Land of the Dead on the murals in many tombs when I would later see a Land of the Second Life and Eternity.

The spring in the Sahara Desert, Ain el Faras, in Ghadames, Libya

Almost immediately on my return from Egypt at the end of February 1970 I travelled in a Jeep through the Sahara Desert to Ghadames, an underground town where little had changed since the Roman times, and the inhabitants still wore togas.

There I sat by a spring, Ain el Faras. It resembled a large square walled-in pool with weed, surrounded by palms. It was around 4,500 years old, and the walls round it had been begun about the same time as the Great Pyramid. I sat and watched bubbles wobble up, and to me, on a Way of Loss, they suggested the cleansing of my heart with inspired energy pouring in from the beyond. I now felt sure of my inspiration from the beyond, and that I had more than 50 works ahead of me, each a bubble wobbling from the beyond up to the surface of the world I occupied. And I did not want to leave.

I was a target and was watched by the Libyan Secret Police. There was always a fawn Volkswagen outside my gate and it followed me wherever I drove. I have described in *My Double Life 1: This Dark Wood* how I was nearly executed by one of Gaddafi's henchmen. I had a Luger pointed at me for an hour in the course of one long night.

Libya was a kind of wilderness. As Tripoli was on the edge of the Sahara Desert I had lived close to the sun and the sand and had purged

Ezra Pound

my self of attachment and had located new depths within myself although I had not been as inward-looking as in Japan. 'The Silence' had been in the Modernist tradition, and aware that I had an epic poem ahead of me, and concerned that the Modernist style – abbreviated narrative in a sequence of images – was not right for an epic, I wrote to Ezra Pound ('Ezra Pound, Rapallo, Italy') and visited his villa on my way home. He had spent 60 years writing his *Cantos* using abbreviation, and had edited down T.S. Eliot's 'The Waste Land', and I wanted to question him now he was 85 and work out if abbreviation was the right way forward. In *My Double Life 1: This Dark Wood* I describe our meeting in full, and how his latest canto was in manuscript on a table in the long room where we sat.

I was driving home, and could not present him with my Modernist poem 'The Silence' (which was still in draft) and my essay written after Eliot's death, 'In Defence of the Sequence of Images', the sequences of images Pound had championed, and I did not then know that shortly before Eliot died Tomlin had arranged for me to visit Eliot when I was on leave in England, so I was able to appear neutral about Modernism and question it from an unpartisan point of view.

I concluded that Modernist narrative would not be right for my epic poem, and that I should return to the narrative of Milton's *Paradise Lost*, Wordsworth's *The Prelude* and Tennyson's *Idylls of the King*; and in *Overlord*, written in the 1990s, my first epic poem about the last year of the Second World War, I turned my back on Modernism for 19th-century narrative.

I ended my time in Libya by carrying forward the Universalism I had developed in Japan as Pound, having edited Eliot's 'The Waste Land', linked me to my work on Eliot in Japan. I saw a thread from Japan that was still with me during my evening with Pound. Both Libya and Egypt were very much a part of my formative years, and helped to shape me into the writer I was to become.

Universalism in the UK

Back in England I was still working for British Intelligence, work that included freelancing feature articles in *The Times* for Charlie Douglas-Home and snippets for *The Times* Diary. I had become Prime Minister Edward Heath's Unofficial Ambassador to the African liberation movements, which were all involved with Russia within the Cold War, and with China. As a cover I worked in an ESN school (a school for educationally subnormal boys) during the day with no homework to set and mark, and began my intelligence work as soon as school ended.

I was living in London in a room at 13 Egerton Gardens near Harrods (where I sometimes met my SIS Controller in the 'Way In' coffee bar on the fourth floor). I was now living self-sufficiently and intensely. It was a dangerous time; every day I was followed by surveillance squads from different countries – menacing nationalism literally behind my back. In April 1971 I had been betrayed to the KGB by the Czech I had persuaded to defect and had introduced to MI6's head of station in Tripoli, and in September I was told Philby might out me as a British intelligence agent to the media.

In *My Double Life 1: This Dark Wood* I have described at length one of the most important experiences of my life which happened that same month, on 10 September 1971: full illumination. In an hour and a half I lay on my bed in my first-floor room (to the right of the two front rooms as you look up from the street) in the late afternoon and opened to the Light and had a most powerful experience of dazzling white Light flooding into my inner darkness, and then many images – visions – that lasted an hour and a half, like the bubbles wobbling up from the Saharan spring. Many of these visions can be found in my *Collected Poems*. My account in *My Double Life 1: This Dark Wood* on pp.372–374 begins as follows:

Illumination on 10 September 1971

I now come to the momentous day, Friday 10 September 1971, the equivalent for me of what Monday 23 November 1654 meant to Pascal, who wrote down his experience and sewed the parchment into his doublet and wore it until he died, so important was his illumination to him....

Experiencing the Flowing Light, an encounter with the metaphysical

I shut out the world, and waited, watching within.... I gave my breathing to the twilight until I fell into a trance. And from behind my closed eyes, looking *into* my closed eyes I saw white light flowing upwards: a tree, white against the black inside me, a bare winter tree of white fire, flowing, rippling as if in water. I put my hands over my eyes, I wanted nothing outside to spoil the brightness of what I saw within. Then a spring opened within me like the spring in the Sahara, and for a good hour and a half visions wobbled up inside me like the wobbling bubbles in Ain el Faras. I remember the first two most clearly: a centre of light shining down from a great height, and then a white flower, like a dahlia or a chrysanthemum, with very detailed, breathtakingly beautiful cells. This was my first glimpse of the celebrated Golden Flower, the centre and source of my being.

There were too many visions for me to remember one quarter of what I saw. But almost immediately a sun broke through my inner dark and hung in the 'sky' with a dazzling whiteness. Then I saw a fountain of light. Then all was dark and I saw stars, then strange patterns, old paintings I had never seen before, old gods and saints. When I came out of my contemplation I was refreshed. I felt turned inside out and wobbly at the knees....

I fell on my knees in the dark. I screwed up my eyes to shut out the outer world, and there was a white point, a small circle of light that went deep up into the heavens behind my closed eyes. I said aloud, "I surrender," and the light moved and changed until it became a celestial curtain blown in the wind, like the *aurora borealis*. I felt limp, exhausted. I had to stop. I was filled with an afterglow, and my fingers were moist. I felt blissfully happy.

For me it was a momentous experience, akin to St Paul's vision on the road to Damascus and Pascal's experience which was so important to him that he sewed a scrap of parchment on which he had written the time and date into the lining of his doublet.

Almost immediately I began my Second Mystic Life. And I went on to have many experiences of the Light over the years. The Appendix lists 112 experiences, their dates and what I saw (see pp.209–215).

My new mystical Universalism had transformed me again, and my unitive vision was greatly strengthened. I wrote an essay which I sent to Colin Wilson, and visited him. My sense of nationhood was already falling away, and I needed to end all deception and pretence in my life and be straightforward. My intelligence work in the UK co-existed with my being illumined, and it now fell away naturally. I terminated my secret work in May 1973 and have had no contact with my former masters since then.

In April/May 1973 I revised 'The Silence' – now that I was clear of intelligence work I had time to return to my writings – and wrote in the lines I quoted on p.40 on the birth of a new Baroque age. I had now entered a Dark Night of the Spirit and was beginning to emerge into instinctive unitive vision, which happens after illumination and towards the end of the Mystic Way, a process that can be found in my diaries and in *My Double Life 2: A Rainbow over the Hills* (see p.45). The unitive vision is Universalist, it instinctively sees the unity behind the universe and humankind, and it also sees the unity and interconnectedness of all disciplines. One's unitive consciousness towards and after the end of the Mystic Way is instinctively Universalist. But then, in 1973, I still saw this vision as Baroque.

While I was writing 'The Silence' in Japan I returned to London on leave in 1966, as I have said (see pp.37–38), and in ten weeks visited as many literary and historical places as I could. I went to Dublin and Sligo and visited places connected with Joyce and Yeats. I wanted to see where Charles I was beheaded, and as I have said (on p.37) I visited the Banqueting House in Whitehall, London, and looked up at the Rubens ceiling showing James I (Charles I's father) ascending to Heaven, which Charles I stood beneath on his way to his execution through an open window upstairs on a raised scaffold outside.

For me in 1966, this painting held all the Baroque features, including the divine soul of James I amid the sensual attention of the angels who were transporting him to Heaven, a perfect blend of spirit and sense. The picture is on the cover of *A Baroque Vision*, 100 selections from 50 of my poetic works, which I had first assembled shortly before I went to Jordan in 2020.

In 1974 I remarried. Ann was a primary-school teacher I had met shortly after my illumination in 1971. I became a Head of English at a large comprehensive in Wandsworth, London, and I was able to teach Milton, Wordsworth and Tennyson for 'A' level, and poems poured up into my consciousness like wobbling bubbles in the Saharan spring. I had long said I would get the equivalent of my grandfather's family business back, and having had two boys I met the now elderly Headmistress of my old primary school, Oaklands School, at the christening of my younger boy in 1977. She asked if I would buy her school and put my wife in as Headmistress. I made arrangements to do this as I saw a chance to escape being a Head of English and create some writing time. The negotiations took five years, and in 1982 I finally bought Oaklands School, which I attended from 1943, and its present site from just after D-Day in 1944. I was not able to retire from my teaching in London until 1985.

My mystical vision had flourished in my poems, particularly in *The Gates of Hell* (1969–1972), *The Pilgrim in the Garden* (1973–1974) and *Visions Near the Gates of Paradise* (1974–1975); and later in *The Fire-Flower* (1980) and *Beauty and Angelhood* (1981). These last two works, written while I was a Head of English, together with my first draft in September–October 1982 of my 'Preface to *Selected Poems*: On the New Baroque Consciousness and the Redefinition of Poetry', completed the forming of my vision and of my formative years.

It would still be another eleven years before I reached the end of my Mystic Way with complete Universalist consciousness (see p.49). A table on p.912 of *My Double Life 2: A Rainbow over the Hills* makes this clear:

Mystic Way behind Works
4 Mystic Lives, Dark Night of the Soul, Dark Night of the
Spirit (new powers/ordeals) and Unitive Life extracted from
Light appendices of *My Double Life 1* and 2, which show
Nicholas Hagger's Mystic Way as a whole

My Double Life 1: This Dark Wood
First Mystic Life: 20 July 1964–18 October 1965
Dark Night of the Soul: 19 October 1965–2 September 1971
Second Mystic Life: 3 September 1971–28 April 1972
Dark Night of the Spirit, new powers: 29 April 1972–12 May 1979

My Double Life 2: A Rainbow over the Hills
Dark Night of the Spirit, new powers: 29 April 1972–12 May 1979
(continued)
Third Mystic Life: 13 May 1979–31 October 1981
Dark Night of the Spirit, ordeals: 1 November 1981–7 April 1990
Fourth Mystic Life: 8 April 1990–6 December 1993
Unitive Life: 7 December 1993 to date

As the table shows, my Dark Night of the Spirit continued until 1990, and my Fourth Mystic Life, which coincided with my intense work on *The Fire and the Stones*, *Selected Poems: A Metaphysical's Way of Fire* and *The Universe and the Light*, was accompanied by 38 experiences of the Light in the four years between 8 April 1990 and 6 December 1993, each listed and dated in *My Double Life 2: A Rainbow over the Hills*, pp.909–910. The end of my Mystic Way and my permanent unitive life which had been instinctively Universalist can be dated to the last of the 38 experiences of the Light I had on 6 December 1993, as the table shows.

However, the turning-point was *The Fire-Flower*, which I assembled in the first half of 1980, together with its 'Preface on the Metaphysical Revolution', my first Preface which signalled that my formative years were over, and that I should now be translating my new Universalist consciousness into works. What followed in the 1980s (see above) was the beginning of this process of assembling Universalism and my 56 works in isolated dedication to my task. Once my 'Preface to *Selected Poems* on the New Baroque Consciousness and the Redefinition of Poetry' was in my mind, a sequel to my 'Preface on the Metaphysical Revolution', then I was already expanding my "new Baroque consciousness" into Universalism in seven disciplines.

In 1980 I still thought of my Baroque vision as blending the spiritual and the sensual, the Romantic and the Classical. It was only later that I came to see that my Baroque vision was an early form of my Universalist vision, which had just formed at the end of my formative years, towards the end of my Mystic Way.

3

The Wilderness Years, 1980–2020: The Unitive Vision, Shaping Universalism and its Structure

Petra

The day after we visited Little Petra we went to Petra, Burgon's "rose-red city half as old as time", which I had first heard of in the staff room at the University of Baghdad when a bespectacled lecturer named Turner announced, "I have just been to a wonderful place, Petra. You must go."

We were up at 5.30am and walked from the Mövenpick Hotel to the Visitors' Centre and then to the gate to Petra. From there it was a walk of several kilometres to get to the meeting place for our tour, so I paid 40 dinars for a horse and cart and we were trotted and galloped through the Siq, a chasm, a very narrow and high red-rose sandstone gorge, sometimes at breakneck speed.

Nabataean Treasury

We eventually emerged from the canyon and stopped at the Treasury, a two-storey façade of columns and

Nicholas Hagger before the Treasury, Petra

statues carved into the rock. It was probably built as a monumental tomb for the 1st-century-BC Nabataean King Aretas III and it featured in *Indiana Jones and the Last Crusade*. We weren't allowed to go inside. The king of the gods, Dushara, peered at us from all the rock-carved tombs as two round eyes on either side of a straight-line nose.

We clopped on along the Street of Façades past the Roman theatre, the Royal Tombs, and then the Nymphaeum, and along the Colonnaded Street to the Great Temple, which may have served as the Nabataeans' forum, and Qasr al-Bint temple, and reached the stopping-point in the basin near a restaurant where lunch would be served. We got out and, being early, sat on a wall and took in the enormous Nabataean town carved from rock in Roman times.

A caveman and a donkey

An elderly Bedouin came with a donkey and asked me persistently in English if I would like to ride up to the monastery at the top of the mountain ahead of us. We had been warned against doing this as the way was precipitous and we would not be covered by our insurance policies, and at first I declined. He talked to us while we sat on the wall in the early sunshine, and said he lived in a village he pointed out on the horizon. Before that he had lived in a nearby cave for twenty years.

I said, "You were a caveman."

He said, "Yes."

So I asked him what it was like being a caveman, how near the entrance he lived, what food he ate and how he prepared it, when he lit a fire. John the Baptist had lived in a cave, and this man I was talking to seemed to have lived in a similar way.

He said, "My son will lead the donkey up to the monastery," so I relented and, putting my trust in a caveman, agreed.

Ann asked, "Have you ever ridden a donkey?"

I said, "Not up a mountain. But if Jesus could enter Jerusalem on a donkey I'm sure I can ride one."

"At eighty?" she asked doubtfully.

I told her to sit in the restaurant over coffee while I was away.

I set off with the caveman's son, who was in his late teens, I judged, and spoke a little English. The path began with steps and was then uneven with boulders, and climbed steeply. There were 800 uneven steps in all on the way to the top. The donkey knew where to tread, and I sat in blind trust, holding on to a handle at the front of the saddle with both hands. I learned to lean the opposite way the donkey was turning to keep us both balanced. We rode higher and higher and the view was more and more dramatic, sometimes plunging precipices on either side, and the ground a long way below. The donkey knew the meaning of "fast" and "stop".

Eventually we stopped in a small village at the top of flights of steps and the boy pointed to the distant summit and said, "Monastery. I wait."

The monastery

I was on foot now, and it took me twenty minutes to reach the 40-metres-high monastery, a 1st-century-BC temple or Royal Tomb. It became a church. Christian hermits and monks, followers of the Desert Fathers

The monastery, Petra

who fled from persecution into the Egyptian desert at Scetis, lived there from ancient times to the 13th century, and scratched crosses on the rear walls. Hence it was called the 'monastery'.

It was carved in the yellow sandstone like the Treasury, it had a central doorway with columns on either side and an upper storey. I walked to a ridge and from a great height looked across the Jordan Rift Valley (which stretches from the Golan Heights to the Gulf of Aqaba) to the Negev desert of Southern Israel 4,000 feet below.

Burckhardt's descendant and two Kings

After a while I retraced my steps and found my donkey and returned to the restaurant, a bone-shaking journey. As I reached the bottom I saw one of our party also sitting on a donkey, just beginning his long ascent. I had chatted to him the previous day. He told me his name was Burckhardt, and when I raised my eyebrows he said, "Yes, I'm a direct descendant of Johann Ludwig Burckhardt, who discovered Petra." Petra was abandoned as a trading centre in the 8th century and sheltered nomadic shepherds until its ruins were rediscovered by the Swiss explorer in 1812.

This Burckhardt had overheard Ann tell a couple she was having coffee with that I had gone up on a donkey, and had immediately announced that that was what he wanted to do. He was crouched over his donkey in a white Panama hat, and holding on for dear life and looking petrified (no pun intended). As we passed I encouraged him: "It's not far now, you can do it." He looked up in terror and waved.

On the way back our horse and cart was stopped in the towering, narrow gorge of the Siq. King Abdullah of Jordan was showing the King of Norway the Treasury, surrounded by attendants. The King of Norway, a tall man in his seventies, had got out of a long open-topped convertible car and was formally dressed in a suit and tie. He looked out of place before the Nabataean monument.

Dushara and Ra

I sat and waited and reflected on Dushara, the king of the gods who was shown as a hemisphere with two circles either side of a line (two eyes either side of a nose). I had read that his name meant 'son of Shara', Shara being a mountain range, but I was sure he was the Nabataean form of the Egyptian sun-god Ra, who each day travelled from east to west. Ra was known at the time of the Great Pyramid, c.2580–2560BC, and the Nabataeans surfaced in the 6th century BC, and their Dushara was like the Egyptian sun-god Ra, all-seeing on top of a mountain but given eyes and a nose as he watched humans from his mountain top. I also saw the Nabataean god al-Uzza as Isis.

The next day we walked across to the Petra Museum and saw

hemispherical stone images of Dushara with eyes and nose. My religious Universalism still regarded the Nabataean hemispherical king of the gods as a form of the Egyptian sun-god.

Hejaz railway

We set off for Wadi Rum. On the way we stopped at a Hejaz railway station in the middle of nowhere. The Hejaz railway was begun in 1900 to take pilgrims to Medina, and from 1916, when he led the Arab Revolt against the Ottoman Empire with Sherif Hussein ibn Ali, Lawrence of Arabia frequently blew up the Hejaz railway (without ever severing the railway lines). We saw a reconstructed engine and original Turkish carriages with wooden slat seats. I clambered into one of them, and was back during the First World War.

Nicholas Hagger in a gun carriage on an Ottoman First-World-War train on the Hejaz railway near Wadi Rum on 5 March 2020

Wadi Rum and "the seven pillars or wisdom"

We stopped at Wadi Rum opposite the seven-pinnacled

A passenger carriage with wooden slat seats on an Ottoman First-World-War train on the Hejaz railway near Wadi Rum on 5 March 2020

Jabal al-Mazmar, known since the 1980s as "the seven pillars of wisdom"

mountain rising from the sand, Jabal al-Mazmar, known since the 1980s as "the seven pillars of wisdom" after Lawrence's book on the Arab Revolt. Lawrence's title referred to the seven great cities of the Middle East: Cairo, Smirna (Izmir), Constantinople (Istanbul), Beirut, Aleppo, Damascus and Medina (in the tradition of Ruskin's *The Seven Lamps of Architecture*).

We all got into several pink-cabined desert Jeeps. In our Jeep I sat in the open back in the warm sun with a view on all sides, concentrating within the moment. All around me was desert, a wilderness with mountainous rocks rising in places. There were shots of where we were going in the film *Lawrence of Arabia*.

We stopped to climb a high rock, and then again at Siq al-Mishran ('20 springs'), and to look at 4th-century-BC instructions to caravans on where to locate water scratched on a wall of rock.

Khazali canyon, a Bedouin, T.E. Lawrence and Peter O'Toole
Then we arrived at Khazali canyon, a curve of sand beneath mountains and a narrow cleft. We were taken into a long black Bedouin tent with a low concrete wall along its back on which there was a long carpet. We were invited to sit on the long carpet, and were served tea by a dozen Bedouin dressed in black.

I spoke to one of them, a man in his thirties, at some length: Awad Zubeidi. He told me in English that he was related to all the Bedouin in the tent, nine of whom were his brothers.

The long black Bedouin tent at Khazali canyon

I asked if he had had a grandfather. "Yes, Sheikh Jaleel." (I asked him to write it, and that was how he spelt it.)

"Did he know T.E. Lawrence?"

"Oh, yes, my grandfather was the top man, he was only under Hussein [the leader of the Arab Revolt]. They blew up trains together. They stole the Turkish gold and brought it here. They distributed it to the villages nearby as thanks for joining the Arab Revolt. Lawrence slept opposite the entrance to this tent, near that rocky mountain you can see." Through the tent's open entrance I could see a

Awad Zubeidi, whose grandfather blew up trains with T.E. Lawrence

mountain rising 200 yards away. "This tent was here in those days. Lawrence had his meals in here. He sat where you are sitting on the low wall. My grandfather died in 1920. Lawrence's descendant, aged 90, came here two years ago." He said he lived in Deesa village, in Orbit, a collection of round tents with air-conditioning.

He added, "The film *Lawrence of Arabia* was here. All the actors were here. O'Toole who played Lawrence was in this tent. He sat near where you are sitting."

I have told in *My Double Life 1: This Dark Wood* how I met Peter O'Toole in Oxford in 1960 and at his request took him and his chauffeur back into Worcester College and discussed *The Merchant of Venice* as he was playing Shylock in Stratford-upon-Avon – he wanted an academic perspective – and how we were so absorbed in Shakespeare we forgot the time, and at midnight, when the College was locked, I had to get him and his chauffeur over a nine-foot-high gate. I have told in *My Double Life 2: A Rainbow over the Hills* how O'Toole turned up on a cruise round Spain and Portugal to Rome I was on in 2010, and how I greeted him, "Peter, may I say hello from fifty years ago," and he had complete recall of the episode, correcting some of my details as I reminded him of what happened with many of the other passengers forming a ring round us and listening.

Still in Wadi Rum, we went on to watch the sun set over a distant mountain range. The sun dropped a diameter every four minutes. I climbed a rock and sat and watched the sun slide behind a mountain peak from 5.15 to 5.30, by which time dusk was becoming twilight. There were tiny mauve irises in the desert as I returned to the Jeep.

We drove to the Captain's Cabin and had open-air tea and then a dinner of lamb and chicken, which had been cooked in hot ashes under the sand. By now the stars shone brightly overhead.

The Middle East in the ruins of the Ottoman Empire

I asked myself what Lawrence had achieved by helping to overthrow the Ottoman Empire. He had contributed to winning the First World War, but also to the chaotic Arab world I had encountered.

I thought of the collapse of the Ottoman Empire following Lawrence's Arab Revolt and the fragmentation of Islam and its sects, and of the Islamic Reformation as Iranian and Iraqi Shiites challenged the traditional Sunni dominance, and I was again reminded of my historical Universalism, of my study of 25 civilisations which showed parallel events in different civilisations. And I mourned the legacy of war and discord throughout the Middle East that had been left behind in the ruins of the Ottoman Empire.

Boarding our ship at Aqaba

We got onto our coach, which had driven by road and waited for us, and were driven for an hour to Aqaba, which T.E. Lawrence's Arabs captured from the Turks. We then had to queue to board our ship.

MS Serenissima

Each of us had a temperature check on a finger for coronavirus. I failed and was directed to a doctor on the quayside, who tried on a finger on my other hand, and I passed.

We were later shocked that a British couple from Wales had been barred from joining the ship for having Covid and had been sent home. That evening it was announced that Israel had denied entry to all on our ship.

*

Shaping Universalism: the progression of my works and of my Universalism during my wilderness years

The wilderness of Wadi Rum set me thinking about my own wilderness years as I developed Universalism in isolation and reflected it in different disciplines in 56 books. Later, sitting on the hind deck of our ship, *MS Serenissima*, in the dark with Aqaba distant from our quay, I reflected on my shaping of Universalism in my wilderness.

Moving away from nationalism and populism

I was aware that I had had to move away from nationalism and populism: the nationalisms that had surrounded me in Iraq, China, Libya and among the African liberation movements, and the populism of dictators like Kaseem, Mao, Gaddafi and the African guerrilla leaders and terrorists I met. I had been working for global Britain while extending British influence in Iraq and in Japan – where I taught English Literature, helped plan Prince and Princess Hitachi's State visit to Britain and promoted British trade during my side-job work with the Ministry of International Trade and Industry (MITI) – and in my intelligence work in Libya. Moving away from my intelligence work and my newspaper articles for *The Times*, another form of nationalism, and from the demagogues of modern political life which I had reflected in works such as 'Zeus's Ass', and towards federalism, sent me deeper into my own wilderness and further from the mainstream of English political life.

I believed that I could see a solution to all the world's problems by wandering in my own wilderness, alone, and that my writings would be inspired from the beyond to say what was needed. I was aware that my view from the wilderness would be unpopular in times of self-indulgence and *faux* populist nationalism, which I would expose in many of my writings, most recently in *Fools' Paradise* and *Fools' Gold*.

My Baroque vision developed into my Universalism, both out of 'The Silence'

After the first of my four drafts of what became the Preface to my *Selected Poems: A Metaphysical's Way of Fire*, 'On the New Baroque Consciousness and the Redefinition of Poetry', in 1982, I carried on my writing while running my own school and staff in Essex and preparing to leave teaching in London, and for two years became a small publisher of books on world issues to get to know the global market.

My 'Preface to *A Baroque Vision*' details the connection between my Baroque vision and my Universalism. The connection can be found in my poem 'Night Visions in Charlestown', first written in 1983, "So hail the Universal Age of Light!.../New rising of Baroque in its own right." Also in my diary entries for 7 April 1985, "Artists create the next age, which will be a Baroque one, uniting Classicism and Romanticism", and on 9 April 1985: "I am a Universalist.... Universalism.... That is the new philosophy, which has characteristics of the Baroque.... A Universal Age." In 1985 I was already turning from "a new Baroque age" to a coming Universal or Universalist Age "which has Baroque features".

In 1987 I attended the Frankfurt Book Fair as a small publisher and spoke with a German representative of Fischers, Reiner Stach. I told him I was now going to be an author writing for another publisher, and I told him about my coming work *The Fire and the Stones*, which sees 25 civilisations growing out of mystical visions, and he said, "You have developed a universalist theory of world civilisations." His use of 'universalist' brought me back to Universalism.

On 29 April 1989 I received much of the 'Preface to *The Fire and the Stones*' in sleep and got up and wrote: "A new baroque Age, an Age of Universalism, is ahead." In my diary for the same day I wrote: "I believe I have devised a new discipline.... I have devised Universalism."

I could now see that my Baroque vision was behind my Universalism and had developed into Universalism, and that both my Baroque vision and my early Universalism had come out of Part III of 'The Silence', written in 1965–1966.

My Universalism, 1991–2000

A look at the chronological progression of Universalism in my works is revealing as at first sight the progression appears haphazard.

The Fire and the Stones, with its Preface entitled 'Introduction to the New Universalism', came out in 1991 together with *Selected Poems: A Metaphysical's Way of Fire*, with its Preface on the New Baroque. There was a launch at the Museum of London, and the historian Asa Briggs and the poets Kathleen Raine and David Gascoyne made speeches. The two books presented historical and mystical Universalism regarding civilisations in relation to the mystical vision of the Fire or Light, and literary and mystical Universalism in relation to *experiencing* the Fire or Light along the Mystic Way.

I then turned to philosophy. *The Universe and the Light* (1993) was subtitled *A New View of the Universe and Reality and of Science and Philosophy, Essays on the Philosophy of Universalism and the Metaphysical Revolution*. I was now openly a philosophical Universalist.

In December 1993 I had reached the end of my Mystic Way, and I returned to literary and mystical Universalism in poetry and autobiography. *Collected Poems 1958–1993: A White Radiance* followed in 1994, along with two statements of my Mystic Way: *Awakening to the Light: Diaries 1958–1967*, and *A Mystic Way: A Spiritual Autobiography*. I was now a literary and mystical Universalist.

I then focused on literature in *A Spade Fresh with Mud*, short stories (1995); *The Warlords* (two verse plays on the Second World War, 1995); and then *Overlord*, an epic poem on the Second World War which came out in four parts between 1995 and 1997. A second volume of short stories, *A Smell of Leaves and Summer*, came out in 1995, and another verse play, *The Tragedy of Prince Tudor*, appeared in 1999, along with two more volumes of short stories: *Wheeling Bats and a Harvest Moon* and *The Warm Glow of the Monastery Courtyard*.

I interrupted this flow of literary Universalist works to bring out *The One and the Many* in 1999, which was subtitled *Universalism and the*

Vision of Unity. This cemented the philosophical Universalism of *The Universe and the Light*.

My Universalism, 2001–2010

The next round of books took me back to historical Universalism: *The Syndicate: The Story of the Coming World Government* (2004), which exposed an attempt to bring in a world government by an undemocratic *élite*; and *The Secret History of the West: The Influence of Secret Organisations on Western History from the Renaissance to the 20th Century* (2005), which focused on all the revolutions since the Renaissance and the involvement of *élites*.

I interrupted my historical Universalism to bring out 'collecteds' within literary Universalism: *Classical Odes* (2006); *Overlord*, one-volume edition (2006); *Collected Poems 1958–2006* (2006); *Collected Verse Plays* (2007), which includes five verse plays (including *Ovid Banished* and *The Rise of Oliver Cromwell*); and *Collected Stories* (2007), which includes five volumes of short stories.

In 2006 I had returned to mystical, religious and historical Universalism. I updated *The Fire and the Stones* in two volumes: *The Light of Civilization: How the Vision of God Has Inspired All the Great Civilizations* (2006); and *The Rise and Fall of Civilizations: Why Civilizations Rise and Fall and What Happens When They End* (2008). Between these two volumes I began my American historical trilogy with *The Secret Founding of America* (2007). My travelogue *The Last Tourist in Iran*, on my visit to the Shiite world to prepare for an epic poem on Islam, appeared in 2008.

The Surfer on the edge of the expanding shuttlecock-shaped universe

My philosophical Universalism was carried to its fullest extent in *The New Philosophy of Universalism: The Infinite and the Law of Order* (2009). It introduced Hagger's paradox, in the tradition of Zeno's paradoxes: a Surfer is surfing on the crest-of-the-wave-like edge of our expanding shuttlecock-shaped universe, his feet are in space-time, where is the rest of him? The answer is, paradoxically: in the infinite.

I then returned to literary and historical Universalism with my travelogue *The Libyan Revolution: Its Origins and Legacy, A Memoir and Assessment* (2009); and my epic poem about Islam *Armageddon: The Triumph of Universal Order, An Epic on the War on Terror and of Holy-War Crusaders* (2010), which I had written in 2008 and 2009 about the events following 9/11.

Armageddon took me on to philosophical and political Universalism. The global sweep of my second epic poem (25,000 lines of blank verse as opposed to the 41,000 lines of blank verse of *Overlord*) led me forward to consider a world government not ruled by *élites*: *The World Government: A Blueprint for a Universal World State* (2010). This was a work of philosophy that focused on political Universalism and its practical expression in a World State.

My focus on a World State was one aspect within my Universalist project, which also included my epic poem on 9/11 and the unity of the universe and humankind and the integration of all disciplines that I had presented in *The New Philosophy of Universalism*.

My Universalism, 2011–2020

I was then back in historical and political Universalism and wrote the second part of my American historical trilogy, *The Secret American Dream: The Creation of a Good New World Order with the Power to Abolish War, Poverty and Disease* (2011).

I swung back to literary Universalism with *A New Philosophy of Literature: The Fundamental Theme and Unity of World Literature, The Vision of the Infinite and the Universalist Literary Tradition* (2012). This identified the fundamental theme of world literature as a quest for the One and a condemnation of social follies and vices, a pair of themes, one of which always predominates in a particular time or era, in accordance with my Universalist reconciliation of opposites expressed in the formula $+A + -A = 0$ (see p.32).

The cover of *A New Philosophy of Literature* shows the pediment of Copped Hall, a local country house, and I was taken into local history and autobiography. I wrote a work of local history, *A View of Epping Forest* (2012), to focus on localism as opposed to globalism, and this led me to my autobiographical Universalism:

My Double Life 1: This Dark Wood, and *My Double Life 2: A Rainbow over the Hills* (both 2015), which described my Mystic Way, my intelligence work and my books; and the pattern behind my life – and all people's lives – based on episodes, which I discovered in the course of writing these two works.

  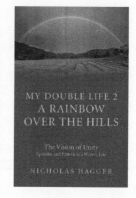

This was followed by a return to literary Universalism, selections from my short stories and poems, *Selected Stories: Follies and Vices of the Modern Elizabethan Age* and *Selected Poems: Quest for the One* (both 2015). These showed that my short stories and poems have followed both aspects of the fundamental theme of world literature, as I set out in *A New Philosophy of Literature.* I then wrote the first of my three masques: *The Dream of Europa: The Triumph of Peace* (2015) and assembled a new volume of poems: *Life Cycle and Other New Poems 2006–2016* (2016). I then brought out my sixth volume of short stories, *The First Dazzling Chill of Winter* (2016).

I now returned to cultural, historical and political Universalism.

The third work in my American historical trilogy came out: *The Secret American Destiny: The Hidden Order of the Universe and the Seven Disciplines of World Culture* (2016). This was on cultural Universalism. I brought out *Peace for our Time: A Reflection on War and Peace and a Third World War* (2018), which includes an account of my speech on political Universalism to 7,000 people in Manila when I received the Gusi Peace Prize for Literature in 2016.

I then carried political Universalism as far as it can go by bringing out *World State: Introduction to the United Federation of the World, How a Democratically-Elected World Government Can Replace the UN and Bring Peace* and its companion volume *World Constitution: Constitution for the United Federation of the World* (both 2018). These two works present the World State, the Promised Land, in as great detail as it is possible to imagine, with all the 850 constituencies for a Lower House to be initially based in the UN General Assembly. The structure and constitution of a new World State are both set out.

I followed this up with literary and political Universalism. I confronted the UK's referendum to leave the EU. I brought out my second masque, *King Charles the Wise: The Triumph of Universal Peace* (2018), about Minerva's visit to Prince Charles to review the way forward after Brexit; *Visions of England: Poems Selected by The Earl of Burford* (2019), 102 poems on places in England; and *Fools' Paradise: The Voyage of a Ship of Fools from Europe, A Mock-Heroic Poem on Brexit* (2020), which deals with Brexit during May's premiership.

My Universalism, from 2021

I followed this up with more literary and political Universalism. A third masque is in production, *The Coronation of King Charles: The Triumph of Universal Harmony* (2021), which looks ahead to the coming Carolingian Age that will begin to bring in a World State. *Fools' Gold: The Voyage of a Ship of Fools Seeking Gold, A Mock-Heroic Poem on Brexit and English Exceptionalism* (2022) is a sequel to *Fools' Paradise* and deals with Brexit during Johnson's premiership.

Further works in different stages of production are five overviews – selections, 'collecteds' or reflections – that focus on my Universalism: *Selected Letters: Nicholas Hagger's Letters on his 55 Literary and Universalist works; Collected Prefaces: Nicholas Hagger's Prefaces to 55 of his Literary and Universalist works; A Baroque Vision: 100 Verse Selections from 50 Volumes; The Essentials of Universalism: A Philosophy of the Unity of the Universe and Humankind, of Interconnected Disciplines and a World State, 75 Prose Selections from 25 Works;* and now *The Promised Land: Universalism and a Coming World State* (all 2022). I was not aware on the ship that I would receive a new title in sleep on 11 February 2021, *The*

Fall of the West: The Story Behind the Levelling-Down of the West and the Shift of Power to the East in the 21st Century (2023), which will take my historical and cultural Universalism to its fullest extent.

This cluster of books shows an 80-year-old looking back on his works: on how they have been reflected in his letters; on the Prefaces he has written; on the evolution of Universalism from the Baroque vision; on the essential principles of his Universalism; and on how his Universalism leads to a World State and the Promised Land.

View from Mount Nebo

Progression as a seeding, propagating process

It is very apparent, when my works are spread out like the kingdoms of the earth and viewed from a great height as from Mount Nebo, that each of the seven disciplines within which I have written – mystical, literary, historical, religious, philosophical, political and

cultural Universalism – has helped bring future works to birth. The chronological progression of my works during my wilderness years is a seeding process in which one inspires and propagates another, which in turn inspires two or three more. But when viewed at the end of the process they seem to be neatly arranged, like the mosaic floors of the early Christian churches in Madaba.

Mosaic in Madaba

Nicholas Hagger's front covers for his 56 books

The structure of Universalism within each discipline following the seemingly higgledy-piggledy, random process of progression
I have reflected on the chronological progression and propagation of my seeded works, which have fertilised new works in a cross-disciplinary process as one discipline interconnects with others and

have collectively developed and shaped my Universalism. Reflecting on the results of this seemingly higgledy-piggledy, random process in each of the seven disciplines – mystical, literary, historical, religious, philosophical, political and cultural Universalism – suggests that far from each of these disciplines being developed in a random way, their progression seems to be inspired and guided, and has resulted in each discipline's having a progressive structure that carries Universalism as far as it can go.

Western society is secular, and to a mystic is therefore wilderness-like, and in each of the disciplines there is a movement away from the purely secular to the consequences of the mystical, of my Metaphysical Revolution.

My mystical Universalism

It can now be seen, when viewed from above as from the top of Mount Nebo, that my mystical Universalism was rooted in my Christian upbringing and church-going and daily chapel at school, and an awakening in London before I went up to Oxford. It grew out of my awareness of the Islamic mystics during my journeys within Iraq, to Fallujah, Babylon and Basra, and my daily walk past the Baghdad libraries and ruins of the Abbasid Caliphs' buildings in Baghdad, the gilded domes of the mosques and the five-times-a-day calls to prayer by the muezzins through the loudspeakers on mosques. In Baghdad I learned about the mystic Suhrawardi. The Ottomans unified the Islamic world, and although Shiites followed their own way they knew their place.

My awareness of mystical Universalism increased in Japan when I visited Zen temples and meditation centres and meditated, and learned about enlightenment and briefly opened to the Light – before I had my breakthrough vision of an inner sun in 1965, as I described in 'The Silence'.

My extreme experiences in Libya put me on a Mystic Way of purgation and a Dark Night of the Soul, which took me to my illumination in London in 1971 while I was involved in dangerous intelligence work; and, after numerous experiences of the Light in the following years and then a Dark Night of the Spirit, to my present unitive vision which instinctively sees the universe and all humankind as a unity, One, and all disciplines as interconnected – as Universalist.

It was as though I was guided by being located near influences that would take me to my predetermined destiny. In *The Fire and the Stones* (1991) I show that all civilisations begin with a mystic's vision of the Light, which passes into a religion that holds so long as the civilisation has a metaphysical vision, but fades when the civilisation turns secular. No religion's dominance lasts for ever and no civilisation lasts forever. I reinforced my statement of the metaphysical vision in *The One and the Many* (1999). I updated the mystical vision of *The Fire and the Stones*  in *The Light of Civilization* (2006) and *The Rise and Fall of Civilizations* (2008).

My literary Universalism

My literary Universalism can be seen to have grown out of my early writings and my extensive reading of European literature in my gap year before I went to university; and my awareness of other cultures which began with my time in Greece and Iraq, the journeys I made through the Middle East and later the Far East, and later again in North Africa.

My early poetic works in Japan, *The Early Education and Making of a Mystic* and 'The Silence' (both 1965–1966), were central to my literary Universalism. My visits to Russia and China in 1966 were particularly productive, and produced 'Archangel' and my vision of a united world in the Cathedral of the Archangel in the Kremlin in 1966. (I told an audience in Moscow in 2019 that I first glimpsed a World State looking at the icon of the Archangel Michael there.)

My literary Universalism began with the poems, verse plays and short stories that were later collected in my *Selected Poems: A Metaphysical's Way of Fire*, *Collected Poems 1958–1993: A White Radiance*, *Collected Poems 1958–2005*, *Collected Verse Plays* and *Collected Stories*;

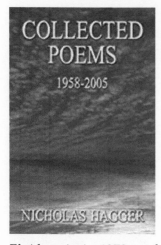

and with a selection from my diaries and an autobiography. It expanded after my 'Night Visions in Charlestown' (1983); and in the course of my writing my first epic poem about the Second World War. My subject was global and my consciousness expanded to include the global material I was presenting.

My early experiences seem to have prepared me for this poem. I had met Churchill (our local MP) and Montgomery while still a schoolboy, I had been to El Alamein in 1970, and I had discussed my coming epic with Ezra Pound and had modelled myself on Homer, Virgil and Milton. After 25 years' research I had a vision in Pisa, Italy of two works completed – my epic *Overlord* and *Classical Odes*, which presents the culture of Europe – and I went to a D-Day celebration in 1994 (50 years after 1944). This took me into *The Warlords, Parts One and Two*, two verse plays, and then, in four volumes (1995–1996), to *Overlord*. My hero was an American, Eisenhower, and I was mindful from my study of civilisations in Japan that epic poems are produced by growing civilisations and that the only major growing civilisation today is the North-American civilisation.

Classical Odes, which I also saw as a finished work in Pisa, contains

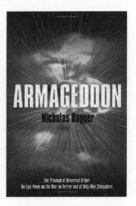

317 classical odes that reflect buildings, ruins and places in European culture. It embodies the European civilisation's cultural tradition, and the great historical wealth that the European Union presides over. This work developed my literary Universalism, and like *Overlord* came from the beyond.

The American vision in *Overlord* took me to Otley Hall, which was on the market soon after I finished the book: a historic house where America was founded from as Bartholomew Gosnold interviewed the crews there for his voyages in 1602, when he named Martha's Vineyard after his daughter, and in 1606–1607, when he was number two during the founding of the colony at Jamestown. I ran Otley Hall as a historic house for seven years and created a knot-garden and other Tudor gardens with the help of Sylvia Landsberg, creator of five of the six medieval gardens in English institutions and author of *The Medieval Garden*, and much of Otley Hall's tradition and history has found its way into *Classical Odes*.

This led me to be interested in an American epic, which the curator of the Richmond Museum, Virginia suggested I should write. I was overtaken by 9/11, and eventually wrote an epic about George W. Bush hunting down bin Laden, which draws on American history. I followed the news and took two years to write my next epic, *Armageddon*, in 2008 and 2009. To obtain local detail for Bush's American war on al-Qaeda, unable to go back to Iraq (a war zone now) I went to Iran and drew on my experiences there.

I also wrote my statement of the fundamental theme of world literature in *A New Philosophy of Literature* (2012).

The backbone of my literary Universalism has been the poems in my four *Selected Poems* (*A Metaphysical's Way of Fire*, *Quest for the One*, *Visions of England* and *A Baroque Vision*) and my two *Collected Poems*, and *Life Cycle and Other New Poems*; my diaries; my two epic poems; my *Classical Odes*; my five verse plays; my three masques; my three autobiographies; my two travelogues; my 1,200 short stories (with another 200 waiting to be published); my *Selected Letters*; and *A New Philosophy of Literature*, my statement of the fundamental theme of world literature. My fourth *Selected Poems*, *A Baroque Vision*, contains 100 verse selections from these works and shows how my Baroque vision became Universalist.

A NEW PHILOSOPHY OF LITERATURE

THE FUNDAMENTAL THEME AND UNITY OF WORLD LITERATURE

The Vision of the Infinite and the Universalist Literary Tradition

NICHOLAS HAGGER

Looking back, I cannot help feeling again that I seem to have been guided to the places I would need for my literary works.

My historical Universalism

My historical Universalism began with my contact with the Greek and Roman civilisations, by which I measured the achievements of the European civilisation, and was followed by my contact with what I came to understand was the Mesopotamian civilisation, all the early historical places in Iraq I used to visit, including Babylon; and then the Arab civilisation. It continued when my journey took me to the Israelite and Syrian civilisations. And later the Japanese, Chinese and Byzantine-Russian civilisations.

In Japan, I was asked in 1966 to teach a year's course to the postgraduate students to be entitled 'The Decline of the West'. I asked, just over 20 years after the end of the war, "What if I don't think that the West is declining?" I was told, "Professor Hagger, we want the course to be called 'The Decline of the West'."

And so I put together a year's course based on Gibbon's *Decline and Fall of the Roman Empire*, Spengler's *Decline of the West* and Toynbee's 12-volume *A Study of History*. I taught a parallel course on world history to Emperor Hirohito's second son, Prince Hitachi.

While doing all this I saw a fourth way in which civilisations begin with a mystical vision round which a religion forms as people gather round it, and it becomes a civilisation. It took me 25 years to research what I had discovered.

The turning-point that made me get on with the writing of it was when, as a small publisher in the mid-1980s, I explained the project to a German at the Frankfurt Book Fair in 1987, and he said, "You have developed a universalist theory of world civilisations." (See p.60.) I gave it the title *The Fire and the Stones*. It was later updated as two volumes, *The Light of Civilization* and *The Rise and Fall of Civilizations*.

My historical Universalism drew strength from my study of post-Renaissance revolutions and secret societies, *The Secret History of the West*, and its sequel about a present-day *élite*, *The Syndicate*. I was dealing with the bad, self-interested New World Order, and this left the way clear for me to research a good New World Order.

Having acquired Otley Hall, where the voyage to Jamestown that founded America was planned, I visited America in 1998 and wrote a poem, 'American Liberty Quintet', which I dedicated to Bill Clinton. Drawn into America by the visit of the Governor of Virginia and the First Lady, for whom I hosted a lunch at Otley Hall, I went on to get to grips with American globalism and wrote my American trilogy about the Freemasonic role in the founding of the

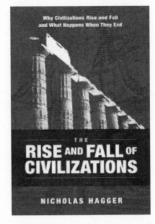

United States, the secret American dream to create a World State and America's destiny to reunite world culture.

Again, it seems as if I was guided to places that advanced my historical Universalism.

My religious Universalism

My religious Universalism began with my church-going and daily chapel at school, and my reading at school of Robert Graves' *The Greek Myths* and his encyclopaedic information on the Greek gods, and my interest in the Egyptian religion of Ra, the Sun-god.

It gathered strength from my daily experience of Islam in Baghdad, and my research into the Mesopotamian gods of Babylon and the myth of Tammuz. It increased during the tour of Amman, Damascus and Jerusalem, where I saw three religions (Judaism, Christianity and Islam) co-existing.

It gathered more strength in Japan where I experienced Zen and went into Buddhism and read extensively from Lin Yutang's *The Wisdom of China and India*, and from my own religious experiences in Japan and later when I visited eleven countries on my way home.

It strengthened even more when I saw a man in the Libyan desert against a backdrop of sky and red earth. By then I was halfway down a Mystic Way of awakening, purgation, illumination, Dark Night of the Soul and Dark Night of the Spirit, before being born anew into an instinctive unitive vision.

I was reminded of my religious Universalism when I passed the hill of Elijah and stood near the River Jordan, which Jesus crossed to meet John the Baptist, who had come from his cave; and in Kerak, when I contemplated the parallel between the cruel Crusaders and the cruel terrorists of Islamic State.

Jerusalem belongs to three religions just as India belongs to six (Muslims, Christians, Sikhs, Jains, Buddhists and Zoroastrians). I came to see that the Light is common to all religions and that in terms of the Light all religions are one. There are many paths up a mountain but there is one God at the top, associated with the sun or Light. As Donne wrote:

> On a huge hill,
> Cragged and steep, Truth stands, and he that will
> Reach her, about must and about must go.
> ('Satire III')

My religious Universalism gathered strength from my visit to Egypt in 1970, and in 2005 from my experience of St Catherine's monastery, Sinai, near where Moses spent 40 years in the wilderness. It found expression in *The Fire and the Stones* and in my two updating works *The Light of Civilization* and *The Rise and Fall of Civilizations*.

My philosophical Universalism

My philosophical Universalism began with my knowledge of Greek philosophy, the Greek texts of Plato and Aristotle I read at Chigwell School and their view of the universe. It continued with my reading of *Great Philosophers of the West* and *Great Philosophers of the East*, two Grey Arrow books I had by my bedside at Oxford. I did not know that the author, the metaphysical philosopher E.W.F. Tomlin, would be my boss as British Council Representative in

Japan and would discuss Western and Eastern philosophy and the Absolute over dinner with me, both as my host and my guest.

It continued again with the Arab metaphysical philosophers I heard about in Iraq, such as Suhrawardi.

The view of my unitive vision that the universe is a unity strengthened until it became *The Universe and the Light* (1993).

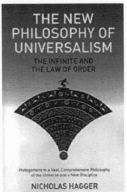

From April 1993 until October 1994 I led the Universalist Group of Philosophers in Uxbridge, at which a dozen philosophers had intensive all-day meetings to develop philosophical Universalism, and out of these meetings came the new perspectives in first *The One and the Many* (1999) and then *The New Philosophy of Universalism* (2009).

My political Universalism

My political Universalism began with my observations of dictatorial nationalism in Iraq and my visit to Jerusalem in 1961, and my growing sense that the world could draw together: my vision in front of the icon of Archangel Michael in the Cathedral of the Archangel on 9 June 1966. It continued in my poem or Prince Hitachi's birthday, 'Epistle to His Imperial Highness, on His Birthday' (August 1966).

My gropings towards a World State continued through the global view of the world during World War II in *Overlord* and *The Syndicate*, which saw a plan for a world government dominated by a self-interested *élite*.

In 2007 I visited Persepolis in Iran – I had it to myself because of a fraught international situation – and pondered on the Grand Staircase of All Nations and the ruins of the Gate of All Nations (or Entrance-Hall of All Countries), built by Xerxes I (who reigned 486–465BC), the successor to Darius I (who founded Persepolis). Xerxes I is mentioned, along with the god Ahura Mazda, on an inscription in the Gate. Soon after the first Persian invasion of Greece in 492BC, the Persians envisaged a Gate through which 'All Nations' could pass – Persia ruled 22 nations under Xerxes I – and I saw this Gate as both reflecting the nations ruled by the Persian Empire, and attempting to create a united world whose nations would come to Persepolis, a unity that would end all conflicts.

The Apadana's East Stairs have walls on either side adorned with carvings (from the reign of Darius I) of Persian soldiers with lances and shields, which anticipate Pheidias's sculptures on the Parthenon, and I passed the huge Treasury (over 120 metres long and nearly 62 metres wide), news of which was brought from Persepolis to Greece during the Persian invasions between 492 and 479BC and led to the building of the Athenian Treasury on the sacred island of Delos from 478BC. In *The Last Tourist in Iran* I saw early Persian culture as having inspired the 5th-century-BC Greek culture which included Pheidias's sculptures and the Athenian Treasury on Delos.

My turning-point was *The New Philosophy of Universalism* (2009), which included a section on political Universalism and other Universalisms. This led me to write *The World Government*, which was on a positive, democratic World State, and eventually (after *Peace for our Time*) *World State* and *World Constitution*. These two works take political Universalism as far as it will go.

My cultural Universalism

My cultural Universalism began with my awareness of many cultures during my journey in 1961, and of my time in the Middle and Far East, especially my journey home when in 1967 I stopped off in eleven countries.

While researching *World State* I wrote *The Secret American Destiny* (2016) about a coming communal world culture in which secular and metaphysical aspects are reconciled. According to cultural Universalism, all cultures contain the two opposites of metaphysical and secular aspects, and a world culture is therefore a crucible that reconciles these opposites: $+A + -A = 0$.

My wilderness years

In each of the seven Universalisms there is a structure within each discipline, and I have developed each as far as it can go. The giants of the Renaissance Leonardo da Vinci and Michelangelo were at home in several disciplines, and I had somehow become a Renaissance man. Yet again I cannot help feeling that I was guided into places and roles that helped me complete my creation of Universalism.

I progressed all these seven aspects of Universalism during my 40 years in the wilderness of a secular culture (1980–2020), while calling for a Metaphysical Revolution that will create an awareness that metaphysical aspects co-exist with secular aspects in world culture, and are reconciled within its cultural Universalism.

My first public call for a Metaphysical Revolution was at the launch of *The Fire and the Stones* and *Selected Poems: A Metaphysical's Way of Fire* in 1991, see my speech in *The Essentials of Universalism*, no.7. The Metaphysical Revolution is mentioned in the Introduction to *The Fire and the Stones* and in the first Preface to *Selected Poems: A Metaphysical's Way of Fire*, 'On the New Baroque Consciousness and the Redefinition of Poetry'; and in its second Preface (later the Preface to *The Fire-Flower*), 'Preface to the Metaphysical Revolution'.

All seven interconnecting disciplines of Universalism can be found in *The Essentials of Universalism: 75 Prose Selections from 25 Works* (2022).

Looking back on the seven Universalisms after emerging from the Jordanian wilderness of Wadi Rum, I was struck by the seven-pinnacled mountain Jabal al-Mazmar ('The Mountain of the Plague'), known since the 1980s as "the seven pillars of wisdom" after T.E. Lawrence's book on the Arab Revolt. Lawrence named his book after seven Middle-Eastern cities, but nevertheless the seven pillars of wisdom on this small mountain can also represent the seven Universalisms in the wilderness in this time of plague.

4

Universalism's Principles: Ten Commandments and the Muses

From Aqaba past Mount Sinai

Next morning we walked in Aqaba. We went to the *suq* and tasted spices. Then we drove round the town, which nestled beneath mountains to its rear and on either side. We stopped at the Fort by the sea, which was occupied by Sharif Hussein bin Ali, the leader of the Arab Revolt, and T.E. Lawrence, a Mamluk Fort built between 1510 and 1517 as a caravanserai for Hajj pilgrims travelling to Mecca and Medina which proved a vital location in the overthrow of the Ottomans.

From Aqaba our ship, *MS Serenissima*, with 90 passengers steamed through the dark along the Gulf of Aqaba, with Saudi Arabia on our port (left) side and the Sinai Peninsula in Egypt on our starboard (right) side. We passed near Horeb, Mount Sinai, in the dark, and rounded the lights of Sharm El Sheikh in Egypt and made our way into the Red Sea. Mount Sinai, where Moses received the Ten Commandments from Yahweh, was beyond Sharm El Sheikh.

Moses receiving the Ten Commandments on Mount Sinai, 1877 lithograph (left), and (right) Moses receiving the Ten Commandments from Yahweh on Mount Sinai, painting by Gebhard Fugel

I thought back to our time in Sharm El Sheikh in 2005, and how we journeyed to St Catherine's monastery, where Yahweh spoke to Moses from the burning bush beneath Mount Sinai. I thought back to the third month after the Exodus from Egypt when Moses climbed to the top of Mount Sinai, and how Yahweh revealed the Ten Commandments to him there.

As the ship steamed on up the Gulf of Suez, with Mount Sinai on our starboard (right) side, I reflected on my own struggle to receive the ten principles of Universalism. In my case it was a process involving a number of attempts, which I saw spread out beneath me as if below Mount Nebo.

*

Attempts to define Universalism's characteristics in earlier works
In the course of my 40 years in the wilderness I came up with several attempts to define Universalism's characteristics and tenets with a view to putting them in a manifesto.

12 beliefs of the Universalist Revolution, which would have 7 consequences in modern European thought and culture
Beliefs are strongly-held convictions, firm opinions.
I first approached the listing of the main features of Universalism from a philosophical angle on pp.132–135 of *The One and the Many* (1999), when I summarised the Universalist Revolution's beliefs in 12 points, which would have 7 consequences in modern European thought and culture; and I repeated them on pp.340–344 of *The New Philosophy of Universalism* (2009):

The Declaration or manifesto summarises what the Universalist Revolution believes, in 12 points. The Universalist Revolution declares:
1. The phenomenal world of the senses is not ultimate reality. There is an invisible infinite world behind the finite one. This perception challenges and sweeps aside humanism, materialism, Rationalism,

Empiricism, scepticism, mechanism, positivism and reductionism in all disciplines.

2.   We can know the One beyond and behind the phenomenal world of the senses, the vision of the metaphysical Reality of Fire or Light.

3.   Each one of us is therefore not a reductionist collection of atoms on a dunghill whose mind is mere brain function, or a solely social ego, but a being with an immortal, invisible body within his or her visible body (as the long mystical Tradition holds), a soul and spirit with consciousness of the infinite.

4.   Universalism, a post-Existentialist development of Vitalism, states the universe in terms of metaphysical Being, or Fire or Light, which manifests into the structure of the universe. It is a science that studies the structure of the universal Whole, which includes every possible concept of the mind and the metaphysical layers of manifesting Being. It also studies perception of the One, the soul's experience of the Fire or Light, which is received in consciousness and can be reported phenomenologically (through a study of consciousness or perception) in 'self-reports' which are quasi-empirical.

It is also a practical contemplative philosophy that 'existentialises' metaphysical Reality, whose universal energy can be known existentially in the contemplative vision. It contacts the universal energy of the Fire or Light, the metaphysical Reality, and applies its consequences to all disciplines. Universalism focuses on all human beings in the world and does not confine its attention to Christians or any one group.

5.   The central idea of our European civilisation and culture, and of all civilisations and cultures, is the metaphysical vision of Reality as Fire or Light which is beyond the world of the senses but knowable within the universal Whole.

6.   This documented vision of Reality should be reinstated in philosophy to sweep away logical positivism, linguistic analysis, structuralism and Existentialism.

7.   This vision of Reality has inspired the growth of all civilisations in history. History studies the universal Whole and should have a

global perspective, and the metaphysical vision which is common to all civilisations is the best basis for a common world culture.

8. This vision of Reality should have a place in the spectrum of literature – novels, plays and poems – and exist alongside and challenge secular, technique-oriented literature which has nothing to say. Literature misleads if it conveys an exclusively surface view of life, if it assumes that appearances are all and does not hint at Reality. Literature should be Truth-bearing and glimpse or reveal metaphysical Reality or Being.

   Universalist literature is neo-Baroque as it combines the metaphysical and secular and unites the world of the senses and spirit by seeking the sunburst experience and unity. It reveals harmony between apparent opposites; sacred and profane, regular and irregular, order and disorder, stillness and movement, Becoming and Being, time and eternity. Universalist literature combines Classicism and Romanticism, statement and image, social situations and sublime metaphysical vision, traditional and organic form.

9. Universalist philosophy, history and literature offer a vision of harmony, meaning and order in relation to the universal Whole after the *Angst* and anxiety of 20th-century thought (Existentialist philosophy and Modernist literature). Universalism emphasises the contemplative gaze, union with the universal Whole and the rustic pursuit of reflection amid tranquillity, the vision of mystic writers, artists and sculptors.

10. European artists – practitioners in painting, music, architecture and sculpture as well as literature – should transmit the sap of the cross-disciplinary vision of the One Fire or Light in their works and connect themselves to the Universalist Revolution's revitalisation of the European civilisation's central idea. They will thereby contribute to the return of a common, unified European culture.

11. European culture needs to be re-formed to restore (to use Arnold's words) the most perfect works from the best self, which constitute the highest expressions of culture, and to reconnect philosophy, history and literature to the Tradition of the unity of vision of the metaphysical Fire or Light. The Revolution should have a hearing,

which will spread awareness of the consequences for European culture of the Revolution's fundamental shift in perception.

12. On the Universalist principle that all the metaphysical ideas of all the 25 civilisations are essentially the same vision, a revival of the common metaphysical vision in the European civilisation and culture will be essentially the same as corresponding revivals in all civilisations and cultures. The revival within the European culture can therefore inspire an international Universalist movement to focus on the common metaphysical ground of all cultures and create a world culture, which would be a force for world peace in the 21st century.

The implementation of this Declaration will have the following consequences in modern European thought and culture:

1. Renewals within our secularised, humanistic culture, which is in terminal decay.

2. Restoration of a vision reflected in all the European arts over hundreds of years, round which all civilisations have grown and whose renewal revives our culture and revitalises our civilisation.

3. Identification of the unifying principle in the universe of physics and formulation of a full Grand Unifying Theory (Form from Movement Theory).

4. Renewal of philosophy through a new metaphysical philosophy of the 1990s, Universalism, which challenges logical positivism, linguistic analysis and Existentialism.

5. Introduction of a new global perspective in history through a new history which takes account of all civilisations and cultures, not just slices of nation-state history, and identifies the unifying principle in all civilisations.

6. Restoration of the essential European vision in literature through a new literature which mixes the metaphysical and secular as did Baroque art (thus neo-Baroque literature), which draws on many disciplines and reflects our Age.

7. Revival of culture by a Group of practitioners who revive the essential European vision in their work, acting like a Pre-Raphaelite Group.

15 tenets reunifying rational and intuitional Universalism

Beliefs become tenets, principles that are held and maintained. In *The New Philosophy of Universalism* (2009), on pp.326–327, again from a philosophical angle, I also listed the 15 main tenets of Universalism in terms of the reunification of rational and intuitional Universalism:

> The reunification of rational and intuitional Universalism… makes possible a manifesto of Universalism, whose 15 main tenets are:
>
> 1. focus on the universe rather than logic and language;
> 2. focus on the universal order principle in the universe, a law which may act as a fifth force;
> 3. the universe/Nature manifested from the infinite/timelessness;
> 4. the universe/Nature and time began from a point and so everything is connected and one;
> 5. the infinite/timelessness can be known through universal being below the rational, social ego;
> 6. reunification of man and the universe/Nature and the infinite/timelessness;
> 7. reunification of fragmented thought and disciplines;
> 8. reunification of philosophy, science and religion;
> 9. focus on the bio-friendly universe, not a multiverse;
> 10. affirming order as being more influential than random accident;
> 11. affirming the structure of the universe as unique, its cause being the universal order principle from the infinite/timelessness/Void/Being/"*sea*" of energy;
> 12. affirming the eventual reunification of humankind;
> 13. affirming humankind as shaped by a self-organising principle so it is ordered and purposive;
> 14. affirming all history and culture as being connected, and one-world government and religion;
> 15. affirming that life has a meaning.

16 goals (restorations, reconciliations, unifications, proposals and revolutions) of Universalist philosophy

I also listed on p.362 of the same work the goals of Universalist philosophy, 16 restorations, reconciliations, unifications, proposals and revolutions *The New Philosophy of Universalism* effected:

1. to return philosophy to its Greek roots in the boundless *apeiron* or infinite;
2. to restore the infinite to philosophy;
3. to restore the finite universe and Nature to philosophy;
4. to restore the scientific view of the universe to philosophy;
5. to restore metaphysics to philosophy;
6. to propose a new Form from Movement Theory to account for the origin and creation of the universe;
7. to reconcile and unite science and metaphysics through metaphysical science which will investigate the universal order principle;
8. to reconcile and reunify science and philosophy;
9. to reconcile and unite the metaphysical and scientific traditions in the history of philosophy;
10. to unite the rational and intuitional metaphysical tradition;
11. to reconcile and unite linguistic and Phenomenological philosophies;
12. to propose that the multi-levelled self has 12 levels of consciousness;
13. to state a new university curriculum for a new discipline, Universalism;
14. to demonstrate how Universalism can transform studies of the past and movements in the present and near-future;
15. to launch a Metaphysical Revolution to bring about these changes in philosophy;
16. to launch a Revolution in Thought and Culture to bring about these changes in culture.

In these 16 restorations, reconciliations, unifications, proposals and revolutions, I have reconciled the contradictions of philosophy by using algebraic thinking: $+A + -A = 0$. Universalism has clear answers to the ultimate questions of metaphysics, seeing them in terms of the infinite and science. I have effected a Metaphysical Revolution to restore metaphysics alongside science in a redefinition of what philosophy should be doing, in a move away from logic and language. It is time for a change of emphasis in philosophy.

I have defined "Universalism" as focusing: on the universe; on a universal order principle; on humankind's place in the universe; on universal cosmic energies which stimulate the growth of organisms and plants; and the universal being or intellect where these energies or rays are received.

10 *primary aspects of Universalism*

Before *The New Philosophy of Universalism* was published, I wrote out 10 points that are primary aspects – particular components or features – of Universalism in an email to the philosopher Christopher Macann dated 23 October 2008 (see *Selected Letters*, pp.474–475):

> Off the top of my head I see the following ten points as being primary aspects of Universalism:
> 1. The universe is central to philosophy, not logic or language;
> 2. The infinite, which is central to Greek philosophy, is a reality and can be confronted (as it is what the Surfer breasts);
> 3. Manifestation – the universe manifests from One to many;
> 4. Metaphysics covers every known concept (and is therefore comprehensive);
> 5. Human consciousness is layered, its links to the manifestation process mean that part-survival is possible;
> 6. Self-improvement is the drive behind evolution;
> 7. Nature is a system that reveals bio-friendly order if it is approached evidentially;
> 8. There are both rational and irrational (intuitive) approaches to the One;
> 9. Universalism reconciles all contradictions as a kind of Theory of Everything;
> 10. It has modern applications in art and thought like Romanticism.

12 *characteristics of literary Universalism*

I listed 12 characteristics – typical features – of Universalism from a literary angle on pp.4–6 of *A New Philosophy of Literature* (2012):

Twelve Universalist characteristics

What are these characteristics? Within literature (and philosophy) the term 'Universalism' incorporates 'universe', 'universal' and 'universality'. It focuses on the universe, on a universal principle of order and on humankind as a whole. It focuses on inner transformation to the universal being, the deeper self below the rational, social ego which is open to universal cosmic energies, the manifesting metaphysical Light. It focuses on universal human virtues, the standard from which writers have ridiculed the follies and vices of humankind.

In all times and ages, Universalist literature seeks confirmation that the universe is ordered by a Reality that surrounds it, which Greek Presocratic philosophers such as Anaximander of Miletus (who flourished c.570BC) described as the infinite, "boundless" (*to apeiron*).

It holds that this Reality is perceived in many cultures as Light or Fire; that all humankind is one; and that there are consequently similarities between cultures and civilisations. It holds that the universal being (or spirit) can know the Reality as the Light and (according to all cultures) achieve immortality; and that there is a universal virtue which measures human behaviour.

This book is a work of literary Universalism. It sets out the long tradition of Universalist literature that reflects this view and adheres to these criteria. In fact, in all ages each particular work of Universalist literature reflects the idea of Reality found in their culture and civilisation, the metaphysical aspect of the fundamental theme; and until relatively recently the outlook of the traditional material could be located within the society and rituals that nourished it. In the interests of clarity it is worth setting out the twelve characteristics by which Universalism can be recognised. Universalism, and the metaphysical aspect of the fundamental theme, focuses on:

1. the infinite (*to apeiron*) that surrounds the universe;
2. the metaphysical Reality perceived in all cultures as Light (or Fire, which is a universal cosmic energy);
3. the universal principle of order in the universe (universal in the sense that its effects are found in all aspects of Nature and its organisms);
4. the oneness of known humankind behind its apparent diversity;

5. the similarities in cultures and civilisations;

6. the universal being (or self) that opens to the Light behind the rational, social ego;

7. universal virtue, a standard by which to measure human follies, vices, blindness, corruption, hypocrisy, self-love and egotism, and [focuses] on vices in relation to an implied universal virtue (when human interaction is considered from a secular perspective, as separated from its context of Reality);

8. the promise of immortality of the universal being or spirit;

9. an inner transformation or centre-shift from ego to universal being;

10. the quest of the purified soul to confront death, in the ancient cultures by journeying to the Underworld, and to receive the secret Light of infinite Reality;

11. a sensibility that approaches Reality through more than one discipline, the sensibility of a polymath; and

12. a new perspective of unity in key disciplines: seeing world history as a whole; seeing the common essence (the inner experience of the Light) of all world religions; seeing the One that can be revealed by philosophy and science; seeing the World State that can unify international politics; and seeing the unity of world literature.

In the ancient world, in which religion was strong, these characteristics dominated society's rituals and were reflected in literature. Despite weakenings of this cultural activity which gave rise to periods of secularisation in literature, this fundamental Universalist and literary perception of the universe can be found in all places and times. It is the archetypal literary theme that has been repeated in each generation. Each generation restates the traditional Universalist theme.

The fundamental literary theme

I went on to outline the fundamental literary theme on p.6 of the same work, beginning:

Outline of the fundamental theme

There are in fact two sides to the fundamental theme: the traditional metaphysical quest for Reality and, in periods of greater secularisation, a more secular view of social reality that focuses on vices in relation to an implied virtue.

5 Universalist reconciliations of contradictory literary traditions

I listed 5 sets of the contradictory traditions Universalism has reconciled on p.347 of *A New Philosophy of Literature*:

> We have seen that Universalism has reconciled and synthesised five sets of contradictory traditions or approaches:
> 1. the metaphysical and secular traditions;
> 2. the classical/Neoclassical and Romantic traditions;
> 3. rational and intuitional approaches within literature;
> 4. linguistic and verbal imitative, and inspired imaginative, traditions;
> 5. mystic and visionary traditions.

10 innovations in stating the fundamental literary theme

I also listed 10 innovations – statements, restorations, unifications and revolutions – in my statement of the fundamental theme on p.351 of *A New Philosophy of Literature* (2012):

> *Ten innovations*
> To sum up, in stating the fundamental theme I have introduced ten innovations. I have:
> 1. stated a metaphysical tradition in literature (the quest for Reality);
> 2. stated a secular tradition in literature (vices in relation to an implied virtue), which co-exists with the metaphysical;
> 3. unified world literature by seeing it as a unity in relation to the dialectic of these two contraries;
> 4. restored the metaphysical infinite to literature;
> 5. restored the vision of the infinite in literature;
> 6. stated a synthesis of the metaphysical and secular traditions, Universalism;
> 7. stated a Universalist literary tradition;
> 8. reconciled classicism/Neoclassicism and Romanticism in the synthesis of Universalism;

9. carried the Metaphysical Revolution, the "Revolution in Thought and Culture", into literature;

10. stated a new direction for world literature.

In these 10 statements, restorations, unifications and revolutions, I have reconciled the contradictions of literature by using algebraic thinking: $+A + -A = 0$.

On the pediment at Copped Hall Light and Shadow sit together [see picture on the cover of *A New Philosophy of Literature*, p.71], two contraries either side of the unifying sundial, two different sensibilities now reconciled. The reconciliation of the two opposites on the pediment and the synthesis of their two sensibilities is a symbol of unifying Universalism.

All these features and characteristics of Universalism came out of my approaching Universalism from a philosophical or literary angle, and do not include the six other disciplines which reflect my Universalism. But they are helpful in throwing light on the beliefs, tenets, goals, aspects, characteristics, fundamental theme, reconciliations and innovations in the different approaches to Universalism.

*

A view from the rear deck

Ten Universalist principles

Now, having come down from Mount Nebo and standing on the rear deck of our ship (up stairs from our cabin) and peering for lights on our starboard (right) side in the slightly chilly night air, I found I had new knowledge. I saw Universalism from all angles and perspectives simultaneously. I recalled my visit in 2005 to St Catherine's monastery under Mount Sinai, on top of which Moses received the Ten Commandments while in the wilderness. Like Moses, I was also waiting to enter the Promised Land of my Universalist world, all nations interconnected and spread out in the plain of a valley before mountains, my Canaan: a coming World State.

In my wilderness years (of seeing beyond nationalism to supranationalist Universalism rejected by nationalist politicians of the UK and seeing beyond the secular to the one metaphysical reality of all religions) I had done the groundwork, and from the new knowledge and perspectives I had after looking at the Promised Land from the top of Mount Nebo, I found I had received ten principles of Universalism:

1. The Universalist knows that the universe is a unity in which all opposites can be reconciled and all humankind can live in harmony.

2. The mystical Universalist knows that the One can be experienced and the unitive vision can become instinctive after one undergoes awakening, purgation and illumination along the Mystic Way.

3. The literary Universalist knows that the fundamental theme of world literature is a quest for the One and condemnation of follies and vices, and that all contradictory literary traditions can be reconciled.

4. The historical Universalist knows the fundamental law of history that civilisations begin with a metaphysical vision that passes into a religion and go through parallel rising and falling stages and turn progressively secular as they decline.

5. The religious Universalist knows that the Light (also known as the Fire) is the essence of all religions, and that all who open to it will instinctively spread the unitive vision in kindness and love.

6. The philosophical Universalist knows that all who open to the unitive vision receive wisdom and understanding in both soul and mind, and that the rational and intuitional approaches to philosophy can be reconciled.

7. The political Universalist knows that the unity of the universe is best expressed in a democratic World State with limited federal powers to abolish war and nuclear weapons.

8. The cultural Universalist knows the cultural unity of the world in which its metaphysical and secular pursuits are reconciled.

9. The harmonious Universalist knows that all the problems of humankind, including war, famine, disease, poverty and the world's financial, environmental, climatic and viral problems, can be resolved.

10. The wise Universalist knows that the best model for a World State is the United Federation of the World and its World Constitution.

My principles speak of "the unity of the universe". I was clear that there is only one universe we know, there is no evidence there are many universes. It is a universe, not a multiverse. On 4 September 1992 I wandered through Jesus College, Cambridge with Roger Penrose discussing his singularity behind the universe and the Big Bang, and he agreed with me then that there is only one universe, the one we know, and not a multiverse of which we have no experience except as a speculative possibility in mathematics. Not long after my voyage on *MS Serenissima* it would be announced that he had won a joint Nobel Prize for Physics for his work on black holes, and would soon be spoken of as being on the level of Einstein. He would soon be saying (speculatively) that the Big Bang was the end of a previous universe as an activity within a multiverse. My Universalist principles stick to what is evidential and speak of "the unity of the [One] universe".

Ten Universalist commandments

I now had it lodged in my mind that the ten principles of Universalism can be turned into ten commandments:

1. Live in harmony with humankind.

2. Seek a centre-shift within yourself and experience the unitive vision.

3. Quest for the One and condemn follies and vices and all foolishness, and reconcile contradictions.

4. Seek out your civilisation's metaphysical vision, even if your civilisation has turned secular.
5. Spread kindness and love to all.
6. Receive wisdom and understanding through the reason and intuition regarding the oneness of the universe.
7. Work for world peace.
8. Seek out the world's cultural unity.
9. Solve the world's problems by approaching them with the unitive vision.
10. Work for a federal World State to replace the UN General Assembly.

These ten Universalist commandments I brought back from the wilderness, and more specifically from the top of Mount Nebo in Jordan. They can create a more just and peaceful world.

Another view of the Promised Land from Mount Nebo

Standing at the back of the *MS Serenissima* in the dark and looking for lights on the starboard (right) side as we headed up the Gulf of Suez, I now saw that the reason for my cruise was to go up Mount Nebo and receive the commandments behind the World State.

My ten Muses and World State
Standing in the dark, I reflected that I am not a patriarch of a people as was Moses. I am a Universalist, having opened to the Light and

the wisdom of the East along the Mystic Way and become an inspired poet with what feels like an attendant Muse guiding me, sending me ideas and words from the beyond.

I have described my Muse in different places in my writings as being one of the nine Muses, daughters of Zeus and Mnemosyne, goddesses who are the source of a poet's creative power and inspire poetry, music and drama and who all seem to have helped me with my books at different times: Erato (lyrical poetry), Polymnia (sacred poetry), Clio (world history and civilisations), Urania (the One, astronomy), Calliope (heroic epic poetry), Euterpe (musical poetry), Melpomene (tragedy), Terpsichore (lyrical dance and choral song) and Thalia (comedy).

Apollo dancing with the Muses (Guilio Romano, c.1540)

Greek vase painting showing the nine Muses, composing music, poetry or drama

Roman mosaic of the nine Muses

If I am writing history, it seems that Clio will help me. If I am writing epic poetry, it seems that Calliope will help me, and so on. There is a mosaic discovered in Sousse, Tunisia (which I saw in 2001), of Virgil seated below the Muses of history (Clio) and tragedy (Melpomene), who inspire historical and tragic literature. Both were beside him while he was writing lines 8 and 9 of book 1 of *The Aeneid*, as can be seen from the scroll spread on his knees.

Virgil between the Muses of history (Clio) and tragedy (Melpomene), who inspire historical and tragic literature. He is holding a papyrus scroll spread on his knees, on which he is writing lines 8 and 9 of book 1 of his epic poem *The Aeneid:* *"Musa mihi causas memora quo numine laeso quidve...."* ("O Muse, remind me of the causes; for what violation of the sacred rites, or what...."). Mosaic discovered at Sousse, Tunisia, in the Bardo National Museum, Sousse, Tunisia. This is the only known likeness of Virgil. Experts have dated it to the 1st century AD, although some prefer the 3rd century. Virgil was popular in Africa because he wrote of the founding of Carthage.

Lines 8 and 9 of book 1 of *The Aeneid: "Musa mihi causas memora quo numine laeso quidve...."* ("O Muse, remind me of the causes; for what violation of the sacred rites, or what....")

Sometimes I do not know which Muse is inspiring me, sending me lines. For example, when I write a masque, is it Erato, Polymnia, Clio, Calliope, Euterpe or Terpsichore, or all of them at different times depending on which part of the masque I am in?

As I wrote in a poem, 'Secret of the Muse', in 1993:

> That you are a sweet Muse, I know
> But which one are you? Which of the nine?
> When I am with you I don't care
> Which as you make me feel fine.
>
> You seem to be the lovely Erato,
> Playing a lyre, smile like a purr,
> Muse of lyric and love poetry,
> And you are erotic enough to be her.
>
> Then you seem to be Polymnia
> Of many hymns with your pensive look,
> Muse of all sacred poetry,
> But then it seems you hold a book

And I think you are Clio, the Proclaimer,
Holding a date-filled chart-like scroll,
Erudite Muse of world history
Who knows how civilisations unroll.

Or are you heavenly Urania,
Holding a globe, a star, a purse,
Muse of astronomy and the One
That is hidden behind the universe?

But I know you are Calliope
The beautiful-voiced, holding a tablet:
Muse of heroic epic poetry
Who tempts me towards the task I was set.

Like a chameleon, my Muse,
You loom and dissolve and change your shape
And are all Muses, each by turn,
And leave their gifts near where I gape –

Even well-pleasing Euterpe,
Muse of music, playing her flutes,
And the songstress Melpomene
With her tragic mask and tragedy's fruits;

Whirler of the Dance, Terpsichore,
Muse of lyre-dance and choral song,
And blooming Thalia, comedy's Muse,
Holding a comic mask in a throng.

Muse, I know you are all nine Muses
And channel their father's power to me,
But most you are Calliope
Who becomes Erato to tempt me with glee

As you know my impossible task ahead,
To think of which makes me feel ill,
Six years of toil on a vast epic
That will be worthy of Homer and Virgil.

And so which Muse inspired my ten Universalist commandments? Probably Clio. But also perhaps my tenth Muse.

Portraits of the nine Muses, mosaic in the Archaeological Museum of Cos

Portraits of the nine Muses, Graeco-Roman mosaic in the Rheinisches Landesmuseum, Trier

Alfred, Lord Tennyson, lithograph 1890

Sometimes my Muse might be Tennyson. It seems I have especially been helped by Tennyson rather than one of the nine Muses. I encountered him at his home at Farringford on the Isle of Wight when I stayed there from 20 to 25 July 2008. As I explained in a letter to the literary critic and leading authority on Tennyson Christopher Ricks on 29 July 2008 (in *Selected Letters*, pp.462–466), I was aware of Tennyson's presence as I worked in his library and slept in his bedroom, and he seems to have followed me home. Ever since my encounter with him at Farringford he seems to edit my work and send me ideas in my sleep, including specific page numbers that need attention: an editorial process that fills me with wonder, which I still do not really understand.

I have come to see Tennyson as my tenth Muse. Besides helping with the seven disciplines and my branches of literature, he seems to take a special interest in the tenth principle and commandment, a World State, as he foresaw it in 'Locksley Hall' (1842):

> For I dipt into the future, far as human eye could see,
> Saw the Vision of the world, and all the wonder that would be;...
> Till the war-drum throbb'd no longer, and the battle-flags were furl'd
> In the Parliament of man, the Federation of the world.
> There the common sense of most shall hold a fretful realm in awe,
> And the kindly earth shall slumber, lapt in universal law.

I named the World State The United Federation of the World after this passage, and the above lines are written into Article 133 of my *World Constitution* as they will be the United Federation of the World's anthem. I know that Tennyson would have been interested in the ten Universalist commandments which urge support for a World State, the United Federation of the World.

Seven of the Muses inspire different aspects of literary Universalism (Erato, Polymnia, Calliope, Euterpe, Melpomene, Terpsichore and Thalia) and the other two inspire historical Universalism (Clio) and philosophical Universalism (Urania). All of them work on all seven Universalist disciplines and my seven branches of literature. Tennyson, who foresaw a World State, seems to reinforce them as my tenth Muse.

The true, inspired poets convey and keep alive the essential reality of their civilisation. Between them my ten Muses seem to have inspired me to write *World State* and *World Constitution*, which sets out the legal framework for a World State, and for all I know they may have made sure I somehow reached the top of Mount Nebo to look at the Promised Land. Having been inspired to be a legislator in *World*

Constitution I now understand what Shelley meant when he wrote in 'A Defence of Poetry' (1821, published posthumously in 1840), "Poets are the unacknowledged legislators of the world." He understood that poets are inspired from the beyond and channel truth and the commandments by which to live.

Universalism proclaims the unity of all disciplines, of which I have focused on seven. These seven disciplines of Universalism are like bands in a rainbow: mysticism; literature; history; religion; philosophy and the sciences; international politics and statecraft; and world culture. There are seven bands but there is only one rainbow, which includes all seven bands. Literary Universalism includes seven branches of literature: poems and poetic epics; verse plays and masques; short stories and novellas; diaries; autobiographies; letters; and the fundamental theme of world literature.

My trademark is a stag with seven-branched antlers. One antler represents the seven Universalist disciplines, the other antler represents literary works within the seven branches of literature. All these disciplines and branches seem to be covered by the nine Muses, and of course by my tenth Muse.

5

A Remarkable Life and its Pattern

Luxor

The next morning I was up at 6am. A medical border unit had come on board and we all had to queue beyond the breakfast area and have our temperatures taken for Covid with a gun-like scanner held to our foreheads.

We had breakfast and then landed at Safaga and were driven through the Eastern Desert by coach for three and a half hours with overnight bags in the hold towards the Valley of the Kings. Our security guard was sitting in front of us, with a gun clearly visible under the right-hand pocket of his suit jacket.

The rugged landscape gave way to the green luxuriance of the Nile Valley as we skirted Luxor. There were regular police checkpoints, and armed militias were on every bridge of a narrow river parallel to the road.

We walked through the St George Hotel, Luxor to the River Nile and got in waiting dhows, boats rigged with triangular lateen sails, eight to a boat, and then zigzagged to and fro across the Nile and back while eating a sumptuous lunch: a starter followed by lamb, chicken, meat and rice, and then baklava and coffee, all cooked and served by a chef-waiter in evening dress.

At one point we were before the Old Winter Palace Hotel, the Winter Palace of the Egyptian royal family in the colonial era, where Agatha Christie wrote *Death on the Nile* while staying there.

We returned to the coach and reached the Valley of the Kings. After a trek we visited the tombs of Ramesses IV and Ramesses III and looked in on Tutankhamun's tomb, which I had visited in 2005. We went on to Queen Hatshepsut's tomb and the Colossi of Memnon, Amenhotep III and his wife guarding their tomb.

We were taken to the Hilton Hotel and, having checked in, went out for a gharry ride. Then we ate by the Nile in the Hotel grounds and open air as dusk fell and it grew dark.

Next morning we were taken to the Temple of Karnak, which was dedicated to Amun-Ra. I was drawn to the many statues of Ramesses II, who had eight wives and over 200 concubines. His left foot out showed him as living, his arms crossed and feet together showed him as dead. I

noticed recurrent hieroglyphs and discussed them with our guide: a plant and bee symbolising lower and upper Egypt, and hieroglyphs showing that the Great Pyramid represented eternity.

I had written my story 'The Riddle of the Great Pyramid', set in c.2580–2560BC, in 1963, before I had been to Egypt, and I had written a second story, 'The Meaning and Purpose of the Great Pyramid', in 2005. Now I realised I had a third story, 'The Great Pyramid as a House of Eternity', which I would write. It is about the same official who narrated the previous stories, and it begins: "I am 80 now, and Khafra is Pharaoh." The three stories may one day appear in a slim book, *The Building of the Great Pyramid*.

Statue of Ramesses II at the Temple of Karnak

We drove back to Sagada filled with images of the after-life. On the coach back to the ship I looked back on my life in relation to the Great Pyramid. Like the builders of the Great Pyramid, all my life I have worked on a vast project, my own pyramid, Universalism. In relation to time, my long effort might seem accidental, circumstantial, a happening by chance, but in relation to eternity it seemed as if my building of my project was always meant to be.

I saw what looked like a clear destiny ('predetermined course of events, fate', *Concise Oxford Dictionary*) and wondered how much was accidental and how much was Providential, guided by the foresight of the beyond, perhaps my Muses.

Looking back on my remarkable life and destiny

The next day was a day at sea. As we chugged up the Gulf of Suez,
sitting on the rear deck, I, an
old man of approximately
Moses' age (see pp.xii, 15),
looked back beyond my
ten Universalist principles
and saw that I have had a
remarkable life. Just consider
what has happened to me in
one lifetime:

View from the ship's rear deck

- I was born just over
  three months before the
  outbreak of the Second
  World War;
- I was presented to Mary,
  Princess Royal, daughter
  of George the Fifth, in the
  London Hospital when I
  was four days old;
- As a boy I lived in Churchill's
  constituency and experienced the
  Second World War under the flying
  bombs and doodle-bugs;
- I experienced bombs blow out our
  windows in March 1943 and (including
  our garage windows) in March 1944;
- I heard Churchill speak at Loughton
  war memorial on 16 June 1945 and
  spoke with him when he signed my
  autograph album in October 1951, and
  I would write about him in *The Warlords*
  and *Overlord*;
- My aunt, Margaret Broadley, was
  Assistant Matron (no.2) of the London

Nicholas Hagger (left) under
blown-out windows of the
garage in Loughton, March
1944

Hospital, and in April 1946, aged 6, I was invited to see Queen Mary visit the hospital;

- I experienced the Oneness of the universe for the first time in late 1946 when taken aback by the brilliance of the stars on a frosty evening in the garden of 24 Ollards Grove, Loughton (where one of the two owners of Oaklands School had previously lived);
- I grew up near Julius Caesar's Loughton Camp (a Bronze-Age camp fortified by Julius Caesar in 54BC and reinforced by Claudius in 43AD, see *A View of Epping Forest*, pp.17–19 and Roger Nolan, *Julius Caesar's Invasion of Britain*, pp.75–76) and Ambresbury Banks, the site of Boudicca's last stand against the Romans in 61AD (see *A View of Epping Forest*, pp.26–38), and at an early age heard stories about the constructive Romans who built roads and the destructive English who burned St Albans, London and Colchester;
- I attended Oaklands School, Loughton, Essex during the war without knowing I would own it from 1982;
- Walking home from school when I was seven I saw a mechanical digger working on wasteland drop a coin, which I picked up and discovered was a Roman coin of Caracalla (198–217), also identified as Elagabalus (218–222), from Antioch, and I went on to collect Roman and Greek coins and visited Jerash/Antioch;
- I attended Chigwell School and there on 18 October 1953 met Montgomery, who I would write about in *The Warlords* and *Overlord*, and in *Montgomery*;
- In September 1953 I had visited France for a week and was taken to all the D-Day beaches, which I would write about in *The Warlords* and *Overlord*;
- I experienced the Oneness of the universe in March 1954, aged 14, while lying among the wild flowers in the long grass of the rough on the Merrow golf-course on the Surrey Downs in warm sun;
- I made my debut as a club cricketer in 1955 at the age of 16 for Alan Lavers' XI against Loughton Cricket Club before a large crowd on the Thursday of Loughton's cricket week in early August;
- In early 1956 I was in touch with the British School of Archaeology at Athens and attended talks chaired by Sir Mortimer Wheeler and Leonard Woolley, and through the Council for British Archaeology

joined a dig at Chester in April 1956, but was put off becoming an archaeologist as I spent a week crouching and trowelling in a Roman sewer;

- I saw the new leaders of the Soviet Union, Bulganin and Khrushchev, arrive for a meeting with Prime Minister Eden in Downing Street in April 1956;

- I attended the Suez debate in the House of Commons on 12 September 1956 when Eden, with Churchill sitting alongside him, unveiled a Suez Users' Association, the collusion which led to the Suez débâcle that destroyed the British Empire;

- I was called to be a poet at the age of 17 while sitting on a wooden bench on Chigwell School's Lower Field reading Hopkins' poem 'Wreck of the Deutschland' shortly before I left school in March 1957, and while visiting Horace's villa at Licenza in the Sabine Hills next month I found what is thought to be Horace's *"fons Bandusiae"*, his Bandusian spring, and cupped my hands in the flowing stream and sipped the clear limpid water and saw it as symbolising my poetic spring;

- I got into Oxford on my Latin, Greek and Ancient History, I believe by describing at my *viva voce* a Corinthian coin I had obtained from a swap at school and contradicting the Senior Tutor's denial that such a coin exists, "Well, I've got it";

- I played club cricket for Buckhurst Hill's 1st XI – an apparent prompt from my destiny as I now live in Buckhurst Hill – and was watched by crowds of hundreds in 1957–1958;

- I experienced the One by the lake at Worcester College, Oxford on a sunny morning in early March 1959 after reading a letter from my father agreeing that I could give up Law, in which I felt trapped, and read English Literature, the path I felt I should follow to advance my destiny – I became the oneness of the trees and sky reflected in the lake (see *My Double Life 1: This Dark Wood*, pp.92–93);

- I studied at Oxford under Christopher Ricks, now the leading authority on Tennyson and Eliot, and corresponded with him as my mentor for more than 40 years;

- I spoke with Jean-Paul Sartre, the French Existentialist, in Paris in April 1959;

- I spoke with Ernest Hemingway in Spain on 30 July 1959;
- I attended a party at Cliveden in May 1960 and spoke with Lord Astor just over a year before the Profumo Affair;
- I met Lord Astor's wife Lady Bronwen Astor (who had had an experience of the Light) at a lecture I gave on 10 April 1992 and, after spending my 65th birthday at Cliveden, had coffee with her on 12 May 2011 (shortly before she died), when she told me that Stephen Ward stole the Skybolt plans from her husband's ground-floor study and passed them to Ivanov of the Soviet Union (see *My Double Life 2: A Rainbow over the Hills*, pp.833–834);
- I spoke with Col. Grivas, the Greek Cypriot leader and terrorist, in Greece in August 1960;
- I met Peter O'Toole, the actor, in 1960 in Oxford, and he asked to come back to my room with his chauffeur and a bottle of vodka, and combing through *The Merchant of Venice* we forgot the time and I had to push him over a locked nine-foot-high gate around midnight, and 50 years later I met him again on a cruise in 2010;
- I was invited for one-to-one sherry on 6 November 1960 with Sir John Masterman, Provost of Worcester College, Oxford and Chairman of the Twenty (XX, Double-Cross) Committee during the war which fed the Germans misinformation on the whereabouts of the D-Day landings, and was asked if I would consider a career in intelligence;
- I stayed with Colin Wilson, the author of *The Outsider*, from 6 to 9 January 1961 and announced that I would lecture abroad for a decade and find wisdom among foreign cultures;
- I taught at the University of Baghdad, Iraq, where the founder of Islamic State later studied;
- In Baghdad I lived out in the sand desert without air-conditioning, and it was so hot I had to sleep with the windows open and sandflies crawled through the mosquito-mesh and I became very ill with sandfly fever – I was delirious and when an Iraqi

Nicholas Hagger with Colin Wilson on 14 August 1991

doctor my aunt had known at the London Hospital visited me I said in a lucid moment, "I've got a temperature of 107," and he said, "You can't, you'd be dead," and after taking my temperature, "Oh," for it *was* 107 – and he later told me I could have died that day;

- In Iraq I visited Babylon, where the one-world Tower of Babel stood, and other Biblical places;

- I drew on Iraq in my later poem written in Japan, 'The Silence' (1965–1966), in references to the legend of Tammuz, the dying god of Babylon, a symbol of my centre-shift as in the Babylonian myth an old self dies and returns as a new self, and Babylon lurks behind 'The Silence';

- I was a Professor at three universities in Japan and wrote speeches for the Governor of the Bank of Japan, including a speech for the Opening Ceremony of the Asian Development Bank in Manila on 19 December 1966;

- At my main Japanese university I was the first Visiting Foreign Professor since William Empson, and I taught in the room where Empson had taught from 1931 to 1934;

- At my main Japanese university I shared a room with my colleague Brian Buchanan, who nicknamed me Shelley and, as Mrs. Patrick Campbell's godson, had known Maud Gonne (whom Yeats admired), met Synge, been dandled on Shaw's knee and met MacBride (who was shot by the British after the Easter-1916 uprising) – and who later encountered Hitler's deputy Hess on the night he landed in Scotland;

- I taught the Vice-Governor of the Bank of Japan, and was in his room when Lord Cromer rang from the Bank of England requesting a loan from the Bank of Japan, and the Vice-Governor asked me if he should agree and I nodded – and secured the loan;

- I was tutor to Emperor Hirohito's second son, Prince Hitachi, and I taught him all world history;

- In Tokyo I lunched with the First-World-War poet Edmund Blunden, who asked me to search for Shakespeare's lost trunk;

- I knew Japan's T.S. Eliot, Junzaburo Nishiwaki, and on 5 October 1965 he wrote out the wisdom of the East on a business-reply card I happened to have: +A + −A = 0, i.e. all opposites and contradictions are reconciled;

- On 12 October 1965 Prince and Princess Hitachi left to make a State visit to Britain, and as I had been involved in planning the visit I was the only foreigner invited to a farewell reception for about 40 at their palace, and after he had appeared, bowed to everybody and shaken hands with me and I had greeted the Princess who was carrying a nosegay all threw their hands in the air and there were collective cries of *"Banzai"* ("[May the Emperor live] ten thousand years", hence "Long life [to the Emperor]", "Victory"), which Japanese troops and kamikaze pilots shouted as they hurtled into battle during the Second World War;

Nicholas Hagger and Prince and Princess Hitachi in their palace grounds, Tokyo, on 5 August 1965

- In Japan I walked to work at my main university under a fierce sun and accompanied by my shadow, and in my poem 'The Silence' I wrote of my Shadow, the wise self I would become when I reached 80, and I now am my Shadow;
- I was the first non-Chinese to discover the Chinese Cultural Revolution when I visited Peking University and spoke to a 5th-year student on 16 March 1966 (see *My Double Life 1: This Dark Wood*, Appendix 4);
- I travelled to London via Moscow, and on 9 June 1966 visited the Cathedral of the Archangel in the Kremlin and, standing in front of the icon of the Archangel Michael, had a vision of a World State and world peace;
- On 28 December 1966 Mao detonated China's fifth atomic explosion and in early January 1967 the fall-out came down on

Japan as light rain 120 times as radioactive as normal rain, and for several days I walked to and from work under an umbrella, careful not to touch wet shrubs;

- On 24 August 1967 I was swimming with my 4-year-old daughter, holding her rubber ring, at Nobe in Japan and a tsunami set off by an earthquake sent rolling waves four feet above the sea's level which crashed down on us and I clung onto her arm and surfaced in boiling foam that rushed over the top of the beach into a field, and then another wave crashed down, knocked me onto my side, and I still held on to her – I had saved my daughter's life from a tsunami but we both nearly drowned that day;

- When I left Japan in 1967 my pupil Prince Hitachi gave me a dark-blue urn for my ashes with a golden imperial chrysanthemum on its side, and a chamberlain explained that as the Prince's father, Emperor Hirohito, had been a god until the end of the

war and in the Shinto religion an emperor has the power to bestow eternal life and Emperor Hirohito had bestowed eternal life on me for teaching his son, this gift of the urn guaranteed my eternal life in the afterlife and my place in Heaven – I had been given entry to Heaven as a leaving present by

Urn with imperial chrysanthemum, enlarged on left, guaranteeing Nicholas Hagger's eternal life

the leader of the Empire of Japan during the Second World War;

- I experienced the mystic Light in Japan and later in London and progressed along the Mystic Way to instinctive unitive vision, which I finally reached in December 1993;

- I lectured at the University of Libya, Tripoli and worked for British Intelligence for four years;
- I was heavily involved in running a *coup* scheduled for 5 September 1969 and was asked by the *coup* leaders to be in charge of all Libya's oil and selling drilling rights to foreign companies;
- To prepare for our *coup* I wrote an article on Libyan–British relations (see *The Libyan Revolution*, p.261) that appeared in Tripoli's English *Daily News* on 24 August 1969 and (I was told by the Libyan Minister of State for Prime Minister's Affairs) in all the Libyan Arabic newspapers, and I was subsequently told by my intelligence contact that this was read by Gaddafi and that my article triggered Gaddafi's Libyan Revolution on 1 September 1969;
- I was an eyewitness of the Gaddafi Revolution – I went to work on the morning of 1 September 1969, found the gates locked and drove home through advancing tanks and armoured cars;
- On 6 November 1969 I persuaded a Czech with nuclear knowledge to defect to the UK, and my ensuing tussle with the Americans close to the Head of the CIA in Tripoli, who also wanted him, cost me my first marriage;
- I saw Col. Nasser, who precipitated the Suez Crisis, ride slowly past me, six feet away on a Jeep with Gaddafi, in Tripoli on 25 December 1969;
- I knocked Col. Gaddafi's peaked cap off his head when he visited the University of Libya on 1 January 1970 (see *The Libyan Revolution*, pp.72–73) – when he died he was the richest man in the world, owning $150 billion misappropriated from Libya's oil revenues and sent to South Africa;
- I located the recent arrival of a Russian SAM-3 missile transporter near El Alamein in Egypt on 19 February 1970, the first confirmation that the Russians had supplied SAM-3s to Egypt;
- I was nearly executed by Mohammed Barassi, a powerful figure behind the Libyan Revolutionary Command Council, on 28 May 1970 – I spent an hour staring at a Luger he was holding, waiting to be shot (see *My Double Life 1: This Dark Wood*, pp.313–320);
- I had been told to return to my 'executioner' and on my way I gatecrashed a large reception for the Queen's birthday at Tripoli's

British Embassy and, holding up his greeting of a long line of guests, spoke with the British Ambassador, Donald Maitland, who told me I must comply with his request and sent me on my way to possible execution, and a month later Maitland became Prime Minister Edward Heath's Chief Press Secretary and on 24 August 1970 I was appointed Heath's Unofficial Ambassador to the African liberation movements;

- I visited Ezra Pound in Rapallo, Italy on 16 June 1970 and turned away from Modernism to 17th- and 19th-century poetry;

- While working in London as Heath's Unofficial Ambassador to the African liberation movements I had to have daytime employment cover that would leave me free to do my real work in the late afternoons and evenings, and I worked in a school for educationally subnormal (ESN) boys in Greenwich, where there was no homework, and, like Fagin with more than 20 Artful Dodgers, drove them on weekly outings into London in a coach – I took my coach driver's test without having driven a coach before and knocked over a bollard in Greenwich High Street as I was not used to the length of the coach, but still passed;

- While working in London as Heath's Unofficial Ambassador to the African liberation movements I was told that I would be outed as a British Intelligence Agent by the defector to the Soviet Union Kim Philby on or soon after 24 September 1971 in retaliation for the expulsion of 105 Russians from the UK as the KGB knew what I was doing, but this did not happen;

- I was Head of English at a London comprehensive, and for 11 years was able to teach the English poets from Chaucer to Tennyson in great technical detail, which helped me as a poet;

- In November 1976 I wrote 'The European Resurgence', and at a dinner told Margaret Thatcher face to face that the East-European nations should be liberated from the Soviet Union;

- I was invited by Frank Tuohy to a dinner he gave on 5 April 1977 for spy Donald Maclean's son Fergus Maclean, who had lived in Philby's household for two years when his mother moved in with Philby, and Fergus rang me at my school to ask me to find him a job in London – and then suddenly returned to Moscow;

- I met a past-life hypnotist in 1978 who took me back to a life as a temple-maiden who was chosen by Ramesses II, Shelley's Ozymandias, to take part in a symbolic ritual to make the Nile flood, and I now have a vivid 'memory' of what he was like;

- In 1982 I bought my old prep school, Oaklands School, in Loughton so I could be independent and have a writing base with an income;

- I wrote *Scargill the Stalinist?*, a short book exposing the Communist links of miners' leader Arthur Scargill, who was trying to overthrow the Government by means of the 1984 miners' strike, and after it was greeted by a long first leader in *The Times* titled 'We Have Been Warned', I met Peter Walker, the minister in charge of handling the miners' strike for the Government, and on 13 December 1984 the National Union of Mineworkers occupied Foyles Bookshop, sat on the floor and demanded that a window filled with my books should be cleared;

- I knew Len Murray, later Lord Murray, the General Secretary of the Trades Union Congress, and often met him in the street and on the tube and discussed politics, including Scargill, and I conducted him as we sang a duet of 'Happy Birthday' to my aunt, and he and I both spoke at my aunt's funeral;

- In 1983/1984 I wrote 'FREE: Freedom for the Republics of Eastern Europe', which was passed to Margaret Thatcher before she met Gorbachev in late 1984; and on 4 November 1986 I broadcast behind the Iron Curtain from the Palace of Westminster and called for the freedom of Eastern Europe – which was achieved after the fall of the Berlin Wall in November 1989;

- I found out that near Sebha, Libya, Gaddafi had missiles that

Nicholas Hagger proclaiming FREE behind the Iron Curtain on the BBC World Service on 4 November 1986, challenging the 1943 Tehran Agreement, with a worried John Biggs-Davison MP looking on aghast

could reach London, Paris and Bonn, and on 24 March 1986 met Shmuel Moyal of the Embassy of Israel in London at the Swiss Cottage Holiday Inn and handed him evidence to be sent to President Reagan, and after Tripoli was bombed on 14 April 1986 I met Moyal again on 7 May 1986 and received confirmation that of the 55 planes involved 20 bombed Tripoli, 20 Benghazi and 15 went to the base near Sebha, disabled the missiles and set back Gaddafi's nuclear plans (see *My Double Life 2: A Rainbow over the Hills*, pp.217–221);

- During his last illness, John Biggs-Davison MP, having heard my call for East Europe to break free from the Soviet Union and join what would become the EU, asked his Constituency Chairman to find out if I would be interested in replacing him, and, knowing I had more than 50 books to write, I declined on 26 February 1988 – Biggs-Davison died on 17 September 1988 and his successor Steve Norris moved into a cottage at Coopersale Hall School as my tenant;

- I bought the Harbour-master's House in Charlestown, Cornwall, which overlooks the sea, made it a writing base six times a year and got to know the sea at first hand;

- I bought Coopersale Hall, Epping, and in 1988 founded a school, Coopersale Hall School, there, which was opened by Lord Tebbit, and Rod Stewart, a parent, opened a new building there in 2011;

- In my study of 25 civilisations, *The Fire and the Stones*, I predicted the end of Soviet Communism and an American-based United States of Europe in the 1990s;

- I had a combined launch for *The Fire and the Stones* and *Selected Poems: A Metaphysical's Way of Fire* at which the poets Kathleen Raine and David Gascoyne spoke along with the historian Asa Briggs (who was then Provost of Worcester College, Oxford);

- I became a full-time writer and visited many countries;

- I established a Foundation of the Light in the autumn of 1991, held meditations to open to the Light at a Mystery School based in Coopersale Hall School's assembly hall on five Sundays in May and June 1992, and opened a Metaphysical Centre in December 1993 before withdrawing to concentrate on my writing;

- I attended a conference at Jesus College, Cambridge, and on 1 September 1992 had a long talk with Roger Penrose, who was an authority on the singularity which sourced the Big Bang and later shared the Nobel Prize for Physics, and we walked round the college late at night looking for a phone and got totally lost;
- I wrote out my Form from Movement Theory on the origin of the universe, which is in the tradition of the Presocratic Anaximander of Miletus, in the packed dining-hall at Jesus College, Cambridge on 4 September 1992 beside a mathematician who wrote out the maths, with Roger Penrose looking on;
- I corresponded with Ted Hughes, the Poet Laureate, for eight years until his death in 1999;
- I followed a Mystic Way from 1957, was fully illumined in 1971, had four Mystic Lives and arrived at instinctive unitive vision in 1993;
- Like Virgil and Milton I had the idea for my epic poem for 25 years before writing it, and in *Overlord* drew on personal meetings with Churchill, Montgomery and his D-Day chef – and would later meet his Liaison Officer, who supplied him with Ultra intercepts on Rommel's army before the Battle of El Alamein;
- Stalin's daughter, Svetlana Stalin, asked me to co-write a book with her on the death of her mother, who, she alleged, was murdered by Stalin, and I met her for five hours on 4 May 1996;
- I bought two more schools, Normanhurst School in Chingford and Braeside School in Buckhurst Hill;
- I bought Otley Hall where Bartholomew Gosnold organised the voyage to Jamestown in 1606/1607 that marks the founding of the United States of America, and ran it as a historic house;
- I arranged for Sylvia Landsberg, designer of five of the six institutional medieval gardens in England, to design the knot-garden at Otley Hall, which shows my Grand Unified Theory of history and religion as 25 herb beds that represent the 25 civilisations of my books *The Fire and the Stones* and *The Rise and Fall of Civilizations* radiating outwards from a suspended point, the singularity from which creation came;
- In Virginia I negotiated twinning between Ipswich and Jamestown

in 1998 at the request of local-government leaders in Ipswich – only for the Ipswich councillors to reject my arrangement when an American deputation arrived to meet them;

- In July 1999 Tony Little, Headmaster of Chigwell School, gave out

The knot-garden at Otley Hall with some of the 25 herb beds (top left), Sylvia Landsberg's drawing for the knot-garden showing the numbered 25 herb beds/civilisations (top right), and (left) the English knot the young Elizabeth I put on her prayer-book in 1544, on which the design is based

prizes for Oaklands School at the Hawkey Hall, Woodford and, sitting next to him, I told him there was a vacancy at Eton and he should apply – and he later told me he had just been appointed Head Master of Eton and sworn to secrecy and he wondered if I was a mind-reader;

- I appointed the Earl of Burford, heir to the Duke of St Albans, as my Literary Secretary in 1999, and he leapt onto the Woolsack in the House of Lords as a protest against the abolition of hereditary peers while working for me;
- I was a Trustee of, and Secretary to, the Shakespearean Authorship Trust, with Mark Rylance as Chairman, and investigated the authorship of Shakespeare's plays by interviewing the most prominent figures in all the societies of Shakespeare's contemporaries (Marlowe, Bacon and the 17th Earl of Oxford *et alia*);

- I housed two libraries on Shakespeare at Otley Hall and had four Globe-Theatre casts to stay for three days each between 1999 and 2000, including Mark Rylance/Hamlet and Vanessa Redgrave/ Prospero, and rehearsed with them and attended their evening banquets;

- I met Jamestown archaeologist Bill Kelso at Jamestown in Virginia on 16 October 1998, sat with him by the River James and told him that I had worked out where Bartholomew Gosnold was buried in Jamestown (at the centre of the old triangular fort), and I was the moving force in Kelso's finding Gosnold's skeleton "about fifty feet" from where we sat, ringing me on 6 February 2003 and saying "Your dead-centre theory was right" and announcing it to the world at a press conference in Virginia, with me sitting by a phone in the UK to answer questions;

- Taking advantage of free movement in Europe I wrote 317 classical odes on European ruins and landmarks – on the European cultural tradition;

- I had 12 properties at one time, and sold the investment properties to bring in revenue for building projects in the schools;

- I moved to Buckhurst Hill, where I used to play cricket, and lived in Connaught House overlooking Epping Forest, with four oak trees on the lawn representing the four schools in the Oak-Tree Group;

- I wrote 56 books (so far) and my literary output includes 1,200 short stories (with another 200 waiting to be published), 2,000 poems including 317 classical odes, 2 epic poems, 5 verse plays, 3 masques, 3 autobiographies and 2 travelogues;

- I wrote three autobiographies, *A Mystic Way*, *My Double Life 1: This Dark Wood* and *My Double Life 2: A Rainbow over the Hills*;

- I wrote two epic poems on war, *Overlord* (41,000 lines of blank verse) and *Armageddon* (25,000 lines of blank verse), in the tradition of Homer, the only other poet to have written two poetic epics, *The Iliad* and *The Odyssey*;

- I visited Iran in 2007 and drove past the nuclear site at Natanz with machine-guns trained on our car, proving that Iran was concealing something nuclear there, and later I looked down the barred well where the Hidden Imam has been hiding since 874AD according to Shia belief, where Government ministers drop written messages to him and where his Second Coming is eagerly awaited;

- In June 2010 I talked with Jonathan Bate, the authority on Shakespeare, outside the Oxford Playhouse and after an email exchange with him received an email on 5 July saying that he had been appointed the new Provost of Worcester College, Oxford, and we had a number of literary discussions during the next ten years;

- I added an Appendix to *Armageddon* (2010) on bin Laden's 69 attempts to obtain nuclear weapons between 1992 and 2005, titled 'Bin Laden's/Al-Qaeda's Historical Attempts to Acquire Weapons of Mass Destruction and Unleash Armageddon in the United States', and replicated it in Appendix III in *The Secret American Dream* (2011), which I sent, flagged, to President Obama (whose face is on the front cover) on 5 April 2011 together with *The Libyan Revolution* and *The World Government*, and it seems that as a result on 2 May 2011, within a month, it was reported that bin Laden had been killed and on 20 October 2011 that Gaddafi had been killed;

- I learned from Eleanor Laing, Deputy Speaker in the House of Commons, on 23 March 2011 that *The Libyan Revolution* was passed to Liam Fox, UK Secretary of State for Defence until 14 October 2011, six days before the death of Gaddafi on 20 October 2011, and was told that the book had influenced the NATO-led deposing of Gaddafi;

- I attended the World Philosophical Forum's annual meeting in Athens and was asked to chair their Constitutional Convention, and on 7 October 2015 I brought in an interim World State, the Universal State of the Earth, and became Chairman of its Supreme Council of Humanity (see *Peace for our Time*, pp.34–50);

- My manuscripts and papers were accepted as a Special Collection by the Albert Sloman Library at the University of Essex in October 2015;

- I received the Gusi Peace Prize for Literature in Manila on 23 November 2016, and I was later nominated for the Templeton Prize;

- In Manila I was asked by a Syrian diplomat Issam Eldebs to visit Assad on a peace mission, and I wrote out a 15-point Peace Plan, which was apparently sent on to Assad with a copy of *The World Government* I was asked to sign to him, and on to Putin (see *Peace for our Time*) – but I could not go into Syria as arranged as in early 2017 Assad suffered an unpublicised stroke and for a while the country was run by his brother;

- I brought out *World State* and *World Constitution* in 2018 about a coming World State, the true Promised Land;

- I was invited to Moscow to make a speech calling for a new era of world peace on 22 April 2019 – the start of the new Mayan Year of the Phoenix, which comes round every 2,000 years and heralds a world empire (the last one being Augustus's Roman Empire) – and I received the Order of the Golden Phoenix from the Russian Ecological Foundation (presented by a Russian cosmonaut) and a silver medal from the BRICS countries (Brazil, Russia, India, China and South Africa) for 'Vision for Future';

- After my speech in Moscow in 2019 an Admiral and Vice-Admiral in full military uniform strode onto the stage and seized my hands and held them in the air in a victory salute for internet cameras;

- I was taken to President Putin's rest-house/sanatorium, which Stalin opened c.1935 and has been used by every Soviet and Russian leader since then, and was sung to by two ladies in traditional costume in a personal concert;

- An exhibition of my works, with glass cases of exhibits and manuscripts and a rolling slide show, was held at the Albert Sloman Library, University of Essex during the last half of May 2019, to mark my 80th birthday;

- I connected my family to the Hagars of Bourn, Cambridgeshire (descendants of Carolus Haggar of Bruges who came to Chelmsford, England in 1366);

- I was awarded my own coat of arms and crest for me and my descendants by the College of Arms;

- I was invited to read a poem and speak on the Commonwealth alongside courtiers at the celebration of the Prince of Wales' 70th birthday;

- I wrote a masque for Prince Charles's coronation, *The Coronation of King Charles*;
- In 2020 I was invited to join the Executive Board of the World Intellectual Forum, which then set up the Global Network for Peace, Disarmament and Development (GNET-PEDAD) to bring in a world government and world constitution largely based on my books *The World Government*, *World State* and *World Constitution*;
- I have known the top figures in cricket, football, politics, history, literature, acting and many other professions, as my *Selected Letters* show;
- I had 93 recorded experiences of the Light (listed in an Appendix in *My Double Life 2: A Rainbow over the Hills*) and another 19 recorded experiences extracted from my diaries, making 112 in all (see pp.209–215);
- I travelled widely – throughout Europe, the Middle East and Arabia, Russia, India and Sri Lanka, China, South-East Asia, North Africa, Tanzania, the USA, South America, the Galapagos Islands and Antarctica (see Visits, **p.206**) – more than could be expected when I was born in 1939;
- I have been blessed in my family who all lived within reach as I wrote my books, and my eldest son Matthew took over the running of the four schools from me.

Sitting on the ship's rear deck in the Gulf of Suez, I saw that I have, indeed, had a remarkable, some might say extraordinary, life. And just about everything that happened to me, seemingly arbitrarily, had later consequences.

How I was shown my future direction and destiny

Looking back, as the ship steamed on its course, I saw there were many pointers to what seemed to be my destiny, and it seemed I was shown my future direction, as if Providence ('the protective care of God', *Concise Oxford Dictionary* – or of angels, or Muses) was nudging me so I would not forget. For example:
- I fell off a bus at the foot of Albion Hill, Loughton as a boy and later owned the school up the hill and built a house next to it

– as though Providence were saying, "Remember Albion Hill" ('Albion' being the name Julius Caesar's Romans gave England in 55BC, and there being evidence of a Roman settlement in the area);

- I was taught about Nature in the grounds of Oaklands School and was well prepared to be a Nature poet interested in the universe, and still use what I learned about birds;

- I was given a book token for my sixth birthday in 1945, walked to Addison's Bookshop in Loughton on my own and was guided by William Addison to buying *The Observer's Book of Trees* – he had just finished his *Epping Forest, Its Literary and Historical Associations*, and after encountering him for the last time when he was in a wheelchair in Queen Elizabeth's hunting lodge in 1988 I wrote *A View of Epping Forest* (2012) in his tradition;

- I recited a poem titled 'The Yellowhammer' by Liza Lehmann (1906), which contains the line "A little bit of bread and no cheese" twice, in a poetry recital contest at school at the age of 10 (which I believe I won), and would write about a yellowhammer's song in relation to Operation Yellowhammer in my poem *Fools' Gold*, one small example of how everything I have ever done has been useful for what was to come;

- When I was 10, my dentist was Howard Carter's brother and he told me the story of the first entry to Tutankhamun's tomb between drillings of my teeth, and captured my imagination – and later being given a *shawabti* (funerary figurine) of Tutankhamun which came from the tomb spurred me on to read up on Egypt and the Pyramids and to write the three stories in *The Building of the Great Pyramid*;

- I read classics and ancient history at Chigwell School and was well prepared for my *Classical Odes*, many of which are of visits to places within the classical world and which collectively reflect the culture of Europe, and, through reading Homer in Greek and Virgil in Latin, for my two epic poems;

- In April 1957 I spent a week in a solicitors' office in Loughton with Mark Liell, who claimed to be a direct descendant of Oliver Cromwell, and in 1966 I wrote 'An Epistle to an Admirer of Oliver Cromwell';

- In 1957 and 1958 I played cricket for Buckhurst Hill ('Buckhurst' means a wooded hill containing male deer or stags) and met for car lifts to away matches at the Bald-Faced Stag public house, and when I was 65 I moved to Buckhurst Hill and my literary trademark was already a stag, whose seven-branched antlers symbolised the seven disciplines and seven branches of literature in which I have written my 56 books;

- I was an articled clerk in a solicitors' office in London for a gap year and read Law during my first two terms at Oxford, including Roman Law and some Constitutional law, and was well prepared to write *World Constitution*;

- I read English Literature under Christopher Ricks, the leading world authority on Eliot and Tennyson, and he became my mentor and advised me as I moved away from Modernism to 17th- and 19th-century literary models, and corresponded with me for more than 40 years;

- In 1959 I met Ernest Hemingway in Malaga, Spain, and became the writer of 1,200 short stories (with another 200 waiting to be published);

- In Iraq I passed Suhrawardi's house every day and was told about his Illuminationism, which prepared me for experiencing the Light;

- On 8 January 1961, having been invited to stay with Colin Wilson in Cornwall, I woke early in his garden chalet and walked to Gorran Haven harbour and made an existential decision to go abroad and quest for Reality and try and get to Japan, and over lunch in The Rising Sun Inn at Portmellon I told him – and I eventually got to Japan, the Land of the Rising Sun, in 1963 and found Reality as an inner sun;

- In the summer of 1963, while waiting to be a Professor in Japan and down to my last £8, I worked as a park gardener in Dulwich Park and learned about the life cycle of plants and shrubs, including rhododendrons, and gardened in three schools (Rosedale Primary, Langbourne Primary and Kingsdale Schools), and acquired knowledge I would need when owning four schools and a historic house for which I was later grateful and which now seems to have been transmitted to me Providentially;

- In Japan my boss as Representative of the British Council was E.W.F. Tomlin, a metaphysical philosopher and friend of the Modernist poet T.S. Eliot – he invited me to lunch soon after I arrived in Japan and I wrote a Modernist poem 'The Silence' and became a metaphysical philosopher;

- I learned the wisdom of the East, *yang* and *yin*, that all opposites are reconciled in a unity (+A + –A = 0), from the Japanese poet Junzaburo Nishiwaki, and all my writings reconcile opposites into a unity;

- My colleague in Tokyo, R.H. Blyth, an expert on Zen Buddhism, arranged for me to attend a Zen meditation just before he died, and set me on my Mystic Way;

- I lunched with Edmund Blunden, a war poet, and later became a war poet in my two epic poems, *Overlord* about the Second World War and *Armageddon* about the War on Terror;

- I went to the Banqueting House on leave from Japan on 8 July 1966 and the ceiling is now on the front cover of *A Baroque Vision* and the throne and room are on the front cover of *The Coronation of King Charles*;

- I knew the short-story writer Frank Tuohy well – he invited me to visit China with him – and I became a short-story writer;

- I went out to the East and in Japan was asked to teach a course on 'The Decline of the West', and I reflected the decline of the West in my poetic works, and (though I did not know this on the ship) my next book will be called *The Fall of the West*;

- In Libya I wrote articles for *The Daily News*, visiting the Roman ruins under the byline The Barbary Gipsy, and they prepared me for my travelogues *The Last Tourist in Iran* and *The Libyan Revolution*, where they can be found in the Appendix – and they prepared me for the travelogue parts of *The Promised Land*;

- I visited the Modernist poet Ezra Pound, and after a long discussion with him realised that Modernism's abbreviated narrative in a sequence of images would not be a good narrative for my two epic poems;

- On 10 October 1987 at the Frankfurt Book Fair I told Reiner Stach of Fischers about my coming work *The Fire and the Stones*, and he said, "You have developed a universalist theory of world civilisations," and his use of the word 'universalist' reminded me I had used it in my diary on 9 April 1985 ("I am a Universalist") and led to my receiving in sleep the beginning of my 'Introduction to the New Universalism' for *The Fire and the Stones* on 29 April 1989.

I could go on; there were many more events in my life that prompted me towards my future direction, and had consequences. Some of these are among the remarkable events I described on pp.103–123. They can all be found in *My Double Life 1: This Dark Wood* and *My Double Life 2: A Rainbow over the Hills*. It seemed as though I had to fulfil a destiny, and I was placed in situations and circumstances that would allow me to fulfil that destiny.

The pattern in my life, in episodes

Sitting near the ship's rail on the rear deck and looking back, I could not help thinking that my life seems to have had a thrust, a curve, a direction (like the ship's direction), a purpose, and a pattern.

I found a pattern in my life in *My Double Life 1: This Dark Wood* and *My Double Life 2: A Rainbow over the Hills*. The 30 episodes in those two works (15 in each) cover 75 years, an average of 2.5 years per episode. So since *My Double 1: This Dark Wood* and *My Double Life 2: A Rainbow over the Hills*

Rear deck of *MS Serenissima*

ended in 2014 I have had two more episodes: 2014–2016; and 2017–2019. And I have started a third episode. These episodes are episodes 31–33.

Episode 31

In episode 31, which covers 2014–2016 and could be entitled Populism and Globalism, the referendum on Brexit took place and populist nationalism won. In October 2015 I had brought in the supranationalistic Universal State of the Earth, an interim globalist World State, for the World Philosophical Foundation (WPF). I had written my first masque, *The Dream of Europa*, on the expanding European Union, and I wrote *The Secret American Destiny* on cultural Universalism. I received the Gusi Peace Prize for Literature in 2016, and I wrote *Peace for our Time* (2018) on political Universalism, which gives a full account of episode 31.

Episode 32

In episode 32, which covers 2017–2019 and which could be entitled Nationalism and World State, I wrote *World State* and *World Constitution* throughout 2017 and I brought them out in 2018, both works of political Universalism which contrast nationalism and a World State. In late 2017 I wrote my second masque, *King Charles the Wise*, which foresees a united world. Just after this came out I spoke on the Prince of Wales' 70th birthday in Canterbury. I also brought out *Visions of England*, on 102 places in England. From August 2018 to May 2019 I wrote *Fools' Paradise*, opposing nationalistic Brexit.

In celebrations of my 80th birthday I spoke on world peace and a World State in Moscow and received the BRICS silver medal for 'Vision for Future'; and went on a cruise of the Mediterranean which took me to Kotor, where I saw what was claimed to be John the Baptist's hand (see pp.25–26). I had my 80th birthday celebrated in an exhibition at the University of Essex, which keeps my archive, and on my 80th birthday I received a coat of arms from the College of Arms full of Universalist imagery. There was also a family gathering for my 80th birthday.

During 2019 I also wrote my third masque, *The Coronation of King Charles*, which carries my vision for the coming Carolingian Age, and began *Fools' Gold*, a sequel to *Fools' Paradise*, which includes my vision for the UK's destiny. All these projects recognised my political Universalism.

To expand on how these events highlighted the theme of episode 32, Nationalism and World State:

Canterbury

On 17 November 2018, just after *King Charles the Wise* came out, there was a celebration of Prince Charles' 70th birthday at the conference hall in the Canterbury Cathedral Lodge Hotel in the Precincts, just opposite Canterbury Cathedral. Prince Charles was involved in the planning and chose the music for evensong in the Cathedral, but was unable to attend as he had to hold an investiture in London. He arranged for the day to be filmed so he could watch.

Ann and I arrived the evening before to stay overnight, and I met the seven other speakers, who were all courtiers, in the library over drinks including the co-author of Prince Charles's book *Harmony* and speech-writer for 20 years, Ian Skelly.

The next day, after a welcome by the Dean, we all spoke to about 200, and Skelly left a copy of *King Charles the Wise* for all to look through. Immediately before evensong I read my 1975 poem on Canterbury Cathedral, 'Pilgrims' Pavement'. It refers to God sitting on a rainbow, an image I took from the painted tester above the recumbent Black Prince in the Cathedral. Later I spoke of the Prince's being the next Head of the Commonwealth of (then, before the Maldives joined in February 2020) 53 nation-states. I said he would be second only to the UN Secretary-General, who oversees 193 nation-states, in the size of the supranationalist organisation he would head. At the end of my speech I turned and looked to camera and said, "Happy birthday, sir."

Between June and October 2019 I wrote my third masque, *The Coronation of King Charles*, which foresees work on a World State progressing during the coming Carolingian Age.

Moscow

I was invited to Russia for ten days by the Russian Ecological Foundation as a special guest (all expenses in Russia paid).

I was told my visit was to celebrate my 80th birthday, but in fact I was to speak about *World State* and bring in a new era of world peace on 22 April 2019, Earth Day, which – unbeknown to me but known to the audience of 250 in Moscow's semi-governmental Civic Chamber – was also the beginning of the Year of the Phoenix in the Mayan calendar which comes round every 2,000 years. The last Year of the Phoenix was around the time of Augustus, when the phoenix symbolised the birth of the Roman Empire from the ashes of the infighting during the Republic, ending with the Battle of Actium. This Year of the Phoenix of 2019 symbolised the birth of a democratic World State from the ashes of Europe, and the world, after the Second World War.

The invitation was issued by Svetlana Chumakova-Izmaylovskaya, and I was driven to the Civic Chamber by Igor Kondrashin of the World Philosophical Forum. When I arrived I was greeted by a Colonel in uniform.

I had been asked to bring greetings from Prince Charles, but the Foreign Office blocked the idea. I received a letter from Sir Alan Duncan, who was then in charge of Russia for the Foreign Office, setting out in six paragraphs what I could and could not do in Russia following the Salisbury Novochoking, and making it clear that my visit was a personal initiative. I operated within his guidelines, but nevertheless began my speech, "Greetings from the UK, Russia's wartime ally," which, when it was translated by the translator standing at my elbow, was warmly applauded.

The speech covered my political Universalism and is in *The Essentials of Universalism* [extract 71], and there is coverage in *Selected Letters*, where all the events of episode 32 and the early events of episode 33 can be found.

Nicholas Hagger speaking on his Universalist theme of One Earth, One Humankind in Moscow's semi-governmental Civic Chamber on 22 April 2019

At the end of my speech, which called for a World State and universal peace I was presented with a Golden Phoenix lapel badge (one of only two made) by a Russian cosmonaut wearing a Hero-of-Russia badge, Aleksandr Lazutkin (who spent 184 days in space), to mark my inauguration of a new age of world peace on the first day of the Year of the Phoenix.

The golden phoenix is a symbol of the World State rising from the ashes of the Second World War, and set my greetings "from Russia's wartime ally" in context. It made me again wonder if I had been sent down to earth months before the outbreak of the Second World War to create a World State that would rise from its ashes. Were invisible angels or Muses involved in this completely unexpected award?

The Russian Ecological Foundation's highest award commemorating the first cosmonaut Yuri Gagarin, a gold breastplate (or badge) of the Golden Phoenix, an ecological, spiritual and Universalist symbol. It is shaped like a drop of water, symbolising the universe, and shows a phoenix rising from the Fire of eternal life, its head haloed by the sun (the Light), its wings shaped like a bowl to receive inspiration from the wind and air, each wing containing seven feathers which can be seen as the seven disciplines and the seven branches of literature. The phoenix is also a World State rising from the ashes of the devastation of nation-states at the end of the Second World War.

I was also awarded a BRICS silver medal for 'Vision for Future'. BRICS stands for Brazil, Russia, India, China and South Africa, and I was honoured that these countries had been watching and were now recognising my calls for a World State.

Later I was called back to the stage. An Admiral and Vice-Admiral in full military uniform seized my wrists. For a moment I thought I was being arrested and hustled away for speaking too freely just down the road from the Kremlin, but then they raised my arms and I stood being filmed for the internet holding hands with an Admiral and Vice-Admiral in Russia's navy.

It was extraordinary that I, who was nearly outed as an intelligence agent by Kim Philby, should have received these awards and held hands with the Russian military. Somerset Maugham had been an intelligence agent in Moscow until Lenin's revolution, and no one in the Soviet Union celebrated his 80th birthday by having the military raise his arms. Having an Admiral and Vice-Admiral act in this way could have marked Russia's approval for my long journey from nationalism (which Philby knew) to Universalism and supranationalism.

Next day I was taken to the Russian Academy of Natural Sciences and had a discussion on camera with the top six academics. I showed *The New Philosophy of Universalism, World State* and *World Constitution*, and the Vice-President stood and made a speech to camera, saying that my ideas on Universalism had such quality that she would submit the books for a prize, and I was presented with the Academy's silver medal of Vernadsky.

I was taken to the Union of Russian Writers and sat in a room that had been visited by Pasternak and Solzhenitsyn and was given a badge to show that I had been made a member of the Moscow branch of the Union of Russian Writers.

A General who was present asked if he could visit me at my hotel. He told me he was working with a group from the Russian Academy of Sciences, that they had made a discovery as important as Galileo's and Copernicus's and had decided I should front a book about it which had already been written, and that it would be sent to me. I would be made a member of the Russian Academy of Sciences and would be the designated leader of the group. Despite further assurances that the book would be coming, it did not arrive.

I was taken to meet Gorbachev's consultant for half an hour. I was told Gorbachev might want to meet me, but later heard he had been taken to hospital unwell the next day.

I planted a tree, the first of a million Siberian cedars called for by the Mayor of Moscow, and I was told that a plaque with gold lettering would soon be on a wall in Moscow to commemorate the event.

I was taken to a reception for Russian Foreign-Office personnel and ambassadors at the Moscow City Duma, and was on Russian television that evening standing on the stage and chatting to the Chairman.

I was taken to the Cathedral of the Archangel, where (as I said in my speech) on 9 June 1966, standing in front of the icon of the winged Archangel Michael, I had a vision of a World State and world peace, which I wrote into 'Archangel', my poem on Communism.

Ann and I spent Easter Sunday with Igor Kondrashin of the World Philosophical Forum and his family at his country dacha 30kms outside Moscow near a river. After tea I changed into a suit and Ann and I were taken to Putin's rest-house and sanatorium, which had been built by Stalin and used by every Russian leader since then. There were three interconnected buildings and seemingly hundreds of doors for specialists.

After a tour Ann and I were taken to a room where three Russians were sitting on settees and we were sung to by two ladies in Russian costume. We had a personal concert in Putin's rest-house. Putin was in Vladivostok, meeting the leader of North Korea, and was going on to China, but I was asked to write to him and sign *World State* and *World Constitution* to him, and these were conveyed to him by one of three of his assistants I met.

There was talk of my being made Putin's peace consultant, which never came to anything. I have often said Einstein should have sat with Hitler and headed him away from nationalistic war, and it would have been good if I could have sat with Putin and made it clear that it would be counter-productive for him to disturb Europe's peace by invading Estonia in the same way that he moved into the Crimea. My message would have been that the needs of setting up a peaceful World State should have precedence over nationalistic adventures that could lead to war.

The next day I was asked to give an interview to a Russian TV station, which turned out to be a two-hour interview with the station's owner.

Cruise
From 12 to 24 May I celebrated my 80th birthday by going on a cruise of the Mediterranean, from Barcelona to Venice via Florence and Pisa; to Rome, Naples, Santorini, Athens, Mykonos for Delos; and to Kefalonia, Kotor in Montenegro and Dubrovnik.

The highlight after Kotor (see pp.24–25, 76) was my visit to Delos, the uninhabited island sacred to Apollo where the Athenians kept the tribute collected from the Cycladic islands to protect them from the Persians in the early 5th century BC.

I had tried to reach Delos in 1958. I had just ordered breakfast on the Mykonos waterfront – bread, butter and honey, for which I paid – when a boatman shouted, "Delos." Without hesitation my travelling companion and I left our breakfast untouched and jumped down into the boat and crossed the two-and-a-half miles to Delos. But it then became clear that the boatman would not wait while we walked to the ruins, and that he would not be returning, leaving us stranded on the uninhabited island if we stayed. So we had to return with him.

It took 61 years for me to return to Delos and visit the bank of the Athenian Empire, the five Treasury buildings within the oldest of the three temples to Apollo, and the Sacred Way where there was once a 9-metre-high statue to Apollo, and ponder on Athenian nationalism and imperialism, and the growth of the Athenian Empire, under the gaze of Apollo in the 5th century BC among the ancient white stones. I had waited 59 years to visit Petra, and now I had waited 61 years to revisit Delos.

Exhibition at the University of Essex

From 20 to 31 May 2019 there was an exhibition of my life and works with manuscripts from my archive and a slide show at the Albert Sloman Library, University of Essex. It was in honour of my 80th birthday, and I visited with Ann and my two sons and my PA on 31 May.

There were three glass cases of exhibits and my manuscripts, themed to feature *Collected Poems*, *Overlord* and *World State/World Constitution*, and the rolling slide show repeated itself every five minutes. I was told it had been very successful, there had been a lot of visitors. I peered into a glass case at a draft outline of *World Constitution* they had found in one of (then) 58 boxes of my archive. I had no recollection of having written that manuscript outline. *Overlord* and *World State* summed up the theme of this episode: Nationalism and World State.

Nicholas Hagger peering at a draft outline of *World
Constitution* at the exhibition of his life and works at the
Albert Sloman Library, University of Essex, on 31 May 2019

Crest and coat of arms

I had been interrogated by Garter Principal King of Arms, Thomas
Woodcock, during a visit to him regarding my descent from the
Hagars (as the name was then spelt) of Bourn Hall, sheep-farmers
and Lords of the Manor in Cambridgeshire from the 16th to the
18th centuries. They were descended from Carolus Haggar, who left
Brugge (Bruges), a European centre for sheep-farmers, in 1336 and
settled in Chelmsford, Essex.

To my astonishment he announced that he was awarding me my
own crest and coat of arms, which my descendants will be able to use
for ever. Details of how I formed the crest and coat of arms can be
found in *Selected Letters*. The patent was deliberately dated 22 May
2019 in honour of my 80th birthday, and the crest is topped by a stag,
my trademark as the two seven-branched antlers reflect the seven
branches of literature and the seven disciplines I have written within.
The shield shows three diagonal lions from the Hagars' 1605 coat of
arms, but brandishing quills to represent my works.

Shakespeare went to the College of Arms building on the same site
to arrange details of the coat of arms awarded to his father in 1597,

and I was honoured to have received my own crest and coat of arms on my 80th birthday. Coats of arms were worn in battle at Agincourt and had national associations then, but now, like Shakespeare's arms, span several centuries and have a Universalist application.

Family gathering

Finally, on Sunday 2 June 2019 there was a family gathering of 35 to celebrate my 80th birthday at our fourth school, Braeside School, Buckhurst Hill, where my sister was Head Girl in 1967.

We sat at tables under awnings in the garden on a warm day and ate a lunch prepared by the school kitchen staff, and the children played football in the tennis-court and grappled with giant chess. There was live background music from a couple of musicians under a tree, and there was a cake with a book motif: a brown 'leather-bound' volume and a pen.

I spoke. It was not an appropriate setting to tell them that Garter had awarded me my own crest and coat of arms, which my descendants could use, and had dated it on my 80th birthday, but I did dwell on my Universalist Latin motto (which is on the coat of arms): *fortis, perspicax, innovans, diligens* – be courageous, perspicacious (or discerning), innovative and hard-working (or diligent).

Sitting in the garden of our fourth school next to the Buckhurst Hill cricket field where I once batted before a crowd of hundreds sitting three or four deep, some in deck-chairs, in 1957 and 1958, I was amazed that these birthday events had brought me face-to-face with the post-Suez nationalist world of my youth and with the unique structure of the supranationalist world of the tenth Universalist commandment without my seeking them. Again I detected the hands of my Muses – or perhaps of angels, Providential activity from the beyond that somehow happened to me and carried me forward through each episode.

Episode 33

And now episode 33 has begun, which covers from 2020 and which could be entitled Vision and Legacy. It began with the coronavirus, Covid-19, which has brought back nationalistic borders and made the

Promised Land recede for a year or two – but the virus has opened up a new interest in a world government that can control all viruses. The virus has been seen as a bio-weapon and now there is a call for a one-world approach to viruses and for the equivalent of a World State that can deliver it.

As if the Muses were putting me in positions where I could carry forward my call for a World State I was invited out of the blue, without any prior contact or indication, to join the Executive Board of the World Intellectual Forum, which soon afterwards set up the Global Network for Peace, Disarmament and Development to bring in a world government and world constitution largely based on my books *The World Government, World State* and *World Constitution*.

During 2020, part of which was spent under lockdown, I assembled my legacy, focusing on the works I have written in *Selected Letters* and *Collected Prefaces*, in *A Baroque Vision* and *The Essentials of Universalism* – and of course in *The Promised Land*. The theme of this episode, Vision and Legacy, is in the vision in *A Baroque Vision* and in the presentation of my legacy in these five works. I have given an account of some of the events of episode 33 in this book, *The Promised Land*, most notably my vision of world unity at the top of Mount Nebo.

A slave of the Muses

Looking back as the ship chugged through the early dark, maintaining its clear direction towards Suez, I saw that my life had a direction that situations, events and circumstances assisted. And deep down I could not see this assistance as random chance; rather as the workings of Providence, in the sense of the protective care of the Muses.

It was as if my soul had been given a blueprint of my life before it incarnated, similar to souls choosing their lives in book 10 of Plato's *Republic*, and as if from time to time my soul had recalled what it should be doing and had sensed if it was on the wrong path. It was as if my soul had sometimes changed direction – from Law to English Literature, for example – if it felt it was on the wrong path, and it was as if events, in conjunction with the Muses, had guided my soul into sticking to my right path.

It was as if my Muses wanted me to undertake a project and long task on their behalf and act as a kind of intelligence agent operating for the beyond, and so long as I worked for them like a kind of slave, channelling their new ideas, they would assist me in bringing my work to birth. I wondered whether, having been a British intelligence agent at the time of my illumination and having become an intelligence agent operating for the beyond, I had defected to the Muses just as Philby had defected to the Russians.

In the dark, progressing towards Suez, it seemed I had been a willing channel and slave of the Muses, like Sisyphus rolling my 56 boulders uphill in the hope of making a hilltop cairn of Universalist works, and that events and circumstances in my early life had put me in positions in which I could serve them.

Denied access to the Promised Land, like Moses
With this perception still in my mind, we were summoned to the lounge on deck 5 for an emergency briefing, and were told that Israel had closed its border with Egypt that afternoon because of Covid. We would not be able to visit Israel.

Our ship had been denied access to the Promised Land of Israel in 2020 just as Moses was denied access to the Promised Land after seeing it from Mount Nebo c.1235BC. Like Moses I had been allowed to look, but could not get in. Instead we would head for Alexandria. Events had seen to it that I would not be describing Israel in the service of the Muses on this voyage.

6

Conclusions on a Providential Life and Works, and on European Civilisation

Cairo and the pyramids

At 8am next morning we were driven through Suez to Cairo with a police escort and armed guards. We stopped behind the pyramids of Khufu (the Great Pyramid), Khafra (or Khafre or Chephren), and Mycerinus in a viewing area.

Nicholas Hagger with the Great Pyramid (left) and the Pyramid of Khafra (right)

We went on to the Boat Museum by the Great Pyramid and saw Khufu's solar ship, one of five barques buried near the Great Pyramid that had been unearthed in 1954, perhaps the oldest boat in existence. It has been restored from 1,200 pieces of Lebanese cedar.

The five solar barques carried the mummy of the dead pharaoh across the Nile to his Valley Temple, and from there it was brought up the causeway into the tomb chamber. The five barques were then buried to provide transport for Khufu in the next world, where Khufu would be living in Ra's eternal sunshine.

We went on to Khafra's Valley Temple, where Khafra was mummified and where there were originally 23 statues of him.

The Sphinx, with the Great Pyramid (left) and the Pyramid of Khafra (centre)

The Sphinx

We went on to the Sphinx (so named by the Greeks after the Sphinx in Greek mythology) and walked as near to it as we could on the long viewing platform. I looked at its alignment. It was clearly aligned with Khafra's pyramid,

and was sideways-on to the Great Pyramid of Khufu, and I was sure it had the face of Khafra, Khufu's son. This was in keeping with Egyptian practice among pharaohs: the son always took the credit and discredited his father. I could see the Sphinx, an

The Sphinx in front of Khafra's Pyramid

embodiment of Khafra, was peering at the horizon, seeking the power of the Sun-god Ra and the second life.

Having researched Khufu and Khafra and written about them in 'The Riddle of the Great Pyramid' and 'The Meaning and Purpose of the Great Pyramid' I now had a third story which would reveal the key to the pyramids: 'The Great Pyramid as a House of Eternity', written by the same official who wrote the previous two stories between 2580 and 2560BC. (All three stories are in *The Building of the Great Pyramid*.) It begins, "I am 80 now and Khafra is Pharaoh."

We lunched at the Mena House Hotel (Khedive Ismail's hunting lodge, built in 1869) in a huge room with gold decorations on the walls and enormous chandeliers hanging from a high ceiling. There were many dishes.

The Egyptian Museum of Antiquities and Ramesses II
Then we went on to the Egyptian Museum of Antiquities. We walked through the Tutankhamun galleries and saw the death mask again. We then had free time. So we went to the Royal Mummies Halls.

I immediately saw Ramesses II and stood beside him. I knew Ramesses meant "Ra is the one who bore him". Like Khafra's face in the Sphinx, he looked for Ra on the horizon. He was lying on his back with a hooked nose (despite his flat conventional nose in his huge statues), and a haughty profile, a bald head with grey side hair tinged with henna, a thin neck and arms with his hands and long fingernails in the air, his right one pointing at his heart and his left one above, so he was like a baby discovering his fingers. He was about 90, and reigned for 67 years. Some records say he lived to be between 90 and 96, but there is a consensus that he was around 90 (c.1303–1213BC).

I recalled that he had eight wives, over 200 concubines and over 100 children (48 to 50 sons and 40 to 53 daughters). (In 2005, at a *Son et Lumière* at the temple of Karnak, it was said that Ramesses II had fathered 92 boys and 106 girls.)

He looked very dark-skinned, and I noticed that the mummy of his father Seti I was very black. Science has confirmed that as a young man Ramesses II was fair-skinned with wavy ginger hair – microscopic inspection shows his hair was originally red – and his mummy has fractures and shows arthritis (he walked with a hunched back in later life), an abscess by a hole in a mandible tooth (which may have killed him), and poor circulation.

I stood and looked at the man who was reputedly the pharaoh who would not let the Hebrews leave Egypt. I studied the face, the nose and the lips that had haughtily told Moses he could not leave Egypt. There is a tradition that Moses was his half-brother or step-brother (as maintained in the film *Exodus, Gods and Kings*) as Moses was taken from the bulrushes by Pharaoh's daughter and adopted. However, it is unlikely that Moses was in fact related to Ramesses II. He looked frail and strangely shorn of authority.

Then I recalled that I was supposed to have met him in a former life. I had met a past-life hypnotist Maurice Blake at a conference in July 1978. He told me he hypnotised people and got them to experience a former life, and asked if I would visit him. I was apprehensive, but also curious about the after-life – like Faust, I sought "beyond the threshold of death" – and open-minded on reincarnation. I saw the invitation as an opportunity I should not refuse. So I made an appointment, drove to Norwich, lay on his sofa with my left arm raised, was hypnotised and taken back through a series of clear images to the life of a young

English Jesuit priest, John Barfield, who left the Vale of Esthwaite in the Lake District, went out to Canada and died of cholera in 1836. Blake took me through my last moments.

There were more things that I wanted to know, to test whether this had actually happened, and I went back four weeks later on 31 August 1978, revisited that life for more clear images, and was then taken further back, to a new regression.

I – in that life, a temple-maiden – had been lined up as one of at least ten women to be inspected by Ramesses II when he came to my temple. He was reasonably young and had a high gold head-dress, and he chose me. This mummy of Ramesses II did not have the authority I remember from my regression. I wrote about my regression in *My Double Life 2: A Rainbow over the Hills* (pp.75–76):

Blake took me back a long time and I surfaced under a huge temple statue of a man I pronounced to be "Ramesses the Second as a Sun-god". I was a woman and lay a garland at his feet at the top of the steps. I lived in the temple. Outside the temple a philosopher sat on a stool, naked above the waist and sporting a black beard, before a group of ten temple-maidens who sat on sand before him. One of them was me. I wore a dress with one shoulder bare and sandals with a twined thong between each big and second toe. The image of the philosopher and his class was so vivid and colourful that I could almost put my hand in and grab a handful of sand. It was like seeing a scene from c.1300 BC [actually c.1270–1260BC] on live TV. I knew the philosopher was a healer and taught occult arts, and that the maidens made the Nile flood by taking part in a public ritual involving the Sun-god.

This ritual involved Ramesses II coming into the temple and choosing one of us for ritual love-making. I saw the beginning of such a ceremony. It was a hot day with a blue sky, and all those who lived in the temple were on parade. The young Ramesses arrived with a tall and shining gold head-dress and gold armour. He was surrounded by his entourage and we were thrilled to see him. He looked magnificent. He came down the line and stopped at me and touched his heart. Recounting this to Blake under hypnotism I dissolved into tears, which can be heard on the tape. I was choking with emotion at the honour, for I was the "Chosen One" and he would take me within and make love to me and make the Nile flood. My name was Nebhotep, and I was ecstatically happy.

Blake brought me out of my trance. In the ensuing discussion I recalled having seen the mummy of Ramesses II in the Cairo Museum [in 1970]. I had looked at the mummy for a long time without realising that I was gazing at the corpse of my former boyfriend. Later I wrote a poem about my two visits to Maurice Blake: 'A Temple-Dancer's Temple-Sleep'. I again pondered whether I had a spirit that can survive death and take memories with it. Had I had far memories or just day-dreams? I knew that if my spirit had lived many times before and brought memories of past lives with it to my present life, then I would want to know this and know my past lives as such knowledge would affect my view of what a man is and of his place in the universe, which would have to be measured over many centuries and not just one lifetime. I knew that if this was the case I would have no fear of death, and that after dying I would be conscious in a mist of light. If, on the other hand, I had merely been day-dreaming then I received some very vivid poetic images which had the force of memories.

I looked again at Ramesses II's right hand, still pointing to his heart, that had picked me out when (if my regression was more than a day-dream) I was a woman and pointed to his heart. It was a strange experience. I felt recognition, but this recognition was tempered by my male revulsion at his lifestyle and treatment of women – or was this a far memory of my later revulsion towards him in that lifetime?

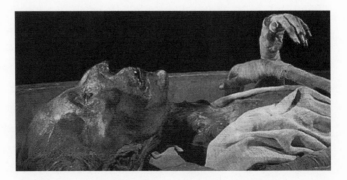

Mummy of
Ramesses II
in Cairo's
Egyptian
Museum of
Antiquities

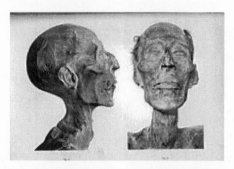

The mummy of Ramesses II

A colossal granite head of Ramesses II from the Ramesseum mortuary temple in Thebes, upper Egypt, c.1270BC, in the British Museum; and a portrait of Shelley who wrote 'Ozymandias' in 1818 by Alfred Clint, 1829

I recognised his type. He was an imperial nationalist, and from my encounters with nationalist leaders during my intelligence work and my familiarity with how their attitudes led to conflict I recognised his type. He reminded me of Johnson, who had similarly followed nationalism and rejected Universalism (and when Foreign Secretary had declined – I suspected on principle – to give me a bodyguard when I collected my award in Manila in 2016). Ramesses II needed his high head-dress to bolster his authority so he could be arrogant towards Moses and ask scornfully and contemptuously, "Who is Yahweh?"

The Greek historian Diodorus Siculus marvelled at the gigantic temple, the Ramesseum, and colossal sculptures of Ramesses II, which I saw in 2005. Diodorus Siculus described a cartouche ('an oval ring including Egyptian hieroglyphs, usually representing the name and title of a king', *Concise Oxford Dictionary*) on the shoulder of this colossal sculpture (see p.142): "King of Kings am I, Osymandias [a transliteration of his throne name into Greek]. If anyone would know how great I am and where I lie, let him surpass one of my works."

In 'Ozymandias' Shelley paraphrased this inscription:

'My name is Ozymandias, king of kings:
Look on my works, ye Mighty, and despair!'

Shelley was writing of a ruined statue of "two vast and trunkless legs of stone" (poetic licence as these are not there) and "a shattered visage" (see pp.140–141) in the Ramesseum across the Nile from Luxor. Shelley wrote of Ramesses II's "frown,/And wrinkled lip, and sneer of cold command", which Moses encountered before the Exodus. The head and chest of another colossal statue of Ramesses II is now in the British Museum (see p.140), and its imminent arrival, together with Diodorus Siculus's description of the inscription, inspired Shelley's poem in 1818. (Shelley died in 1822.)

The Ramesseum, mortuary temple to Ramesses II across the Nile from Luxor, and (overleaf) the fallen Colossus there with a cartouche on its shoulder (in close-up on p.142) bearing Ramesses II's throne name, which Diodorus transliterated into Greek as 'Osymandias' and which, along with the statue in the British Museum, inspired Shelley to write 'Ozymandias'

The shattered visage of the statue in the Ramesseum, Luxor, Egypt, with
the cartouche visible on the back of its left shoulder

The Ramesseum, the mortuary or memorial temple to Ramesses
II, god on earth, to keep alive his memory after his death, was begun
soon after the start of his reign in 1279BC and construction lasted 20
years. The statue of Ramesses II in the British Museum was 19 metres
high, and rivalled the Colossi of Memnon and the seated statues of
Ramesses II carved into the mountain at Abu Simbel as one of the largest

surviving colossal statues in the world. It weighed 1,000 tons and was transported over land. If Nebhotep was living there, then she met Ramesses II when he was visiting to inspect the progress in the construction of his memorial temple during its later stages when the statue I saw at the beginning of my regression, of "Ramesses II as a Sun-god", the statue of

Two feet of Ramesses II at the Ramesseum

Shelley's 'Ozymandias', was in place. (In my regression I saw, and may have a far memory of, the statue of Ozymandias.)

During my visit in 2005 I found the two bare feet of the statue of Ramesses II, and I picked up an earthenware pottery wine cup with a pointed base that could be stuck in the sand, and which I had perhaps drunk from in that early life.

I discussed Ramesses II (Ozymandias) with our guide. I asked him if Ramesses II picked out a woman, a temple-maiden, when he visited temples. He said, "Yes, certainly, but not a temple-maiden. They had to remain virgins. There were concubines attached to the temples, he picked out a concubine."

I was taken aback. In my regression I had clearly seen myself in a former life as a temple-maiden, so was Ramesses II breaking with convention and going for a temple-maiden rather than a concubine? Or was I a temple concubine in that former life? I was not certain the clear images I saw during my regression were anything more than day-dreams, but supposing they were in fact far memories.... I knew my name, Nebhotep, and my tearful reaction was that of a temple-maiden and Ramesses II's consort rather than of a concubine. I knew that the first of Ramesses II's eight wives is listed as "possibly" Nefertari or Nebettawy; could I have been saying her name and wrongly transcribed it phonetically after my regression as Nebhotep? Queen Nefertari or Nebettawy, Mistress of Upper and Lower Egypt (the plant and the bee), had six children by Ramesses II and died c.1255BC.

Small statue of Khufu in the Egyptian Museum of Antiquities, Cairo

Later I went downstairs to the Egyptian Museum of Antiquities' ground floor, and after a hunt in different rooms of the main gallery I eventually found (in room 37) the only known statue of Khufu, only 7.5cms high. It was hard to check his face against the Sphinx without a magnifying glass. Then (in room 42) I found the statue of Khafra (or Chephren), a black life-size statue whose face, I thought, *did* resemble the face of the Sphinx looking at the rising eastern sun.

We returned to the coach and were driven back to the ship. My head was

Life-size statue of Khafra in the Egyptian Museum of Antiquities, Cairo (left), and, for comparison, the face of the Sphinx from the front, which looks identical (above)

full of the Sphinx with the face of Khafra (or Chephren) looking for the rising sun, and of the statues of Ramesses II with a conventional flat, not hooked nose. And I was thinking of the four external seated statues of Ramesses II in Abu Simbel (see p.145), and the splendid young man I met in his gold head-dress and gold armour some time between c.1270 and 1260BC, soon after his encounter with Moses and the beginning of the Exodus, in a temple, perhaps the Ramesseum.

I thought back to Moses, aged about 40, meeting Ramesses II, aged about 28, in c.1275BC, and I thought of the conclusions that they would have drawn from their lives in c.1235BC: Moses after 40 years in the wilderness, that the Promised Land was ahead; and Ramesses II shortly before his death in 1213BC, that his three campaigns in Canaan and Syria against the Hittites and his campaigns in Nubia and Libya had glorified his nation and spread his nation's influence as 'Egypt-first'. Both of them were nationalist leaders

Close-up of colossal statue of Ramesses II wearing the double crown of Lower and Upper Egypt and showing an idealised unhooked nose, at the Great Temple of Ramesses II in Abu Simbel, Egypt

– Moses of the Hebrews, Ramesses of the Egyptians – but Yahweh universalised Abraham's descendants and gave Moses a Universalist perspective in his Ten Commandments, which went way beyond national considerations.

Views from the ship in the Suez Canal

As I sat later on the deck of the ship, waiting to enter the Suez Canal, I wondered what conclusions I would draw from my life.

*

Conclusions on the Providential direction of my life and destiny
This brought me back to the Providential nature of my life (see pp.103–119 and 119–123).

Now, sitting again on the rear deck as the ship headed for the Suez Canal in twilight and again looking back, I could see very clearly the Providential direction of my life, which has perhaps been guided by the foresight of my Muses:

- It felt as if I chose, or was sent down, to be born in May 1939 to experience the war, call for world peace, and leave a blueprint for a World State;

- I moved to Loughton in 1943 to live in Churchill's constituency and experience the bombing there, which I would need for my understanding of war and yearning for peace, and for my epic poem *Overlord*, which is about the last year of the Second World War, from D-Day to the fall of Berlin and the dropping of the first two atomic bombs;

- I was to go to Chigwell so I could meet Montgomery for *The Warlords* and *Overlord* and (under a young classics master, David Horton) get into Oxford on my classics;

- I was interested in the universe and journeying to another planet, and after research in my local library, in a school exercise book (now in my archive) in 1953 I wrote a novel about a journey to the moon and on to an imaginary planet called Holacanthus, which I had to abandon to take my 'O' levels – and the whole-universe perspective of Universalism is rooted in this early work, which put me in touch with the universe;

- I was to meet my early friends John Ezard so he could introduce me to new works in English and European literature; Colin Wilson so he could introduce me to new works in European literature; and Ricky Herbert so he could introduce me to new works in

French, German and Russian literature at Oxford, as I would need to absorb all these works and their challenging perspectives before my coming writing career;

- I was at Oxford so I could meet Christopher Ricks, who would become one of the world's leading critics and an authority on Tennyson and Eliot, and have a lifelong association with him in which he would act as my mentor during forty years of correspondence while I charted a good direction for my writing;

- I was introduced to the heroic couplet in 1960 and wrote 'Zeus's Ass', 'Zeus's Emperor' and *Fools' Paradise* in heroic couplets;

- I was in Baghdad to get to know the Iraqi desert as a foretaste of the wilderness where, like Moses, I would be spending much of my life, and to get to know the Muslim world I would write about in *Armageddon*, my second epic poem about the War on Terror from 9/11 to the departure of George W. Bush, which included an Appendix listing bin Laden's 69 attempts to obtain nuclear weapons that I replicated in *The Secret American Dream* and sent, flagged, to President Obama – and a month later, on Obama's orders, bin Laden was dead;

- I was in Japan to meet E.W.F. Tomlin, who set me on my metaphysical course when I was teetering on being sceptical; to meet Junzaburo Nishiwaki, who introduced me to Eastern wisdom that transformed my approach to writing, the Taoist reconciliation of all opposites and contradictions, *yin* and *yang*, in what became my trademark algebraic formula $+A + -A = 0$; to meet R.H. Blyth, who sent me to meditate in a Zen temple and set me on my Mystic Way; to meet Frank Tuohy who inspired me to write short stories in 1966; to meet Brian Buchanan, who, while sharing a room with me, talked about the famous Irish writers he had met as a boy and by nicknaming me Shelley sent me back to Romantic poets; to have my first experiences of the Light; and to become tutor to Emperor Hirohito's second son Prince Hitachi, and see a new way of considering all history as a whole;

- I was in Libya to write weekly two-page features on the country's Roman ruins and historical features under the byline The Barbary Gipsy, an approach I would need for my two travelogues *The Last*

Tourist in Iran and *The Libyan Revolution*, and this work, *The Promised Land*; to experience the nationalistic perspectives of Gaddafi's revolution and of the UK's Secret Intelligence Service (MI6), in the course of which I lost my first wife, and as a result of which, while working in Greenwich at the urging of the Secret Intelligence Service, I met my second wife (who I would not have met without being in Greenwich as part of my intelligence work); and to put myself firmly on the Mystic Way and progress towards full illumination;

- Back in London I was a British intelligence agent working as an Unofficial Ambassador to the African liberation movements for Prime Minister Edward Heath, and following my full illumination in 1971 I might have become an intelligence agent for the Light working as an Unofficial Ambassador to the Muses, who are bringing in a Universalist World State;

- I wrote on international politics for *The Times* in the early 1970s and wrote poems about international politics to protect the cultural health of Europe, including 'Zeus's Ass', 'Zeus's Emperor', *Fools' Paradise* and *Fools' Gold*;

- I left overseas universities for schools in the UK in 1971 so I could focus on my poems and my Baroque vision, and my short stories, in London, and to meet my second wife in Greenwich, with whom I would create the Oak-Tree Group of Schools;

- I was a Head of English in Wandsworth so I could teach set books of poets (Chaucer, Milton, Wordsworth, Tennyson) that would help my own work;

- I acquired my old school, Oaklands School, in 1982 and put my wife, a teacher, in as Headmistress, to give me time to write my works;

- I became a small publisher for a couple of years to learn how books are produced, as the knowledge would help me when I was ready to be a full-time author;

- I began to be published in 1991, and met established figures who helped me in different ways: the poets Kathleen Raine and David Gascoyne, the historian Asa Briggs, a Universalist Philosophy Group of a dozen philosophers I chaired, and many others who can be found in my *Selected Letters*;

- While visiting my wife's aunt in Porthleven, Cornwall, I was given a large lump of local iron pyrites by a neighbour, and years later, in 2020, supplied a picture of it for the front cover of *Fools' Gold*;
- My 56 books within seven disciplines seemed to be fed to me from the beyond during my Providential journey.

I knew that those who seek to change the world's existing structures are in the wilderness, but that the wilderness is where many solitary geniuses have lived. They have developed their unique vision apart from others until it has grown and bloomed in significant works. I knew before I left England to go to Iraq (and later to Japan, and to Libya) that talent is formed in groups, whereas genius (in the sense of originality) is developed in solitude and isolation, in the wilderness.

In Iraq I discovered the wilderness in the desert all round Baghdad, which I crossed to reach Jordan in early 1962. My decade abroad began my time in the wilderness, and as Christopher Ricks pointed out when I chatted to him at Worcester College, Oxford on 1 July 2019, I had been on a mission to bring Universalism to birth, an entirely new approach to the world, ever since leaving Oxford.

Looking back over my Universalism, I again wondered if I was sent down to the earth by the angels in 1939, shortly before the outbreak of the war, to draw up a plan for world peace so there would be no more wars. If so, I have done my best to deliver this. In Manila I was approached by a Syrian diplomat who wanted me to take a peace plan for Syria to Assad, and I wrote a 15-point peace plan which is in *Peace for our Time*. Assad fell ill, and I was unable to visit him.

If I *was* sent down to the earth in 1939 with a mission, I am sad at some of the pivotal situations I encountered along the way, including the loss of my first marriage. However, the ensuing Dark Night set me on my Mystic Way to full illumination and then to the instinctively unitive vision that permeates my 56 books and that – in the tradition of Dante, Kant and world leaders from Truman to Gorbachev – led me to call for a world government that can bring in a new era of peace.

Conclusions on how my works came out of my Providential life
Now, looking back in the ship's deserted library on a swell that had made some queasy, I could see how my works came out of my Providential life:

- My concern for peace was born in the war years when I lived under Nazi bombing;
- My poetry came out of my observations of Nature when I was a pupil at Oaklands School and kept a bird diary, and out of my Latin and Greek verse at school;
- My short stories came out of my collection of Roman, Greek and old English coins, which taught me to study the faces of the past Roman Emperors and English Kings;
- My Universalism grew out of my after-lunch coffees in fellow undergraduates' rooms at Worcester College, when I sat with undergraduates reading philosophy, history, different European literatures, international politics and other disciplines, and in the course of our post-prandial discussions it seemed natural to be cross-disciplinary;
- My writing life was shaped by my 1960 letter to Intelligence Corps at the War Office (see *Selected Letters*, p.3), and subsequent signing of the Official Secrets Act, which took me deep into nationalism, and although I countered this with supranationalism entrammelled me in restrictions for my entire writing life;
- My sense of unity began in the stone garden at Ryoanji Temple in Kyoto, Japan;
- Japan turned me into a writer – I sat day after day at my desk in sweltering heat in 1965–1966 and wrote 'The Silence' over 18 months;
- The nationalism I encountered in Iraq and Libya (both Gaddafi's and British Intelligence's) sowed seeds that turned me against nationalism and towards a conglomerate that can keep peace (the EU); and
- I went into the negative side of world government (self-interested *élites*) and came out supporting the positive side (a democratic World State solving all the world's problems).

Looking back for the context of how my works came out of my life, I again fixed on my tenth conclusion about the Providential direction of my life (see pp.146–149), which gives a Providential – guided – slant on how my works came out of my life: that at the time of my full illumination in 1971 I was a British intelligence agent working as an Unofficial Ambassador to the African liberation movement for Prime Minister Edward Heath, and that following my illumination I might have become an intelligence agent for the Light, working as an Unofficial Ambassador to the Muses, who are bringing in a Universalist World State – and who might have fed me my works. To put it in more straightforward language, my allegiance changed from nationalist work to opening to the universal images and works that bubbled up in my inner spring.

Conclusions on my Providential life and people I knew appearing at the right time

I found I had reached conclusions on my Providential life and the people I have known:

- I followed the course I wanted – I wanted to write, and I evaded the Law by crucially meeting Christopher Ricks and devoted my time to getting my books written;
- Outwardly my life was bitty – lecturing abroad, working for British Intelligence, writing for *The Times*, teaching at schools in London, running schools in Essex – but the bits were crucial to creating my inner unity that produced my works;
- It seemed I was in a wilderness, but (with hindsight) the right people appeared at the right time who would stimulate my thinking and help bring my writings to birth: Christopher Ricks, E.W.F. Tomlin, Frank Tuohy, R.H. Blyth Brian Buchanan, Edmund Blunden, Ezra Pound, Colin Wilson, Asa Briggs, Kathleen Raine, David Gascoyne, Ted Hughes and others;
- In the same way the right people appeared at the right time who would enable me to own four schools and have 330 staff, and fund the acquisition and building programmes of the schools by buying and selling properties;

- Had I stuck to my original path of Law and politics, I would not have lived abroad, would probably not have undergone the development I underwent in Japan, Libya and London, and would not have written my works, so I was right to evade the Law and choose bittiness – and inner unity of purpose;
- As a general rule, in life the people one needs to help one discover one's course and destiny appear at the right time, suggesting that our lives *are* Providential – guided from the beyond – rather than accidental and the products of random chance.

I had sought out the desert wildernesses of Iraq and Libya to advance my self-development, just as early Christian hermits and mystics had sought out the Egyptian desert at Scetis where they could advance along the Mystic Way without the distraction of complex civilisation. Even now, on this journey and voyage, I had sought out the wildernesses round Mount Nebo, Bethany, Wadi Rum, and the deserts on either side of the Gulf of Suez, and my memories of the wilderness round St Catherine's monastery. I reflected that, like John the Baptist's, mine was a voice crying from the wilderness – even from the wildernesses of Jordan and Egypt in this book, which has turned out to be a reflection on how the wilderness leads to unitive living as well as on how my Universalism developed and turned into a lifelong project.

Conclusions on the European civilisation and my approach to it

Looking back, I could see that my view of the European civilisation was exactly as I had described it in *The Fire and the Stones* (1991), updated in *The Rise and Fall of Civilizations* (2008):

- The United Kingdom has been a part of the European civilisation since the Roman time of Julius Caesar;
- The central idea of the European civilisation has been the centrality of the Christian Light in first Catholicism and then Protestantism, see *The Fire and the Stones*;
- The European mystical tradition was strong during the Classical Middle Ages and weakened after the Renaissance, but strengthened during the Baroque Age and was preserved in Romantic poetry,

and I kept it alive in my post-Romantic, neo-Baroque poetic works such as 'The Silence' and in my classical odes, see *The Universe and the Light* and *The Light of Civilization*;

- The European literary tradition has weakened since a breakdown of certainties and Europe's secularisation, and I kept the central idea alive in my writings, and reflected the fundamental theme of world literature (a Universalist concept) in *A New Philosophy of Literature*;

- European philosophy is rooted in the ancient Greek philosophy's view of the universe in the 5th century BC, and my philosophy carried forward the Presocratic Greek philosophers' intuitional grasp of the unity of the universe – my Form from Movement Theory (see p.114) looks back to Anaximander of Miletus's view of the universe – and reflected the Universalist oneness of the universe and humankind, see *The New Philosophy of Universalism*;

- European history has emerged from the history of ancient Greece and Rome, and my history continued the universal perspective of Gibbon, Spengler and Toynbee, and reflected the Universalist perception of all history as one flow in works, see *The Fire and the Stones*, updated as *The Rise and Fall of Civilizations*;

- European religion has centred round the Light of Christianity, and my religious works saw the Light as being common to all religions and showed that all religions have a common Universalist essence in the mystic Light, see *The Light of Civilization*;

- European international politics developed from Greek democracy through city-states, unstable nation-states, nationalist dictatorships and wars to its present liberal democracy and peace, and my political works showed that a Universalist World State is ahead that will include all civilisations and end all warfare, and that the European conglomerate (the European Union) has collected together European states to enable this to be formed, see *The World Government*, *The Dream of Europa*, *World State* and *World Constitution*; and

- European culture was unified round the European civilisation's central idea of the Christian Light, as religious paintings, music and literary works such as Dante's show, and my cultural works showed that a Universalist world culture that reconciles the mystical and the secular in all living civilisations will be a consequence of a Universalist World State, see *The Secret American Destiny*.

Power seems to be shifting from the West to the East as the US economy has been more affected by Covid than China's economy, and Europe has been more affected than some Far-Eastern countries. At the end of the Cold War there was one superpower, the US. Under Trump the US drew back from world leadership, and there are now three superpowers, the US, the EU and China, with authoritarian China set to be expansive and dominant by 2030 unless the world can bring in a federal World State.

Conclusions on the stages of European civilisation I have lived through
Looking back, I could see that in my life I lived through a tumultuous period: the Second World War, the melting away of the British Empire, participation in what became the European Union and departure from it. In my study of civilisations, *The Fire and the Stones*, updated as *The Rise and Fall of Civilizations*, I have shown that 25 civilisations go through 61 parallel stages.

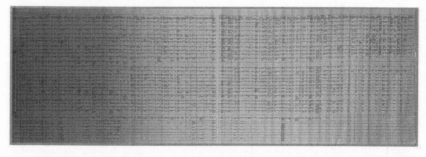

The 7-foot-long chart that accompanies *The Fire and the Stones* (1991) showing 25 civilisations rising and falling through 61 stages. The book predicted the end of Communism in the Soviet Union, and forecast the conglomerate that became the European Union.

I could see that in the last tumultuous 80 years I have lived from the end of stage 37 to the beginning of stage 46 in the European civilisation

Nicholas Hagger shows Iain McNay the 7-foot-long chart of 25 civilisations each going through 61 stages while being interviewed by him on Conscious TV on 14 April 2015

as set out on my seven-foot-long chart; and that the consequences of the events in stages 37 to 44 could still be felt, and that stages 45 and 46 were already making their presence felt even though, despite being expected, they had not yet happened:

37. The breakdown of certainties that began in 1870 and was intensified in 1914;

38. The weakening of the European civilisation's central idea and religion, which has left the visual arts restless and secular;

39. Philosophy dominated by a rationalism that was realistic and secular (logical positivism and linguistic analysis);

40. Imperial decline of the British Empire as a result of overextending itself, from c.1914 to the present;

41. Colonial conflict leading to decolonisation, from c.1914 but especially c.1940 to the present;

42. Proletarianisation and egalitarianism following the decline of an authoritarian empire, socialism in 1945, 1964, 1976 and after 1997;

43. Loss of national sovereignty to an inheriting secularising foreign conglomerate, in the case of the UK the loss of British sovereignty to what became the European Union as a result of the colonial

conflict and decline (as I forecast in *The Fire and the Stones*);

44. Drawing together of syncretism and Universalism as religious sects draw together with the Fire or Light as a common essence, a new prevailing philosophy and view of the universe;

45. Rejection of the conglomerate and yearning for the cultural and religious purity of the lost past of the European civilisation;

46. An attempted counter-thrust through a foreign federalism to replace the conglomerate, in the UK's case a coming Federation of the British Isles after the end of the United Kingdom, but also an international move towards a federal World State.

As regards stages 45 and 46 of the European civilisation in the UK's case, after Brexit there has been a revival of the sovereignty and independence of the UK to what it was in the reign of Queen Victoria and the rise of the British Empire, a revival of national cultural purity to decontaminate the foreign influence of the EU's conglomerate (the European Union) suggesting the beginning of stage 45. But there has not been a revival of the UK's national religion, of the medieval Fire- or Light-based medieval vision and of the Baroque vision and outlook of the 17th-century Metaphysical poets' Protestant Light (both of stage 28), which will co-exist with Universalism. If the UK stays out of the EU and there is a revival of its national religion, perhaps as a reaction to Covid deaths and echoes of the 17th-century Great Plague, then Brexit marks a beginning to stage 45. But if the UK returns to the EU then Brexit will be a short-lived nationalist movement and the UK will return to stage 43 of the European civilisation (the European Union) and the federalism of stage 46 will be postponed.

Looking back, I could see that I have lived through a collapse of standards (the breakdown of certainties) and a weakening of religion and a time of aridness in philosophy, through the decline of the British Empire and colonial conflict, increasing proletarianisation and egalitarianism, loss of sovereignty to a conglomerate and a move to cultural purity that seems likely to end in federalism (the loss of Scotland and Northern Ireland), alongside Universalism and a coming World State (stages 44 and 46). Stages 44–46 are a new working of my algebraic formula, +A (Universalism, stage 44) + –A (cultural purity, stage 45) = 0 (federalism, stage 46 – which we have not yet reached).

Conclusions on the UK's place in the world

Looking back, I reached conclusions on the UK's place in the world:

1. I was born into a UK that had an Empire that covered a quarter of the world and was more of an Asiatic power than a European power; that was engaged in Europe in nationalistic wars but was as much within the European civilisation as other countries on the Continent. Having lived through the bombing of the war I am with Churchill who, in his Zurich speech in 1946, called for "a kind of United States of Europe" that would bring peace to the warring countries of Europe, and with Thatcher, who did much to create the single market. The UK has always been independent, but I saw the merits of the 75 years of peace that the new European arrangements brought, ending in the European Union, and even though it appears (to the British Brexiteers) to be a foreign conglomerate I am sorry the UK has split from Europe.

2. Time will tell whether the UK prospers or whether it has made its greatest mistake since the Second World War. Covid will blur the final reckoning as some of the GDP lost to Brexit can be misattributed in the news to Covid, and this will disguise some of the loss of GDP to Brexit. And the general outcry against the slowness and expense of new trading paperwork and hankering to go back to the cheapness of bulk purchases may be outweighed in UK voters' minds by what would soon be seen as the evident slowness of the EU's ordering process of anti-Covid vaccines while it consulted 27 member-states, which would leave the EU way behind the UK in securing sufficient supplies of vaccines.

3. In 1962 the American statesman Dean Acheson, who was Secretary of State in Truman's administration, said that "Great Britain has lost an Empire but not yet found a role". Sixty years later, after leaving its membership of the EU (its substitute role), the UK is about to find out that it has still lost its Empire and is not a great power: that it has lost a role and not found an empire. After a while there will be a clamour for the UK to return to its substitute role in the EU.

4.   The UK's separation from Europe has come at a time when China is being expansionist in the Pacific and Russia is provocatively sending its warships into the English Channel, and the UK will be dependent on the US and NATO for protection as its military is too small to make headway against the great powers, despite announcing that it will increase its Trident nuclear arsenal from 180 to 260 warheads (which will be situated in Scotland, further alienating the Scots and straining the Union). The most influential blocs are the three superstates, the US, the EU and China, and the UK's global outlook seeks to trade with the Commonwealth rather than Europe and restore the links the UK had 47 years ago.

5.   The UK is no longer a global power. It runs the risk of falling between three stools (the US, Europe and the Commonwealth) and does not recognise that since the time of the Romans the UK has been a European nation and a member of a European civilisation that is currently in a conglomerate phase (stage 43).

Conclusions on Western civilisation

Looking back on the rear deck in the dark as the ship approached the Suez Canal, I reached conclusions on Western civilisation:

1.   My conclusions on Western civilisation (European and North-American civilisation) were that it is declining (contrary to how many would like to see it), and that I have been the poet of its decline.

2.   I concluded (see p.154) that power is shifting from the West to the East as a result of the rise of authoritarian China.

3.   Just as the Athenian Empire was plunged into decline by the plague (typhoid or viral haemorrhagic fever) that killed up to 100,000 Athenians including Pericles between 430 and 426BC, and devastated the Athenian army and ended Athenian supremacy; and just as the Roman Empire was plunged into decline by the plague (smallpox) that killed 5 million Romans including Marcus Aurelius between 165 and 180AD, and devastated the Roman army and ended the *Pax Romana*; so Western civilisation has been plunged into accelerated decline from 2020 by Covid.

4. Covid, which began in China, has temporarily ended Western civilisation's old liberal era of capitalist globalisation and replaced the old certainties of travelling to places like Jordan and Egypt with travel bans and quarantine. The banning of our ship by Israel was the first surfacing of this new Covid-driven era. Western civilisation is now temporarily in a time of borders and competitive protectionism.

5. Covid has had the same effect as the Great War of 1914 in demolishing a sunny Edwardian-style existence, where products could be ordered from anywhere on earth and businesses could be invested in worldwide, and the old certainties of visiting family and freedom of movement outside one's home, and replaced them with huge debt and never-ending recessions. The old world has gone and has temporarily been replaced by nationalistic borders, quarantine, distancing and masks. The question is, how permanent will this new temporary state of affairs turn out to be?

6. In Japan in 1966 I was asked to teach 'The Decline of the West'. Now, the West was being levelled down by revolutions, wars and independence movements against its empires, and by division – Brexit and 'America First', which meant less funding for NATO and, ahead, the mob's invasion of the US Capitol, for which Trump would be impeached and acquitted. The West was splitting asunder, and would collapse under Covid and the colossal debt Covid would cause – the West would suffer worse economically than the East, and be levelled down. The West has fallen from the height it enjoyed at the beginning of the 20th century.

7. The West has fallen apart, from within. To put it more simply, the West has fallen. I did not know on MS Serenissima that on 11 February 2021 I would receive the title of my next work in sleep – more sleep inspiration from the Muses: The Fall of the West.

8. The West has fallen, and power has shifted to the East, and it is now ready for a democratic, Presidential federal world government that can replace the UN. As the North-American civilisation is the youngest (still in stage 15, the stage the Roman civilisation was in when it had the Roman Empire), the US may take the lead in organising this world government, which will be formed in stage

46 (the federal stage) of many of the world's living civilisations.

9.   I have said (see p.132 and point 5 on p.159) that Covid has brought back nationalistic borders and made the Promised Land recede for a year or two, but that it has opened up a new interest in world government that can control all viruses. Ahead is such a federal World State that can organise the parameters of a new global normal.

10. The central idea of both the European and the North-American civilisations, which together form Western civilisation along with those nation-states that have adopted the Western way of life, is living in relation to the Light and the teachings in the Bible about the life of Christ, the Light of the World. When as a boy I was taken to church every Sunday and attended chapel every school morning, the hymns and prayers regularly mentioned the Light and reminded me of my spiritual path which would lead on to the Mystic Way and illumination when I was 26, and more fully when I was 32. Church and chapel connected me to the civilisation's central idea and were an excellent preparation for my later metaphysical living. Human beings need to locate the Light, and through it live in unitive harmony.

11. The central idea of the Light of the World is no longer strong. The pointers to it have weakened since my boyhood, a weakening that happens during a civilisation's decline. Times of silence and reflection in the 1950s when I was a boy have been filled with today's television programmes, mobile phones, social media, computers and computer games, and leave little time for the development of unitive consciousness that is alert to Nature and the universe – as was Wordsworth's during his long walks in the Lake District, during which he composed and recited his poetic works-in-progress – and to the Light.

12. At every level – standards, behaviour, honesty, principles – the world is not such a good place in 2020 as it was in my boyhood around 1950. Of course materially things have improved, and computers have opened new vistas and brought a World State closer, but the essential values and recognition of the Light have receded, and the Western decline at every level is as Arnold said

in his poem 'Dover Beach':

> The Sea of Faith
> Was once, too, at the full, and round earth's shore
> Lay like the folds of a bright girdle furled.
> But now I only hear
> Its melancholy, long, withdrawing roar,
> Retreating, to the breath
> Of the night-wind, down the vast edges drear
> And naked shingles of the world.

People simply knew more when I was young. Before I went to Oxford I read *The Times* each morning on my way to London and back, and the articles on different parts of the British Empire on the centre page were daily and often in two or three parts and filled with detail one was expected to know. I have continued as I was then and now feel something of an exception as people today are different and generally do not delve deeply, read widely and attempt to have the vision of a Renaissance man. Or seek the wilderness and have a vision like Moses' that can lead a people – or that can lead humankind towards a federal World State.

Looking back as the ship entered the Suez Canal in the dark, I saw clearly that in my youth I had opened to a power, the Light, that used to be widely known and is not widely known today, and that during my journey along the Mystic Way it guided my life, gave me unitive vision, shaped my works often through sleep inspiration, and, through a seemingly random order of tackling my books, guided me into carrying seven disciplines, and seven branches of literature, as far as they could go, and enabled me to arrive at the Ten Commandments of Universalism. It also gave me the foresight to see the future direction of Europe, and that fallen Western civilisation has a world government ahead that will arrest its further decline for a while.

7

A View of the Promised Land: A World State and a Golden Age

The Suez Canal and the Suez Crisis 1956
Early next morning I went up on deck and had a view of the walls of the Suez Canal on either side, the Egyptian side on our left and the Saudi-Arabian side on our right.

Going through Suez to Cairo and then steaming through the Suez Canal now brought back memories of the Suez Crisis in 1956. Egypt's leader, Col. Nasser, nationalised the Suez Canal, which had been constructed by the Western Suez Canal Company between 1858 and 1869 to connect the Mediterranean and the Indian Ocean via the Red Sea. I followed the 1956 Suez Crisis avidly while still at school, and took cuttings from my parents' *Daily Telegraph*. I half-expected to be called up to take part in the coming military action and be one of the troops keeping order in Suez.

The Suez Canal

I wrote to my MP John Biggs-Davison, asking if I could attend one of the Suez debates and he sent me a ticket to the Strangers' Gallery for the debate on 12 September 1956 when Prime Minister Eden, standing alongside a seated Churchill, unveiled a three-power plan for a Suez Users' Association, the beginning of the collusion between Britain, France and Israel that led to the Suez débâcle (see p.105).

I saw the situation in terms of the challenges to the Athenian and Roman Empires I was reading about in ancient history at school: the challenges had to be put down if the empires were to survive. The British Empire could not allow its assets to be seized by a local dictator if it was to survive.

I spoke for Eden's Suez policy at the school's Debating Society with John Ezard, later of *The Guardian,* as my opponent, and we cycled home together afterwards.

In 1970 I would see Nasser, who had precipitated the Suez Crisis, drive past me in a Jeep alongside Gaddafi, and by then the British Empire was melting away.

My journey along the Suez Canal reminded me that my Universalism was rooted in, and grew out of, my turning against the Egyptian and British nationalism at the end of the British Empire in 1956, which the media at the time referred to as "the Suez Crisis".

The structure of The Promised Land *received in sleep*
Ahead was a day at sea and as Ann was still asleep I breakfasted alone.

I knew I would be writing *The Promised Land* as I stood on Mount Nebo on 1 March, and later as I sat on the coach. I knew I had to structure the book during the previous day at sea (on 9 March), and now, on 11 March, wrote in my diary: "It's now 8.35, and I have a day at sea ahead – to think out *The Promised Land.*" I checked a fact in the ship's library and began a plan.

There was a briefing at 12.30. We were told that a massive storm was crossing Egypt behind us. It covered half Egypt, and it was chasing us, and the harbour at Alexandria had been closed. We would be racing ahead of the storm to Port Said, the other side of the Suez Canal, and would be heading for the safety of Antalya, a port in Southern Turkey, where we would visit Roman ruins.

Ahead would be a second day at sea, keeping ahead of the storm and making for Turkey, and I wrote in my diary, "Worked fitfully on *The Promised Land* plan."

I have often received key ideas in my sleep (see *My Double Life 2: A Rainbow over the Hills*, pp.910–911, 'Sleep inspiration' [and pp.216–218]) from the idea for *The Fire and the Stones* (1991) – the concept of my study of 25 civilisations as "Light-bearers" (on 24 August 1979) and the beginning of its Preface 'Introduction to the New Universalism' (on 29 April 1989) – to the idea for *A Baroque Vision* (2021) and its theme of the Baroque as the source of Universalism (received in sleep on Christmas morning, 25 December 2019). I attribute this sleep inspiration to the Muses.

On the morning of Friday 13 March 2020 I woke at 3am with the structure of *The Promised Land* in my mind. I later wrote in my diary:

> Woke in the middle of the night and scribbled out notes on the structure of *The Promised Land*. Put this into a plan during the journey home [from Perge and Aspendos, see below]. Had lunch later and sat on the back deck for a short while looking at the cranes with magnetic grasps and dozens of containers and then returned to my cabin [419T on the *Serenissima*] and worked on *The Promised Land*. I have finished the plan in draft, incorporating all the bits and pieces I have written at different times and also the restructuring I saw I needed to do between 3 and 3.30am, writing under the small torch light above my bed in my cabin while Ann slept. It's in five parts. Pt 1, The Promised Land. Pt 2, The Formative Years, 1960–1980, The Mystic Way and the Baroque Vision. Pt 3, The Wilderness Years, 1980–2020, The Unitive Vision and Universalism. Pt 4, Ten Commandments: Ten Universalist Principles. Pt 5, A View of the Promised Land.

It seemed that the Muses might have woken me, their slave, in the middle of the night to tell me what they wanted me to say in response to Israel's closure of its border to our ship.

Other works of mine that came through sleep inspiration include: 12 stanzas of 'Night Visions in Charlestown', the turning-point and link between the Baroque and Universalism (on 6 August 1983); the word Universalism in the title of *The New Philosophy of Universalism* on the morning of 28 February 2007 (see letter of 28 February 2007 in *Selected Letters*); and the structure of *The Secret American Dream*, an early statement of the World State (on 3 December 2009), which I would send to President Obama with the Appendix on bin Laden's 69 attempts to buy nuclear weapons flagged.

I see this ability to see important original ideas in my sleep as being a consequence of my full illumination on 10 September 1971, which opened me to unitive vision and many powers from the beyond, including second sight, the ability to foresee and anticipate future historical events like the Delphic Oracle, such as: the collapse of Communism with the fall of the Berlin Wall; the creation of the European Union as a stage-43 conglomerate; and the break-up of the United Kingdom into a Federation of the British Isles.

I am full of admiration and wonder at the power of inspiration that derives from metaphysical living, which I once described to Colin Wilson as opening one's soul to a spring like the one in Ghadames, and allowing bubbles to wobble up into consciousness from the beyond. I was also thinking of the spring near Horace's villa in Licenza, northeast of Rome, which is thought to be Horace's *"fons Bandusiae"*, his Bandusian spring, and which I squatted next to in 1957 when I was 17 and scooped up water in my cupped hands to sip, and put in my 1973 poem 'Ode: Spring', which refers at the end to "the gushing of this spring between my sleeves".

I said to Colin Wilson that the ability to open to this spring may be what genius was traditionally supposed to be able to do, and that the inner nature of this inspiration explains why geniuses such as Blake and Van Gogh have often been neglected as their ideas are too new and unfamiliar to attract a great following during their lifetime – and so they willingly spend much of their lives in the wilderness to be near their spring, getting inspiration for original work that will be better understood by a future generation. He said, "Yes," and lapsed into a thoughtful silence.

Flower of the Pax Romana *at Perge, Turkey*

A few hours after my sleep inspiration we landed at Antalya, Turkey. We walked past a camera on a tripod that was measuring our temperatures, and I was struck by how advanced Turkey was in testing for Covid. We were taken by coach to Perge (or Perga) 15 kilometres east of Antalya, an ancient Greek city founded in Anatolia by 1209BC.

We began a long walk through the ruins at Hadrian's Gate. I immediately saw a circle with a six-petalled flower in it, the same circle I saw on Hadrian's Arch in Jerash (Antioch, see p.4), but with petals like slender blue-eyed grass.

I asked our guide what it represented. He did not know, and he rang a contact in the museum at Ephesus, who said the petals were olive leaves on a shield with two spears at the bottom, laid down and not being used as arms, signifying Hadrian's *Pax Romana*. But the petals did not look like olive leaves. According to the contact in Ephesus the citizens of both Antioch and Perge were saying to Hadrian: we have no need to defend ourselves under your *Pax Romana*, so we are leaving our shields and spears outside the city walls.

Hadrian's Gate, Perge

The six-petalled flower over Hadrian's
Gate in Perge

I worked out that the six petals stood for the six main regions in Hadrian's *Pax Romana* in the 120s: Britannia (where Hadrian built Hadrian's Wall to keep out the Picts or Scots); Gaul (France); Hispania (Spain); North Africa; Asia Minor; and Italy. The capitals were: Londinium; Lugdunum (Lyon); Tarragona; Carthage; Ephesus; and Rome. The *Pax Romana* covered the whole of the known world during early Roman times.

Flower of the Pax Romana *at Aspendos, Turkey*

The idea of a Roman peace had appeared in the Republic and was associated with the spreading of peace between 210 and 100BC. It was associated with Sulla and Julius Caesar. But the Roman peace, the *Pax Romana*, traditionally commenced from the accession of Caesar Augustus, who defeated Mark Antony and Cleopatra in the Battle of Actium in 31BC and founded the Roman principate in 27BC. He became the first Roman Emperor and was responsible for the *Ara Pacis Augustae*, Altar of Augustan Peace. The *Pax Romana* ended in 180AD with the death of Marcus Aurelius. It lasted roughly 200 years.

We walked on past the baths to the agora, which reminded me of the white Roman cities of Sabratha and Leptis Magna in Libya. Then we returned to the coach and went on to Aspendos, about 40 kilometres east of Antalya, to see the Roman theatre built in 155AD, which is three storeys high and in good condition, the best-preserved theatre of antiquity, with 12,000 seats in tiers.

Two views of the Roman theatre at Aspendos, c.155AD

On the way out of the theatre I found a stone tablet on its side, below knee-height, that appeared to show Medusa with her mouth curled down and a six-petalled flower (see **p.4** and front cover). It had rounded petals, like blue cohosh. Again, the six main regions of the *Pax Romana*, which lasted from 27BC to 180AD, were symbolised as a six-petalled flower that represented peace.

Six-petalled flower on stone tablet at the Roman theatre at Aspendos, Turkey (see p.5 and front cover)

We went on to look at a Roman aqueduct before we returned to Antalya and the ship. I sat on the back deck and then went to my cabin and worked on what I had received in my sleep.

At the briefing later we were told that Cyprus had closed its archaeological sites and tourist places because of Covid, and so we were going to Alanya in Turkey the next day.

Alanya and Istanbul

The next morning we landed at Alanya and set off by coach to Sidé, which was founded in the 7th century BC. We saw the Vespasian Gate and the Roman theatre, and then walked to the 1st-century-BC Temple of Apollo and Temple of Athena (which was rebuilt in the 2nd century AD) at the end of Sidé's peninsula.

We returned to the coach and drove to Cleopatra's beach, where the Egyptian Queen Cleopatra is thought to have swum during a voyage on the Mediterranean, perhaps on her way to or from Actium. We went on to Damlataş Cave, which is full of stalactites and stalagmites that have formed during the last 15,000 years.

Back on ship we heard that Cyprus had now blocked all entry because of Covid, and that we were hoping to fly from Alanya to Istanbul.

The next morning we were taken by coach to Alanya airport. I asked our guide about the flower of the *Pax Romana*. He insisted there were six olive leaves, as the guide at Antalya had also said. I repeated that the petals did not look like olive leaves.

Having been denied access to, and shut out from, Israel and the Promised Land, I was flown to Istanbul, a four-hour flight. We were driven to the Marmara Pera Hotel and arrived at 3.30pm.

The Bosphorus: seeing a World State ahead

The rest of our party sat in the Hotel foyer, chatting to pass the time. Ann and I took our luggage up to our room, and, having heard that we would be flying back to London the next day, 17 March (which turned out to be seven days before the UK's lockdown), we left the hotel, found a taxi and for 50 euros went on a tour of places I wanted to see in Istanbul.

The speed of our tour reminded me of when we were in Munich. Our coach took us to a beer hall where Hitler had made a speech and we were given pints of beer. Ann and I left, and I found a taxi, said to the driver, "All the Hitler places," saw the lot as research for my epic poem *Overlord*, and returned to find the group still sipping the same pints of beer.

We drove over a bridge to the Sea of Marmara and stopped to view the distant bridge over the Bosphorus, which connects Europe and Asia. We drove on through the old city to view the Topkapi walls (the Sultan's palace) and the Blue Mosque (built between 1609 and 1616), Hagia Sophia (which opened in 1537) and the Suleymaniye Mosque, the Ottoman imperial mosque inaugurated in 1557.

We drove round the Roman walls of Constantinople that had Roman tiles in them, the walls of the Eastern Roman emperors from Constantine to Justinian which signified the beginning of the end of the Roman civilisation in the West, and then at my request we returned to the Bosphorus and got out to saunter along the sea wall.

Jerusalem used to be the centre of the world in Crusader times, and in Jerusalem in 1961 I thought about what could unite the world. More vividly, I had seen a World State ahead in Moscow in 1966. And now in 2020, having gazed in first Jerash (Antioch) and then south

Turkey on a forgotten symbol of the *Pax Romana* and having retrieved its lost knowledge, standing by the Bosphorus with Europe on my left and Asia on my right, I saw a World State ahead, a democratic World State with enough supranational authority to abolish war, enforce disarmament, combat famine, disease and poverty, and solve the world's financial and environmental problems – including its medical problems.

A view of the Bosphorus Bridge which connects Europe and Asia

I looked across the Bosphorus where Europe and Asia meet, which Lord Byron swam, and, thinking of Roman Constantinople, the capital of the Roman Empire from 330 to 395 – like Rome, Constantinople had seven hills – and then of the Byzantine Empire, I saw a World State that united Europe and Asia, and that could regulate and eliminate all hostile viruses and pandemics, especially those that may have come into existence as a consequence of military research like Spanish flu in 1918 (which may have begun in an American laboratory as a contribution to germ warfare to end the First World War) and now coronavirus (which may have begun in a research laboratory in Wuhan in China).

Standing by the Bosphorus in Istanbul, where Europe and Asia meet, I saw a world ahead with all problems solved, the vision I had had from the top of Mount Nebo, standing where Moses stood.

*

171

The World State fleshes out the tenth Universalist commandment
I had seen from the top of Mount Nebo, and saw again by the Bosphorus in Istanbul, a world of separate nation-states with borders, each trying to cope with the same problems like Covid-19, and just as each country was thinking of itself and seeking protection from the virus, so each country was thinking of itself and seeking protection from the world's military, economic, medical, financial and environmental problems. The solution to all these problems could be found centrally by regarding humankind as one political entity and all nation-states as part of one landscape, like the distant towns and settlements within Canaan, the Promised Land, seen from Mount Nebo.

I saw that life under the World State will be good for all humankind. Life under the World State fleshes out the tenth Universalist principle and tenth commandment, "Work for a federal World State to replace the UN General Assembly", and I had glimpsed it in the Epilogue on pp.207–214 of *World State*.

The seven goals of the World State fulfilled
I had seen the seven goals of the World State:

1. bringing peace between nation-states, and disarmament;
2. sharing resources and energy so that all humankind can have a raised standard of living;
3. solving environmental problems such as global warming, which seem to be beyond self-interested nation-states;
4. where possible, ending disease;
5. where possible, ending famine;
6. solving the world's financial crisis; and
7. where possible, redistributing wealth to eliminate poverty.

And in the Epilogue of *World State* I had seen the seven goals of the World State as having been fulfilled:

Global Democracy and a Golden Age
Life under the World State
War has been abolished, peace is enforced by the World Court of

Justice and the World Armed Force and its international bases on every continent. The World Commission moves in a regular roster between 11 cities. Television comprehensively shows the activities of the World Commission, the World Senate and the World Parliamentary Assembly. Gas and oil pipelines supply gas and oil to all nation-states and there is a network of nuclear power stations. The World Cabinet (the World President and Council of Ministers) controls pollution. Diseases are under control, the world's citizens are being moved from conditions of squalor, rehoused and guaranteed access to pure water and medical care. There is no military expenditure; annual world budgets finance economic growth and public spending. There is one global currency and one world-wide central bank. Access to mortgages and jobs is universal. Migration is freely conducted, subject to quotas. The 13 regions based on the world's living civilizations send regional leaders to the Regional Leaders' Meeting, but the main world regions are now: the American Union; the European Union; the West Asian (or Middle Eastern) Union; the Central Asian Union; and the East Asian-Pacific Union.

Life in a sample of regions and nation-states
What is it like to live under a global democracy? Let us consider how people might live in some of the regions and nation-states of the World State, taking account of how they will be represented. (See table on pp.166–170 [of *World State*] for individual nation-states' representation in the World Parliamentary Assembly.) The picture is as follows:

- *North America*. The United States has 30 World Representatives in the World Parliamentary Assembly and eight World Senators (two per zone in four zones). As the World State was US-inspired and created as the result of a US initiative, many Americans are in the World Commission's bureaucracy and World Armed Force. There is no stockpile of nuclear weapons, all have been destroyed. Poverty within the United States was abolished soon after the advent of universal health care. All Americans are entitled to a minimum standard of living (dollars per day/housing). Canada has six World Representatives in the World Parliamentary Assembly, six World Senators and one World Commissioner. Canada has moved closer to North America in lifestyle and outlook.

- *Central America/Caribbean.* The region has four World Senators and one World Commissioner. There is no poverty.
- *South America.* There are six World Senators and two World Commissioners. All South-American citizens are entitled to a minimum of $10 per day.
- *China* has 30 World Representatives in the World Parliamentary Assembly, eight World Senators and one World Commissioner. Communism is officially dead and China is now a liberal democracy. The death penalty has been abolished. There is a minimum entitlement of $10 per day for all Chinese citizens.
- *India* has 30 World Representatives in the World Parliamentary Assembly, six World Senators and one World Commissioner. There is no famine.
- *Africa* has eight World Senators and two World Commissioners. AIDS and malaria have been eliminated.
- *Europe* has 30 World Representatives, 12 World Senators and four World Commissioners. All European citizens have a minimum entitlement per day/housing.
- *The Russian Federation* has 15 World Representatives in the World Parliamentary Assembly, six World Senators and one World Commissioner. There is no stockpile of nuclear weapons, all have been destroyed.
- *Afghanistan* is within the South-Central Asia region. It has six World Representatives in the World Parliamentary Assembly, shares four World Senators with Central Asia, and shares one World Commissioner with Pakistan. There is a minimum entitlement of $10 per day for all Afghans. Minimum-standard housing has replaced mud huts. All Afghan citizens receive full education.
- *The Middle East.* The region, which includes Syria, has eight World Senators (if Israel and Iran are included) and three World Commissioners. There are no local wars.
- *Central Asia* has four World Senators and one World Commissioner.
- *South-East Asia/Asia* has seven World Senators (one for South-East Asia, two for Central Asia, two for East-Central Asia and two for

East Asia) and access to three World Commissioners (for West-Central/South-East Asia, East Asia, and Indonesia).

All of the world's citizens live under conditions of liberty. There are no tyrannies under the World State. There is no elitist Syndicate tyranny of any kind. The New World Order's dream of federal tyranny has been controlled. There is a Universalism (which focuses on all humankind) of minimum standards of living and a context of peace.

A new Golden Age

In the Epilogue at the end of *World State* I had foreseen a new Golden Age of peace and prosperity:

Towards a Golden Age

I have set out a conception of a World State that is rooted in the history of the last 5,000 years. I have seen the supranational authority and World State as being *partly* federal in limiting itself to seven goals, and loosely allowing nation-states and civilizations to continue at local, regional level. Such a loose structure will allow a high degree of democracy, with the higher Senate and lower Assembly both directly elected. It will avoid the more drastic United States of the World in which there would be upheavals at the local/regional level, and the New World Order's federal Union of the 13 regions that would be controlled by the élitist Syndicate whose agenda is universal world dominance with very little expansion of democracy.

Such a loose federal model limited at the supranational level to seven goals will leave nation-states and civilizations free to run themselves outside the areas of the seven goals through the democratic process via the World Senate and World Parliamentary Assembly. The loss of sovereignty and disturbance to existing nation-states and civilizations will be minimal. Life outside the areas of the seven goals and elections to the Senate and Assembly will continue, allowing nation-states and civilizations the maximum amount of continuity with their local and regional traditions.

They will surrender sovereignty in the areas of the seven goals, but their minimal loss of sovereignty will be amply compensated for by a gain in a share of world sovereignty and a maximal increase in democracy via the directly-elected Senate and Assembly.

A Golden Age of Universalism

We can glimpse the future again. A new Golden Age has dawned. It is a Golden Age of peace, promise, and prosperity. State persecution is unknown – it is of the past. All the bad things of history – plunder, pillage, rapine, air raids, invasion, missile attacks, barbaric hordes, poverty, squalor, disease, blighted crops – have been abolished.

True political Universalism, which sees all humankind as belonging to one political entity, has arrived. No one in the world falls below a minimum standard of living and housing, and there are no avoidable diseases caused by poor environmental conditions. In the past, wars created refugees living in tented squalor that bred diseases. Such conditions no longer apply.

With political Universalism linking all the Earth's regions into a World State, all religions are drawing together. There will be a religious Universalism, uniting within diversity the essence of Christianity, Islam, Buddhism, Hinduism, Taoism, and other world religions. There will be a spiritual revival. And there will be no wars between religions. Paradise has truly arrived on earth.

However, a World State cannot be built and a Golden Age cannot happen unless the process is set in motion. Someone has to address the UN and propose a World Constitutional Convention to create a new supranational system.

And so I appeal to the UN. Members of the General Assembly, do your duty. Give up a little sovereignty to the supranational level in respect of the seven goals, so there can be universal peace and disarmament on a legally enforceable footing. You will still retain your national or regional sovereignty outside the areas of the seven goals. Have courage and be forward-looking. Bring in the Universalist World State.

The nationalistic and Universalist visions

I stood by the Bosphorus and thought myself back on Mount Nebo. Moses had stood on Mount Nebo and seen Canaan. I had stood on

Mount Nebo and seen the future world. It is as I have shown in *World State* and *World Constitution*, its companion volume. Now, like Moses, after 40 years in the wilderness (1980–2020) I have seen from my Mount Nebo and can hand the vision on and die serene.

Ramesses II, Moses' counterpart (and some say, without good evidence, half-brother, on the unevidential assumption that Moses had been legally adopted by Pharaoh's daughter after he was found in the bulrushes), lived for personal aggrandisement and buildings that contained colossal statues of himself, and he died around 90 leaving a nationalistic vision, hook-nosed but idealised in his colossal statues with a perfect nose. Moses led his Hebrew people nationalistically, but he also had a larger vision of serving Yahweh, and his larger Universalist vision for humankind has outlived Ramesses'.

The way out of the wilderness

Standing on Mount Nebo like Moses I had seen that someone should point the way and lead the world out of the secular, nationalist wilderness of declining civilisations and inward-looking bordered nation-states. I had seen that a vision of the future is essential. To continue as we are would mean that all problems would be tackled on the same basis as Covid was being tackled, by separate nation-states coming up with solutions in their areas and failing to address the root cause of the problem. This was the case with war, nuclear weapons, famine, disease (including viruses), poverty, banking crises and environmental problems such as climate change. Each of these problems could be solved with one global solution, instead of being fudged with 193 solutions by 193 nation-states, each concerned only about itself – the UK announcing it will increase its nuclear arsenal from 180 to 260 nuclear weapons – and not about humankind as a whole.

The Promised Land

Standing by the Bosphorus at the end of my long journey from nationalism to supranationalist Universalism and from secular living to a unitive vision of one metaphysical reality, I recalled that on Mount Nebo I wished I could address the UN General Assembly and show what I had seen, the Promised Land (from which I had subsequently been shut out) below the hills of Gilead all divided and at war, Palestine against Israel, separate zones which blocked transport from the Dead Sea (under Israel) to Jericho (under the Palestinian authority) – when it could all be one unified land of milk and honey, breeding cattle and growing wild flowers for bees, one Promised Land fully in charge of its own destiny with a prosperous future for a while.

It seemed like a dream of Paradise but it could actually come to pass. I did not then know that in February 2021 the World Intellectual Forum (WIF) would set up the Global Network for Peace, Disarmament and Development to bring in a world government that is democratic, Presidential and federal, and will replace the UN, largely based on my books *The World Government, World State* and *World Constitution*.

I did not know that I would be asked to be on the Board of the World Intellectual Forum (WIF) in 2020, and (after my Zoom presentation on a supranational democratic world government within a partly-federal World State confined to seven goals) would be made Chairman of a WIF working group on a supranational partly-federal World State confined to seven goals and give a PowerPoint Presentation to groups from different world regions, socialise their feedback on a website I would launch and lay it before the UN. I did not know that ahead was the possibility of asking the UN to set up a UN working group to study the feasibility of bringing in a World State based on my three books.

I did not know that I would amend the seven goals to:

1. Creating supranational legal powers to abolish and end war, keep a rules-based peace with human rights between nation-states with the aid of a world peace-keeping force, and achieve universal disarmament for the benefit of all humankind;

2. Sharing resources and energy supplies, and redistributing wealth to eliminate poverty and hunger and to supply basic needs for the benefit of all humankind;

3. Solving environmental problems caused by climate change such as global warming and famine while respecting all life forms and avoiding violent farming methods, for the benefit of all humankind;

4. Ending disease, including eradicating Covid, and promoting wellness and good health in all for the benefit of all humankind;

5. Extending education, science and skills development for the benefit of all humankind;

6. Delivering a growing world economy and solving all financial and funding crises for the benefit of all humankind; and

7. Raising awareness of universal spirituality and global ethics, and ending all friction between religions so all religious leaders can co-operate, for the benefit of all humankind.

Standing by the Bosphorus, in my mind I stand again on Mount Nebo and look across the Promised Land and see the view that is on the front cover of this book. Like Moses I raise my right arm and point, and my finger extends from Hebron, Herodium beyond the Dead Sea, Bethlehem, Qumran, Jerusalem, Ramallah beyond Jericho, Nablus beyond Lake Tiberias, the Sea of Galilee, to the distant hills of Amman. My finger points from Hebron to Nablus and the land in between, and I figuratively point to six continents, America (North and South America traditionally seen as one continent), Europe, Asia (Europe and Asia traditionally seen as two continents rather than as Eurasia, one), Africa, Australia and Antarctica, like the six regions of the known world of the *Pax Romana* represented by a six-petalled flower.

There is a Zen saying in the East, which I quoted in *The Universe and the Light* (1993): "Show a fool the moon and he looks at your finger." A variant of this saying could be: "Show a fool the Promised Land and he looks at your finger."

My finger points across 193 nation-states and with one sweep of my right arm like a cosmonaut on the moon I encircle and transform the world into a World State. Look at the coming World State, not at my finger.

Timeline

List of dates of key events in Nicholas Hagger's life, referred to or relevant background in *The Promised Land*

22 May 1939	Born.
2 Jul 1939	Christened.
Mar 1943	Bombs blow out windows of 52 Brooklyn Avenue, Loughton.
May 1943	Attends Essex House School.
Sep 1943	Starts at old Oaklands School.
Mar 1944	Bombs fall on cricket field and blow out windows of 52 Brooklyn Avenue again, including garage windows.
Sep 1944	Starts at new Oaklands School.
16 Jun 1945	Hears Churchill speak at Loughton war memorial.
Sep 1947	Starts at Chigwell School.
25 Oct 1951	Encounters Churchill in Loughton.
Sep 1953	Visit to France and D-Day beaches.
18 Oct 1953	Meets Montgomery.
Jul 1954	Experiences Oneness of the universe.
Apr 1956	On archaeological dig at Chester.
12 Sep 1956	Attends Suez debate in House of Commons as guest of John Biggs-Davison MP.
Mar 1957	Call to be a poet.
4–25 Apr 1957	Visit to Italy and Sicily.
Jul 1957–Jul 1958	Articled clerk at Gregory, Rowcliffe & Co., solicitors.
11 Aug–14 Sep 1958	Visit to Greece.
Oct 1958–Jun 1961	At Worcester College, Oxford.
Mar 1959	Changes from Law to English Literature.
1–10 Apr 1959	Visit to France.
23 Jul–23 Aug 1959	Visit to Spain.
Jan 1960	Visit to Colin Wilson.
14 Jul 1960	Writes to Major Goulding.
end of Jul/Aug 1960	Visit to Greece, encounters Col. Grivas.
6 Nov 1960	Sherry with Sir John Masterman.

1 Dec 1960	Meets Admiral Sir Charles Woodhouse.
6–9 Jan 1961	Stays with Colin Wilson and announces he will lecture abroad and find wisdom among foreign cultures.
16 Sep 1961	Marriage to Caroline.
30 Sep 1961–4 Jun 1962	Lecturer at University of Baghdad, Iraq.
13 Dec 1962	Birth of Nadia.
15 Oct 1963	Death of father.
6 Nov 1963	Visit to Dick Paul.
15 Nov 1963–18 Oct 1967	Professor at Tokyo University of Education and Keio University, Japan.
21 Dec 1963	Visits Junzaburo Nishiwaki.
22 Apr 1964–Mar 1965	Lecturer at Tokyo University.
26 Apr 1964	Lunches with Edmund Blunden.
Apr 1964–Oct 1967	Speech-writer for Governor of Bank of Japan.
10 Jul 1964	Visits Ichikawa City Zen meditation centre.
20 Jul 1964	Visits Zen Kogenji temple.
20 Jul 1964–18 Oct 1965	First Mystic Life.
5–6 Jan 1965	First visit to Kyoto (including Ryoanji Stone Garden) and Nara.
1965–1966	Writes *The Early Education and Making of a Mystic*.
Jan 1965–Jun 1966	Writes 'The Silence'.
1 Jul 1965–18 Oct 1967	Tutor to His Imperial Highness Prince Hitachi.
26–27 Jul 1965	Visits Zen Engakuji temple, Kitakamakura, with Frank Tuohy.
11–12 Aug 1965	Second visit to Kyoto (including Ryoanji Stone Garden) and Nara.
11 Sep 1965	Visions: images.
5 Oct 1965	Junzaburo Nishiwaki writes out $+A + -A = 0$ to describe the manifestation of the Absolute and the wisdom of the East.
11 Oct 1965	Golden light.
17 Oct 1965	Centre-shift.
18 Oct 1965	Round white light, Zen enlightenment (*satori*).
19 Oct 1965–2 Sep 1971	Dark Night of the Soul.
3–23 Mar 1966	Visits China with Frank Tuohy.

19 Mar 1966	Interrogates Vice-President of Peking University and is first to discover Cultural Revolution.
Apr 1966–Oct 1967	Selects interpreters at Ministry of International Trade and Industry.
7–10 Jun/25–29 Aug 1966	Visits Soviet Union twice.
11, 20 Jun–23 Jul 1966	Writes 'Archangel', poem about Communism.
20 Dec 1966–13 Mar 1967	Writes 'Old Man in a Circle'.
18 Oct–6 Nov 1967	Tours South-East Asia and India, and parts of Europe.
25 Oct 1968–1 Jul 1970	Lecturer at University of Libya, Tripoli.
3 Nov 1968	Visit to Sabratha with Ben Nagy, discussion on a revolution in Libya.
15 Nov 1968	Visit to Leptis Magna with Ben Nagy.
3 Apr 1969	First article as Barbary Gipsy for *The Daily News*, arranged by Shukri Ghanem (later Prime Minister).
Apr 1969	Ben Nagy hosts parties for ministers.
30 May 1969	Is approached by SIS.
6–10 Jul 1969	Visit to Djerba.
18, 22 Aug 1969	Interviews Dr Muntasser, Libyan Ambassador to London.
24 Aug 1969	Article on Libyan-British relations appears in English and Arabic in Tripoli, read by Gaddafi.
28, 30 Aug 1969	Dinners with Beshir al-Muntasser, Minister of State for Prime Minister's Affairs.
1 Sep 1969	Gaddafi's *coup*.
5 Sep 1969	Scheduled date of pro-Western *coup*.
14 Sep 1969	Last article as Barbary Gipsy for *The Daily News*.
1969–1972	Writes *The Gates of Hell*.
6 Nov 1969	Viktor agrees to defect.
4 Dec 1969	Is separated.
25 Dec 1969	Sees Col. Nasser ride through Tripoli with Gaddafi and Numeiri.
1 Jan 1970	Knocks off Col. Gaddafi's peaked cap.
12–23 Feb 1970	Visit to Egypt.
19 Feb 1970	Locates SAM-3 missile transporter near El Alamein.
24–28 Feb 1970	Visit to Sahara and Ghadames.
11–14 Apr 1970	Visit to Malta.

27–28 May 1970	Is nearly executed.
28 May 1970	Holds up reception line for Queen's birthday to inform British Ambassador Donald Maitland.
28 May–3 Jun 1970	Return visits to 'executioner'.
1–20 Jul 1970	Drives through North Africa and western Mediterranean.
16 Jul 1970	Visit to Ezra Pound in Rapallo.
30 Jul, 8, 17 Aug 1970	Visits to John Heath-Stubbs.
Aug 1970–15 Apr 1972	Lives at 13 Egerton Gardens, London.
24 Aug 1970	Becomes 'unofficial Ambassador' to Edward Heath, Prime Minister.
29, 30 Aug 1970	Articles on Libya in *The Times* and *The Sunday Telegraph*.
3 Oct 1970	Article on World Council of Churches' grants to liberation movements in *The Times*.
Jan 1971–Aug 1973	Teaches at Riverway ESN School, Greenwich.
21 Apr 1971	"Exposed to Czech intelligence and KGB" by Viktor.
May 1971–Nov 1972	Margaret Riley in 13 Egerton Gardens.
May 1971	Pussy-cat becomes landlady, chef and chambermaid at 13 Egerton Gardens.
3 Sep 1971–28 Apr 1972	Second Mystic Life.
5 Sep 1971–28 Apr 1972	Visions reflected in poems.
10 Sep 1971	Illumination.
24 Sep 1971	Told will be publicly exposed by Philby in retaliation for Heath's expulsion of 105 Russians.
1–4 Mar 1972	Attends symposium on Cunene Dam near Frankfurt for *The Times*.
15 Apr 1972	Moves into newly-purchased Flat 6, 33 Stanhope Gardens.
24 Apr 1972	Visit to Colin Wilson in Cornwall.
29 Apr 1972–12 May 1979	Dark Night of the Spirit: new powers.
25–29 May 1972	Attends SWAPO conference in Brussels for *The Times*.
10–27 Sep 1972	Visit to Tanzania and Zanzibar for *The Times* and *The Guardian*.
19 Sep 1972	Interviews Jumbe.
20 Sep 1972	Asks Nyerere for permission to visit Makumbako

	(restricted area).
22–23 Sep 1972	Visit to Mlimba-Makumbako section of the Tanzam railway.
24 Apr 1973	Visit to Colin Wilson.
17 May 1973	Discontinues with SIS.
3 Jul 1973	Ends all connection with SIS.
15–20 Aug 1973	Visit by Margaret Riley, first inklings of a neo-Baroque movement.
31 Aug 1973	Leaves Riverway School.
1 Sep 1973–31 Aug 1974	Second-in-command in the English Department, Henry Thornton School.
24, 28–29 Oct 1973	Writes 'In Marvell's Garden, at Nun Appleton', reworked in 1980 as 'A Metaphysical in Marvell's Garden'.
24 Dec 1973	Agrees sale of 9 Crescent View, Loughton to tenant.
1974–1975	Writes *Visions near the Gates of Paradise*.
22 Feb 1974	Marriage to Ann.
20 Mar 1974	Moves out of newly-sold flat 6 in 33 Stanhope Gardens.
4 Apr 1974	Moves into newly-purchased flat 5 in 10 Brechin Place.
1 Sep 1974–31 Dec 1985	Head of English and Senior Teacher, Garratt Green School.
3 Oct 1974	Birth of Matthew.
27 Oct 1975	Matthew's christening.
1976–1979	Writes *Whispers from the West*.
6–7 Nov 1976	Writes 'The European Resurgence'.
24 Nov 1976	Tells Margaret Thatcher face-to-face in the Waldorf Hotel that East-European nations should be liberated from the Soviet Union.
4 Feb 1977	Moves to 100A Stapleton Road.
5 Apr 1977	Dinner with Donald Maclean's son, who spent two years in Philby's household.
26 Apr 1977	Birth of Anthony.
25 Sep 1977	Anthony's christening, Miss Lord offers Oaklands School.

undated 13–26 Nov 1977	Attends poetry reading by David Gascoyne and Kathleen Raine with Frank Tuohy.
25 Apr 1978	Moves out of newly-sold flat in 10 Brechin Place.
15 Aug 1978	Moves into newly-purchased 46 Ritherdon Road.
undated 25–30 Sep 1978	Encounters Colin Wilson.
7, 20 Oct 1978	Asa Briggs urges the writing of *My Double Life 1: This Dark Wood*.
18–20 Feb 1979	Christopher Ricks considers as Metaphysical poet.
13 May 1979–31 Oct 1981	Third Mystic Life.
24 Aug 1979	Idea of *The Fire and the Stones* received in sleep.
Oct 1979–Apr 1980	Revises Elegies for *The Fire-Flower*.
Sep 1980–Jul 1981	Discussions with Tom Dyer, Brain of Britain.
1981–1985	Writes *A Rainbow in the Spray*.
14 Apr 1981	Miss Lord agrees to sell Oaklands School.
1 Nov 1981–7 Apr 1990	Dark Night of the Spirit: ordeals.
1 May 1982	Christopher Ricks considers as Romantic poet.
1 Sep 1982	Principal of Oaklands School, with Ann as Headmistress.
17–29 Oct 1982	Christopher Ricks considers as Baroque poet.
1 Nov 1982	Death of mother.
12 Feb 1983	ILEA inspectors ban marking.
Apr–Jun 1983	Sells 46 Ritherdon Road to Norman Rodway.
11 Nov 1983	Explains FREE (Freedom for the Republics of Eastern Europe) to Lord Whitelaw.
12 Nov 1983–May 1984	FREE.
21, 22 Feb 1984	Meets Brian Crozier and Josef Josten through John Biggs-Davison.
Mar 1984	Miners' strike begins.
4 Jun 1984	Diagnosed with bronchiectasis.
15 Jun–2 Jul 1984	Subversion of FREE by Josten.
12 Jul 1984	Receives material on Scargill.
18–19 Jul 1984	Writes article on the miners' strike for *The Times* at the invitation of the Editor, Charlie Douglas-Home.
29 Jul–11 Aug 1984	Visit to Lake District and Scotland.
9 Aug 1984	Josten blocks article.
22–23 Sep 1984	Writes *Scargill the Stalinist?*

12 Oct 1984	Brighton bomb injures Tebbit.
15 Nov 1984	Scargill at Soviet Embassy.
23 Nov 1984	Invited to meet Peter Walker, Secretary of State for Energy.
29 Nov 1984	Launch of *Scargill the Stalinist?*
13 Dec 1984	NUM sit-in in Foyles.
Feb 1985	Founding of the 'Heroes of the West'.
22–26 Feb, 11 May, 14 Jun, 19–30 Jul 1985	Visits to France.
3 Mar 1985	End of miners' strike.
15–29 Apr 1985	Five neo-Baroque Universalist poems.
12 Aug 1985	Idea for *The Fire and the Stones* again received in sleep.
12 Aug 1985	Death of John Cameron.
11–13 Oct 1985	Visit to Frankfurt.
29 Oct 1985	Death of Charlie Douglas-Home.
29 Nov 1985	Death of Josten.
Dec 1985	Voluntary severance from ILEA.
1986–1988	Writes *A Question Mark over the West*.
27 Feb 1986	Meets Lord Whitelaw.
24 Mar, 7 May 1986	Meetings at Swiss Cottage Holiday Inn, operation to eliminate Gaddafi's missiles near Sebha.
14 Apr 1986	News of operation to eliminate Gaddafi's missiles near Sebha.
30 Apr 1986	Meets Lord Whitelaw in Lord Privy Seal's Council office about Victor, Lord Rothschild, and terrorism. Recommendations photocopied.
5 May 1986	Thatcher uses Recommendations to end Soviet terrorism at Tokyo Summit, 4–6 May 1986.
1 Jul 1986	Launch of McForan's *The World Held Hostage*.
8–16 Jul 1986	Norris McWhirter's investigation.
1–7 Aug 1986	Tour of Europe.
2 Sep 1986	Launch of Tomlin's *Philosophers of East and West*.
1–5 Oct 1986	Visit to Frankfurt.
21 Oct 1986	News of Krassó's petition for democracy in Eastern Europe, inspired by FREE.
4 Nov 1986	Launch of Gorka's *Budapest Betrayed*, broadcast

	behind Iron Curtain and challenge to Soviet sphere of influence agreed at 1943 Tehran Conference.
7 Dec 1986–11 May 1989	Writes *The Fire and the Stones*.
21 Jan 1987	At 10 Downing Street.
22 Jul, 7 Aug 1987	Asked to export satellite dishes behind the Iron Curtain.
31 Jul–4 Aug 1987	Visit to Denmark.
7–11 Oct 1987	Visit to Frankfurt.
15 Dec 1987	Acquires Harbour-master's House, Charlestown.
16 Jan, 25 Feb 1988	Death and memorial service of Tomlin.
26 Jan 1988	Kathleen Raine consults about obituary.
17 Feb 1988	Suspected TIA.
26 Feb 1988	Declines to be considered to replace Biggs-Davison as MP.
17 Sep, 4 Nov 1988	Death and memorial service of John Biggs-Davison.
26 Sep 1988	Eliot's centenary service, meets Laurens van der Post.
3 Nov 1988–9 Mar 1989	Founds Coopersale Hall School.
19 Apr 1989	Coopersale Hall School opens.
2 Jun 1989–6 Oct 1990	Assembles *Selected Poems: A Metaphysical's Way of Fire*.
7 Sep 1989	Full opening of Coopersale Hall School.
1 Sep 1989–31 May 1994	Steve Norris MP lives at Coopersale Hall School as tenant.
28 Oct 1989	Visit to Laurens van der Post.
28 Oct 1989,	
13, 21 Sep 1990	Visits to Kathleen Raine.
1990–1992	Building of Coopersale Hall extension.
Feb 1990	Gorka becomes Coopersale Hall School's architect.
8 Apr 1990–6 Dec 1993	Fourth Mystic Life.
23–30 Apr 1990	Visit to Hungary.
9 Jul 1990	Lord Tebbit formally opens Coopersale Hall School.
10 Aug 1990	Visit to Kathleen Raine.
7–9 Dec 1990	Visit to Prague.
22 Apr 1991	Launch of *The Fire and the Stones* and *Selected Poems: A Metaphysical's Way of Fire*. Speakers Asa Briggs, Kathleen Raine, David Gascoyne.
1, 12 May 1991	Asked to lecture at Temenos Academy by Kathleen Raine.

8 May 1991–17 Aug 1992	Writes *Awakening to the Light*.
31 May 1991	Break with Kathleen Raine.
6, 14, 22 Aug, 22 Oct,	
18, 20 Dec 1991	Visits to Colin Wilson.
27 Sep, 2 Oct 1991	Establishes Foundation of the Light.
9–12 Oct 1991	Visit to Frankfurt.
31 Dec 1991–9 Sep 1992	Writes *The Universe and the Light*.
27 Mar 1992	Visit to David Bohm.
10 Apr 1992	Winchester lecture, 'The Nature of Light'.
14 Apr 1992	Visit to Colin Wilson.
9, 17 May,	
7, 14, 21 Jun 1992	Mystery school.
31 Aug 1992–30 Dec 1993	Writes *A Mystic Way*.
1–5 Sep 1992	Conference on reductionism at Jesus College, Cambridge.
4 Sep 1992	Form from Movement Theory drafted in Jesus College's hall.
27 Oct 1992	Death of David Bohm.
2 Jan 1993	Death of Miss Lord.
9–10 Jan 1993	Global Deception Conference, meets Eustace Mullins.
27 Jan 1993	Meets Christopher Ricks.
27 Jan 1993–2 Feb 1994	Assembles *Collected Poems: A White Radiance*.
7, 10, 13 Apr 1993	Visits to Colin Wilson.
14 Apr 1993	Visit to Frank Tuohy.
16–18 Apr 1993	Addresses Quaker Universalists in Birmingham.
27 Apr 1993	Metaphysical Research Group retitled Universalist Group of Philosophers.
29 Apr–4 May 1993	Conference on Ficino in Florence.
3 May 1993	'Sees' finished *Overlord* and *Classical Odes* in Pisa.
21 Jun 1993	Decision to use blank verse for *Overlord*, made with Christopher Ricks.
8–29 Jul 1993	Visit to USA.
5 Aug 1993	Nadia's marriage.
18 Aug 1993	Last visit to Colin Wilson.
6 Dec 1993	Metaphysical Centre opens.
7 Dec 1993 to date	Unitive Life.

1994–2004	Writes *A Dandelion Clock.*
7 Feb–14 Apr 1994	Assembles *Awakening to the Light.*
27 Feb, 16 Apr 1994	Visits to Mary Seal.
14 May 1994–10 Jan 1995	Assembles *A Spade Fresh with Mud.*
28 May–4 Jun 1994	Visit to France.
2 Jun 1994–23 Nov 1996	Writes *Overlord.*
2 Jun 1994–17 Feb 1995	Writes *Overlord* books 1 and 2.
18 Jul–1 Aug 1994	Tour of Europe.
26 Jul 1994–3 Mar 2005	Writes classical odes.
1–31 Aug 1994	Writes *The Warlords.*
6–9 Oct 1994	Visit to Germany.
15 Oct 1994	Lecture on Intuitionist Universalism at Regent's College.
15 Oct 1994	Break with philosophers.
8 Feb–17 Mar 1995	Assembles *A Smell of Leaves and Summer.*
31 Mar–6 Apr 1995	Tour of Germany.
10 Apr–27 Sep 1995	Writes *Overlord* books 3–6.
27 Apr–1 May 1995	Tour of Europe.
18 May 1995	Lecture on Universalism at Alister Hardy Research Centre.
26 May 1995	Purchases The Bell, Great Easton.
14–25 Jul 1995	Tour of Turkey and Greece.
22 Jul 1995	Sees undecomposed body of St Gerasimos in Kefalonia.
25 Sep 1995	Steve Norris reveals he is discontinuing as MP.
14–21 Oct 1995	Tour of Bay of Naples.
24–28 Oct 1995	Tour of Russia and Ukraine.
13 Jan–4 Jun 1996	Writes *Overlord* books 7–9.
4 May 1996	Visit to Svetlana Stalin.
24–26 May 1996	Visit to Hay-on-Wye.
25 May 1996	Meets Charles Beauclerk, Earl of Burford.
6 Jun, 1 Jul 1996	Death and memorial service of Mabel Reid.
15 Jun–23 Nov 1996	Writes *Overlord* books 10–12.
12–27 Jul 1996	Tour of Greece and Turkey.
9–12, 19 Sep 1996	Acquires Normanhurst School, forms the Oak-Tree Group of Schools (Oaklands, Coopersale Hall and Normanhurst).

24–26 Sep 1996	Visit to Rome.
20 Jan 1997–7 Oct 1998	Assembles *The One and the Many*.
24 Jan 1997	Acquires Otley Hall.
6 Jul 1997	Opens Otley village fête.
18 Jul 1997–17 Feb 1998	Assembles *Wheeling Bats and a Harvest Moon*.
3 Aug 1997–22 Mar 1998	Writes screenplay, *Gosnold's Hope*.
3 Oct 1997	Lecture at Aldeburgh, 'Revolution in Thought and Culture'.
10 Nov 1997	Death of Ann's mother.
24 Jan 1998	Meets Mark Rylance at the Globe.
28 Jan 1998	Lecture on 'The Garden of the One', Cambridge.
28 Jan 1998	Visit to Bourn Hall, seat of the Haggers.
5, 18 Feb 1998	Death and funeral of Argie.
9 Mar 1998	Charles Beauclerk becomes Literary Secretary.
3 Apr–28 Jun 1998	Writes *The Tragedy of Prince Tudor*.
24–25 Apr 1998	Globe cast of *As You Like It* stay and rehearse at Otley Hall.
15–31 May 1998	Becomes a trustee of SAT, houses Shakespearean Authorship Trust library.
4 Jul 1998	Opens Otley village fête.
20–24 Jul 1998	Visit to Venice.
27 Jul–23 Nov 1998	Assembles *The Warm Glow of the Monastery Courtyard*.
4–28 Aug 1998	Abridges *The Warlords* Parts One and Two into a one-performance version.
9–21 Oct 1998	Tour of USA's east coast.
15 Oct 1998	Lecture on Bartholomew Gosnold in Richmond, Virginia.
29 Oct 1998	Mark Rylance lunches at Otley Hall.
Nov 1998	Lord Tebbit distributes Normanhurst prizes.
9 Dec 1998	Questions Martin Taylor about earth-dollar.
13 Dec 1998–3 Apr 1999	Writes *Ovid Banished*.
29 Mar, 24 Apr 1999–9 Jun 2000	Writes *The Rise of Oliver Cromwell*.
28–30 Apr 1999	Globe cast of *Julius Caesar* stay and rehearse at Otley Hall.
30 Jun 1999–29 Mar 2000	Writes *The Secret History of the West*.

13 Jul 1999	Tony Little, later Head Master of Eton, distributes Oaklands prizes.
17–20 Jul 1999	Tour of Cathar France.
26 Oct 1999	Charles Beauclerk, the Earl of Burford, leaps onto the Woolsack in the Lords.
2000–2005	Writes *Summoned by Truth*.
12–14 Apr 2000	Globe cast of *The Tempest* including Vanessa Redgrave stay and rehearse at Otley Hall.
14–21 Apr 2000	Tour of Iceland.
26–28 Apr 2000	Globe cast of *Hamlet* stay and rehearse at Otley Hall.
28 Apr 2000	Charles Beauclerk leaves Otley Hall.
1 Jul 2000	Opens fête at Bourn Hall.
14–20 Jul 2000	Tour of Sicily.
5 Aug 2000	Matthew's marriage to Melanie.
28 Sep–5 Oct 2000	Visit to Turin and Rome.
19 Nov 2000	Patricia Cornwell lunches at Otley Hall.
13–15 Feb 2001	Visit to Lisbon.
14 Mar 2001	Jamestown deputation to twin with Ipswich lunch at Otley Hall.
30 Mar–6 Apr 2001	Visit to Spain.
2 May 2001	Virginia's First Lady and twinning deputation at Christchurch Mansion and Otley Hall.
2 May 2001	Visits US Embassy and Governor Gilmore.
6–20 May 2001	Mediterranean cruise.
10–12 May 2001	Revisits Libya.
Jul 2001	Matthew Hagger becomes Managing Principal of Oak-Tree Group of Schools.
12 Jul 2001	Birth of Ben, first grandson.
6 Sep 2001	With "thirty-four-generationed" Lord Tollemache at Helmingham Hall.
24 Nov 2001	Iain Duncan Smith MP distributes Normanhurst prizes.
7 Feb 2002	Lord Braybrooke shows Cornwallis's surrender sword over lunch.
23–28 Mar 2002	Visit to Cyprus.

21–24 Jun 2002	Visit to Heidelberg and Freiburg, Heidegger and Husserl places, with Christopher Macann.
9–23 Nov 2002	Visit to China.
6 Feb 2003	Kelso claims to have discovered Bartholomew Gosnold's skeleton in Jamestown Fort.
28 Feb 2003	Acquires Connaught House.
17 Oct 2003	Iain Duncan Smith MP opens new block at Normanhurst School.
11 Nov 2003	Meets John Hunt.
17–22 Nov 2003	Visit to Gran Canaria.
Jan–Mar 2004	Assembles *The Syndicate*.
Jul–Nov 2004	Assembles *The Secret History of the West*.
15 Jul 2004	Sells Otley Hall.
2–4 Aug 2004	Visit to Scilly Isles.
Aug 2004	Works on first two of trilogy of novellas.
Oct 2004–19 Aug 2005	Assembles *The Rise and Fall of Civilizations*.
Nov 2004–15 Dec 2005	Assembles *Collected Poems 1958–2005*.
30 Nov–2 Dec 2004	Visit to Brussels.
1 Jan 2005–16 Jul 2005	Assembles *The Light of Civilization*.
31 Jan–8 Feb 2005	Visit to Egypt.
9 Feb–30 Apr 2005	Assembles *Classical Odes*.
20 Feb, 9 May,	Attends Christopher Ricks's Professor-of-Poetry
20 Nov 2005	lectures at Oxford.
23 Feb 2005	Leaves the Shakespearean Authorship Trust.
13 Jun 2005	Kelso digs up Shelley church for Gosnold DNA.
9, 26 Sep 2005	Death and funeral of John Silberrad.
4 Dec 2005	Addresses Harry Beckhough's intelligence group.
19 Dec 2005–18 May 2006	Writes *The Secret Founding of America*.
15 Jan–27 Apr 2006	Assembles *Collected Verse Plays*.
27 Apr 2006	Lyme disease suspected.
5 May–5 Jun 2006	Assembles one-volume *Overlord*.
21 Jul–13 Oct 2006	Assembles *Collected Stories*.
12–14 Aug 2006	Visit to Dartmoor.
13–20 Jan 2007	Visit to Iran.
23 Jan–16 Feb 2007	Writes *The Last Tourist in Iran*.

Jan–Aug 2007, May 2008	Works on trilogy of novellas.
18 Feb 2007	Sells The Bell.
8–11 Mar 2007	Visit to Vienna.
9, 17 Apr 2007	Death and funeral of Ricky Herbert.
8 May–15 Jul 2007	25 radio broadcasts to USA.
14 May 2007	Attends Christopher Ricks's Professor-of-Poetry lecture at Oxford.
23 Jul–11 Aug 2007	Visit to Galapagos Islands and Peru.
27 Aug–4 Nov,	
27 Nov 2007–1 May 2008	Writes *The New Philosophy of Universalism*.
5–26 Nov 2007	Visit to Argentina, Falkland Islands, South Georgia and Antarctica.
16 Dec 2007	Ken Campbell's 'School of Night' actors read *The Warlords*.
16 Dec 2007–2 Sep 2008	Abridges *The Warlords* Parts One and Two into *Montgomery*, a one-performance version focusing on Montgomery.
22 Mar 2008	Matthew's marriage to Kate.
12 May, 24 Nov 2008	Attends Christopher Ricks's Professor-of-Poetry lectures at Oxford.
14 May 2008	Visit to Wilton House.
22 May–5 Sep 2008,	
21 Jan–22 Jul 2009	Writes *Armageddon*.
15 Jun 2008	Tony Hagger, Young Filmmaker of the Year.
10 Jul 2008	Nadia's marriage to Ian.
20–25 Jul 2008	Stays at Tennyson's Farringford.
26–28 Aug 2008	Visit to Totnes.
31 Aug, 8 Sep 2008	Death and funeral of Ken Campbell.
1 Sep 2008–5 Feb 2009	Writes *The Libyan Revolution*.
21 Sep–18 Dec 2008	Writes *The Revolution That Didn't Happen*.
28 Jan 2009	Eric Galati reads from *Overlord* in London.
6–8 Feb 2009	Visit to Paris, recital in Saint-Sulpice.
26 Feb–1 Mar 2009	Visit to North Norway.
28 Feb 2009	Sees Northern Lights.
1 Apr 2009	Birth of Alex, second grandson.
3 May 2009	Coopersale Hall School's 20th anniversary.

11 May 2009	Attends Christopher Ricks's Professor-of-Poetry lecture at Oxford.
24 May 2009	Revisits Otley Hall.
23–26 Jul 2009	Visit to Eastbourne.
17 Aug–23 Nov 2009	Writes *The World Government*.
3 Dec 2009–19 Apr 2010	Writes *The Secret American Dream*.
20 May 2010	Sees the sundial at Copped Hall.
18–19 Jul 2010	Ann's 60th birthday at Le Manoir aux Quat'Saisons.
22 Jul 2010–31 Mar 2011	Writes *A New Philosophy of Literature*.
26 Aug–10 Sep 2010	Mediterranean cruise, encounters Peter O'Toole.
11 Dec 2010, 6 Jan 2011	Death and funeral of John Ezard.
9 Feb 2011	Birth of Olivia, first granddaughter.
21 Mar 2011	Interviewed on Gaddafi by Adam Boulton.
13 Apr 2011–30 Apr 2014	Assembles *Selected Stories: Follies and Vices of the Modern Elizabethan Age*.
19 Apr 2011	Lecture on *The New Philosophy of Universalism* for internet.
4 May–8 Nov 2011	Writes *A View of Epping Forest*.
1–4 Jul 2011	Visit to Hadrian's Wall.
19–21 Aug 2011	Visit to Gidleigh Park.
31 Aug–3 Sep 2011	Visit to Isle of Man.
30 Nov 2011	Rod Stewart opens new building at Coopersale Hall School.
14 Jan–14 Aug 2012	Writes *My Double Life 1: This Dark Wood*.
7 Mar 2012	Receives *The Victoria and the Triton* from Ricks.
1 Jul 2012	Oaklands 75th anniversary, Haggers' 30th anniversary at Oak-Tree Group of Schools.
19 Aug 2012–7 Sep 2013	Writes *My Double Life 2: A Rainbow over the Hills*.
7 Sep–27 Oct 2012	Assembles *Selected Poems: Quest for the One*.
20 Feb–13 Mar 2013	Visit to India, Sri Lanka and Arabia.
22–23 May 2013	Visit to the Grove before Bilderberg Group meeting.
Apr 2014	25th anniversary of Coopersale Hall School.
22 May 2014	75th birthday.
31 Aug 2014–19 Apr 2016	Assembles *Life Cycle and Other New Poems 2006–2016*.
19 Dec 2014–9 Feb 2015	Writes *The Dream of Europa*.
3 Mar 2015–8 Apr 2016	Assembles *The First Dazzling Chill of Winter*.

19 Apr–14 Sep 2015	Writes *The Secret American Destiny*.
25 May–8 Jun 2015	Voyage in the Baltic.
31 May–2 Jun 2015	Visit to St Petersburg.
28 Aug 2015	Acquires Braeside School.
3 Jun 2015	Visit to Tallinn, Estonia.
4–9 Oct 2015	Attends World Philosophical Forum in Athens.
7 Oct 2015	Chairs a Constitutional Convention and brings in the Universal State of the Earth and becomes Chairman of the Supreme Council of Humanity.
31 May 2016–17 Feb 2017	Writes *Peace for our Time*.
3–9 Oct 2016	Attends World Philosophical Forum in Athens.
18–26 Nov 2016	Visits Manila, Philippines.
22 Nov 2016	Asked by Issam Eldebs, Syrian Consul General in Manila, to undertake a peace mission to President Assad in Syria.
23 Nov 2016	Receives Gusi Peace Prize for Literature in Manila.
26–27 Nov 2016	Writes 15-point Peace Plan for Syria to Eldebs.
9 Feb–10 Aug 2017	Writes *World State*.
9 May 2017	Presentation at Loughton Festival, 'Epping Forest and a Literary Life'.
14 Aug–18 Dec 2017	Writes *King Charles the Wise*.
26 Aug–11 Oct 2017	Writes *World Constitution*.
15 Jan–5 Feb 2018	Assembles *Visions of England*. (Selection made by the Earl of Burford in 1998–1999.)
9 May 2018	Presentation at Loughton Festival, 'My World-View'.
Jun 2018	Nominated for Templeton Prize for five years from 2019.
1 Jun 2018–12 Jul 2019	Assembles *Selected Letters*.
7 Aug 2018–29 May 2019	Writes *Fools' Paradise*.
9 Oct 2018	Awarded crest and coat of arms by Garter Principal King of Arms at the College of Arms.
30 Oct 2018	Adviser at Galileo Commission meeting in London.
17 Nov 2018	Reads poem and speaks on Prince Charles' coming role in the Commonwealth at a celebration of Prince Charles' 70th birthday in Canterbury Cathedral Precincts.

21–30 Apr 2019	Invited to Russia by the Russian Ecological Foundation to inaugurate a new era of universal peace.
22 Apr 2019	Awarded BRICS silver medal for 'Vision for Future'.
12–24 May 2019	Mediterranean cruise.
14 May–29 Aug 2019	Assembles *Collected Prefaces*.
20–31 May 2019	Exhibition on NH's life and works with manuscripts from his archive and slide show at the Albert Sloman Library, University of Essex.
22 May 2019	80th birthday.
2 Jun 2019	Family gathering at Braeside School to celebrate 80th birthday.
7 Jun–31 Oct 2019	Writes *The Coronation of King Charles*.
25 Aug 2019–15 Jun 2021	Writes *Fools' Gold*.
10 Dec 2019–24 Feb 2020	Assembles *A Baroque Vision*.
2 Feb–9 Jun 2020	Assembles *The Essentials of Universalism*.
28 Feb–17 Mar 2020	Visits Jordan, Egypt, Turkey.
1 Mar 2020	Ascends Mount Nebo, has the idea for *The Promised Land*.
13 Mar 2020	Receives the structure of *The Promised Land* in sleep shortly before 3am.
23 Mar 2020	First lockdown in the UK because of coronavirus.
6 Jul 2020	Invited to be on the Executive Board of the World Intellectual Forum that is seeking to bring in a democratic, federal world government and world constitution largely based on NH's books.
29 Aug–1 Sep 2020, 22 Nov 2020–30 Mar 2021	Writes *The Promised Land*.
11 Feb 2021	Wakes with the title of his next work, *The Fall of the West*, in his mind after receiving it in his sleep.

Appendices

1

Visits

Visits by Nicholas Hagger to countries/places referred to or relevant
background in *The Promised Land*

1953	Sep	France: Paris, Normandy (Cabourg, Caen, Ouistreham and the D-Day beaches).
1957	4–25 Apr	Italy: Rome, Licenza (Horace's villa), Naples, Pompeii, Herculaneum, Mount Vesuvius, Sorrento, Capri, Paestum, Syracuse, Catania, Mount Etna.
1958	11 Aug–14 Sep	Greece: Athens, Thermopylae, Delphi, Mount Helicon, Thebes, Thespiae and the Veil of the Muses, Sunion, Marathon, Mount Parnassus, Eleusis, Dafni (Daphnae), Megara, Corinth, Patras, Olympia, Pylos, Sphacteria, Kalamai, Tripolis, Argos, Nauplion, Epidavros (Epidaurus), Tiryns, Mycenae. Crete (Knossos, Phaestos, Gourna). Rhodes. Mykonos. Delos. Return via Belgrade.
1959	1–10 Apr	France: Paris.
	23 Jul–23 Aug	Spain: Barcelona, Valencia, Malaga, Coin, Torremolinos, San Sebastian.
1960	end of Jul/Aug	Greece via Belgium, Amsterdam, Yugoslavia: Athens, Spetsai, Spetsopoula, Porto Cheli, Calchis, Sciathos. Return via Skopje, Dubrovnik, Split, Rijeka.
1961–2	30 Sep 1961– 4 Jun 1962	Iraq: Baghdad, Ctesiphon, Basra, Shatt al-Arab, Gourna, Rutba, Babylon. Visit to Holy Land: Bethlehem, Jericho, Dead Sea, Qumran, Bethany, River Jordan, Jerusalem (Mount of Olives, Gethsemane, Calvary, Garden Tomb, Via Dolorosa). Visits to Amman, Damascus, Beirut.

1963–7	15 Nov 1963– 18 Oct 1967	Japan: Tokyo, Hiroshima, Kyoto, Nara, Nikko, Gora, Kurihama/Nobe, Kamakura/Kitakamakura, Karuizawa.
1966	3–23 Mar	China via Hong Kong, Kowloon: Canton, Shanghai, Hangchow, Nanking, Peking.
	5–11 Jun/ 23–30 Aug	USSR: Nakhodka, Khabarovsk, Moscow. London via Brest, Warsaw, Berlin, Flanders. Same route in reverse in August.
1967	18 Oct–6 Nov	South-East and Central Asia, Europe. Hong Kong. Macao. Vietnam: Saigon/Cholon, Bien Hoa. Cambodia: Phnom Penh, Siem Reap/ Angkor Wat. Thailand: Bangkok. India: Calcutta, New Delhi. Nepal: Katmandu. Turkey: Istanbul. Hungary: Budapest. Austria: Vienna. France: Paris.
1968–70	25 Oct 1968– 1 Jul 1970	Libya via Avignon, Marseilles, Tunis. Carthage: Tripoli, Sabratha, Leptis Magna, Gourna (or Suq Al-Jum'a), Ghadames.
1969	6–10 Jul	Tunisia: Djerba.
1970	12–23 Feb	Egypt: Cairo/Pyramids, Memphis, Saqqara, Luxor, Alexandria, El Alamein.
	24–28 Feb	Libya: Tripoli, Nalut, Ghadames.
	11–14 Apr	Malta: Valetta, St Paul's Bay, Sliema.
	1–20 Jul	North Africa and Europe. Tunisia: Medenine, Gabes, Hammamet. Algeria: Souk Ahras, Algiers, Oran. Morocco: Tangier. Spain: Marbella, Barcelona. Italy: Rapallo. Switzerland: Geneva, Annemasse, Mont Blanc/Lake Leman.
1972	1–4 Mar	Germany: Frankfurt, Arnoldshain.
	25–29 May	Belgium: Brussels.
	10–27 Sep	Tanzania: Dar es Salaam, Zanzibar, Tanzam railway (Lugema, Mkera, Iringa), Mikumi National Park. Return via Nairobi.
1976	12–15 Apr	France – D-Day beaches: Cherbourg, Valognes, Ste Mère-Eglise, Utah/Omaha beaches, Bayeux, Arromanches, Juno/Sword beaches, Pegasus

		Bridge, Cabourg, Deauville, Trouville, Caen, Ouistreham; Hill 112, Falaise; Chartres; Versailles, Paris, Rouen.
1985	22–26 Feb	France: Boulogne, Paris (Conciergerie), Versailles, Caen, Rouen.
	11 May	France: Paris.
	14 Jun	France: Rouen via Normandy.
	19–30 Jul	France – Dordogne: Orleans, Blois, Périgueux, Les Eyzies, Sarlat, St Cyprian, Beynac, La Roque, Domme, Gourdon, Rocamadour, Padirac, Souillac, La Madeleine, Les Combarelles, Cap Blanc, St Emilion, Bordeaux, La Rochelle, Nantes, Mont St Michel, Rouen, Boulogne.
	11–13 Oct	Germany: Frankfurt.
1986	1–7 Aug	Europe. Belgium: Dunkirk, Bruges, Ghent, Antwerp, Waterloo, Brussels. Holland: Amsterdam. Germany: Bonn. Luxembourg: Echternach, Luxembourg City, Bourscheid (Ardennes). France: Lille.
	1–5 Oct	Germany: Frankfurt.
1987	31 Jul–4 Aug	Denmark: Esbjerg, Rynkeby, Ladby, Kertminde, Svendborg, Trelleborg, Fyrkat, Nodebo, Gilleleje, Helsingor (Elsinor), Kobenhavn (Copenhagen), Odense, Jelling.
	7–11 Oct	Germany: Frankfurt.
1990	23–30 Apr	Hungary: Budapest, Szentendre, Visegrad, Esztergon, Tura, Kocskemet.
	7–9 Dec	Czechoslovakia: Prague.
1991	9–12 Oct	Germany: Frankfurt.
1993	29 Apr–3 May	Italy: Florence, Pisa.
	8–29 Jul	USA: New York, Boston, Niagara Falls, Washington, Philadelphia, Florida (Orlando, St Petersburg, Daytona).
1994	28 May–4 Jun	France – D-Day beaches via Southwick House, Broomfield House, Fort Southwick, Fort Nelson: Caen, Villers-Bocage, Banville, Pegasus Bridge,

		Ouistreham, Sword and Juno beaches, Arromanches (Gold), Mulberries, Bayeux, American beaches (Omaha, Pointe du Hoc), Colleville, Lisieux, Falaise, Chambois, Montormel (Falaise Gap), St Foy de Montgommery, Rouen, Atlantic Wall, Calais.
	2 Jul	Southwick.
	18 Jul–1 Aug	Europe. Belgium: Brussels. Germany: Hannover, Berlin. Poland: Poznan, Warsaw, Auschwitz, Cracow. Hungary: Budapest via Slovakia. Austria: Vienna, Salzburg. Germany: Munich, Cologne via Rothenburg, Rhine. France: Moselle, Meuse.
	6–9 Oct	Germany: Munich, Berchtesgaden, Dachau, Ingoldstadt, Nuremberg.
1995	31 Mar–6 Apr	Germany: Obersalzburg/Berghof, Dresden, Goslar via Colditz, Brocken, Gottingen, Flossenberg, Weimar, Buchenwald, Wewelsburg, Externsteine, Hermannsdenkel, Padeborn, Verden, Sachsenhain, Belsen, Luneburg, Deutsch Evern.
	27 Apr–1 May	Europe. Holland: Hoek van Holland, Arnhem, Oosterbeek, Nijmegen. Germany: Rheinberg, Büderich, Wesel, Straelen. Holland: Venlo, Maastricht. Belgium: Bastogne. France: Reims. Luxembourg: Clervaux. Germany: Saar. France: Forbach. Germany: Trier. Belgium: Ardennes. Luxembourg: Echternach. Belgium: Oûr, St Vith. Germany: Losheim. Belgium: Elsenborn, Malmédy, Stavelot. France: Calais.
	14–25 Jul	Turkey: Istanbul, Troy, Guzelyali, Kusadasi, Ephesus, Selçuk, Didyma. Greece: Samos, Patmos, Athens, Kefalonia, Ithaca, Athens, Eleusis.
	14–21 Oct	Italy: Sorrento, Mount Vesuvius, Solfatara, Cumae, Avernus, Pompeii, Herculaneum,

		Oplontis, Amalfi, Paestum, Capri, Naples.
	24–28 Oct	Russia: St Petersburg, Moscow, Yalta.
1996	24–26 May	Herefordshire: Hay-on-Wye.
	12–27 Jul	Greece: Athens, Sunion, Thebes, Delphi, Naupactus, Patras, Olympia, Pylos, Sphacteria, Mistras, Sparta, Mycenae, Epidavros (Epidaurus), Peiraeus. Greek islands: Aigina (Aegina), Mykonos. Turkey: Ephesus. Greek Islands: Patmos, Rhodes. Crete (Knossos). Santorini (Akrotiri). Greece: Dafni (Daphnae), Athens.
	22–26 Sep	Italy: Rome, Licenza (Horace's villa), Tivoli, Vatican.
1998	20–24 Jul	Italy: Verona, Mantua, Sirmione, Venice, Padua.
	9–21 Oct	USA: Boston, New Bedford, Martha's Vineyard, Virginia (Richmond, Jamestown, Pamplin Park civil war site, Yorktown, Monticello, Tuckahoe plantation), New York.
1999	17–20 Jul	France: Carcassone, Rennes-le-Château, Montségur, Narbonne, Béziers.
2000	14–21 Apr	Iceland: Reykjavik, Golden Circle, Thingvellir, South Shore whale-watching, Westman Isles, Heimaey, Lake Myvatn, Reykjanes (Blue Lagoon).
	14–20 Jul	Sicily: Palermo, Agrigento, Marsala, Motya, Segesta, Selinunte, Syracuse, Etna, Taormina, Catania.
	28 Sep–2 Oct	Italy: Turin, Rome.
2001	13–15 Feb	Portugal: Lisbon.
	30 Mar–6 Apr	Spain – Andalusia: Madrid, Toledo, La Carlota, Cordoba, Grenada, Seville, Malaga.
	6–20 May	Mediterranean. Greece: Athens. Crete: Chania. Libya: Benghazi, Cyrene, Tripoli, Sabratha. Tunisia: Sousse/El Djem, Tunis, Carthage. Sicily: Selinunte, Agrigento, Trapani, Erice, Segesta. Sardinia: Barumini. Minorca: Mahon. Spain: Barcelona.

2002	23–28 Mar	Cyprus: Pafos (Ptolemaic tombs, Temple of Aphrodite), Nicosia, Famagusta, Salamis, Kirenia, Bellapais, Troodos mountains (Makarios's monastery).
	17–19 May	France: Bordeaux.
	21–24 Jun	Germany: Heidelberg, Freiburg.
	9–23 Nov	China: Shanghai, Suzhou, Yichang, Yangtze's Three Gorges, Shibaozhai, Chongqing, Xian (terracotta army), Beijing (Temple of Heaven, Forbidden City).
2003	17–22 Nov	Gran Canaria: Maspalomas.
2004	2–4 Aug	Scilly Isles.
	30 Nov–2 Dec	Belgium: Brussels.
2005	31 Jan–8 Feb	Egypt: Luxor, Karnak, Sharm El Sheikh, St Catherine's monastery (Mount Sinai), Cairo (Pyramids).
2006	12–14 Aug	Devon: Dartmoor.
2007	13–20 Jan	Iran: Tehran, Shiraz, Persepolis, Yazd, Nain, Isfahan, Natanz, Kashan, Qom, Saveh, Hamadan, Malayer, Arak.
	8–11 Mar	Austria: Vienna.
	23 Jul–11 Aug	Ecuador: Quito. Galapagos Islands: Baltra (South Seymour), Bartolomé, Santiago, Santa Cruz, Floreana, Espanola, San Cristobel, North Seymour. Peru: Lima, Cuzco, Urubamba, Ccaccakoyllo, Machu Picchu.
	5–26 Nov	Antarctica. Argentina: Buenos Aires, Ushuaia. Falkland Islands: Port Stanley. South Georgia: Salisbury Plain, Elsehul, Grytviken, Stromness. Penguin Island. King George Island: Arctowski station. Deception Island. Goudier Island: Port Lockroy. Antarctic Peninsula: Paradise Bay.
2008	22–23 Feb	Essex: Down Hall.
	14 May	Wiltshire: Wilton, Salisbury.
	20–25 Jul	Isle of Wight: Farringford.
	26–28 Aug	Devon: Totnes.

	22 Oct	Hertfordshire: St Albans.
2009	6–8 Feb	France: Paris.
	26 Feb–1 Mar	North Norway: Tromso, Honingsvag, North Cape, Alta.
	23–26 Jul	Sussex: Eastbourne.
2010	26 Aug–10 Sep	Mediterranean via Guernsey. Spain: Santiago de Compostela. Portugal: Oporto. Spain: Cadiz, Granada (Alhambra). Italy: Siena, San Gimignano. Corsica: Calvi. Italy: Rome, Tarquinia, Naples, Pompeii.
	26–27 Nov	Gloucestershire: Painswick, Slimbridge, Tetbury.
2011	1–4 Jul	Northumberland: Hadrian's Wall.
	19–21 Aug	Devon: Gidleigh Park.
	31 Aug–3 Sep	Isle of Man.
2012	22 Nov	Yorkshire: Beverley.
2013	20 Feb–13 Mar	India, Sri Lanka and Arabia. India, Golden Triangle: Old and New Delhi, Agra, Bharatpur, Jaipur. Sri Lanka: Colombo, Kandy. India: Tuticorin, Kochi, Old Goa, Mumbai (Bombay), Porbandar. United Arab Emirates: Fujairah. Dubai. Oman: Muscat.
	19–20 Jul	Hampshire: Portsmouth (*Mary Rose*), Sandbanks.
2014	20–21 Jul	Devon: Sidmouth Ottery St Mary.
2015	25 May–8 Jun	Baltic. Copenhagen, Stockholm, Helsinki, St Petersburg, Tallinn (Estonia), Berlin, Amsterdam.
	4–9 Oct	Greece: Athens.
2016	3–9 Oct	Greece: Athens.
	18–28 Nov	Philippines: Manila. Hong Kong.
2018	6–10 Apr	Spain: Malaga, Puerto Banus, Marbella, Gibraltar.
	16–22 Sep	Yorkshire: York, Yorkshire moors and dales, Whitby, Huddersfield.
	16–18 Nov	Kent: Canterbury.
2019	21–30 Apr	Russia: Moscow.
	21–24 May	Mediterranean. Spain: Barcelona. France: Cannes. Italy: Florence, Pisa, Rome, Naples. Greece: Santorini, Athens, Mykonos, Delos, Argostoli.

		Montenegro: Kotor. Croatia: Dubrovnik. Italy: Venice.
2020	28 Feb–16 Mar	Jordan: Amman, Jerash, Mount Nebo, Dead Sea, Mandaba, Bethany-by-the-Jordan, Kerak, Little Petra, Petra, Wadi Rum, Aqaba. Egypt: Luxor, Valley of the Kings, Karnak, Cairo, Suez Canal. Turkey: Antalya, Perge, Aspendos, Alanya, Sidé, Istanbul.
	30 Oct–1 Nov	Lancashire: Blackpool, Fleetwood.

2

Light

112 Experiences of the Light
93 experiences extracted from Light appendices of *My Double Life 1* and *2*, which show experiences of the Light with page numbers, and 19 experiences since 2011 extracted from diaries (D)

16 experiences in *My Double Life 1: This Dark Wood*

185	11 Sep 1965	First experience of Light as orb of Fire. Visions: scrivenings in foreign language, corn stalks, whirlpool.
187	11 Oct 1965	Golden Light.
187–188	18 Oct 1965	Round white Light, dazzling like a white sun.
373	10 Sep 1971	Light. Visions: white light, bare winter tree of white fire, flowing, rippling (Flowing Light), white flower like chrysanthemum (Golden Flower), sun, stars, fountain of white light, white point, circle of light.
375–377	11 Sep 1971	Light. Visions: dome of light, yellow and purple tomb, old gold death mask, filigree light, face of God, point of white light, egg, Christ on the cross, devil, saint, crown of thorns, Roman robe, yellow rose, black thorns, child, death-mask, frost, white flower, suns, shafts of light, long white-hot line like trunk of tree.
377–378	12 Sep 1971	Light. Visions: (morning) red flower, streaks of white, red lights, prison gates, egg, face of God, white wheel, white light, yellow mountain range, stars with rings, blob of moon, blobs, thorns with light behind, Greek theatre; (afternoon) golden star, golden rays, silver star.
379	24 Sep 1971	Visions: streaks of white light, golden (white) flower like dahlia.

389–390	21 Nov 1971	Visions: Diamond. Fire, golden glow, laurel wreath.
391	3 Jan 1972	Light. Visions: snowflakes, Saints, Pope's head, monk, altar, Cathedral, white light.
401	3 Apr 1972	Visions: Flowing Light, golden head of Christ, crown of thorns in golden light, Roman effigy of God, white sun, two stars, white ageless face.
401–402	8 Apr 1972	Visions: golden furniture, temple columns, brown statue head, celestial curtain, diamond in luminous blue light (first experience of blue Light), Golden Flower, light flashing up.
403	17 Apr 1972	Visions: possessed, in union with the Light, aglow with the mystic Fire.
403	22 Apr 1972	Visions: pale blue light that blended with dazzling white light like a diamond shining in the sun.
404	28 Apr 1972	Visions: white light with blue tints, hoop of light like sun-halo.
443	3–4 Dec 1972	White light, white sun, dim.
468	31 Jul 1973	Visions: Greek temples, African mask, light nearly breaking.

77 experiences in *My Double Life 2: A Rainbow over the Hills*

12	24 Jan 1974	Fire and vision: great fire in a grate.
12	27 Jan 1974	Blue Light.
22–23	28 Aug 1974	Light.
25	13 Oct 1974	Blue Light.
28	1 Dec 1974	Blue Light.
31	9 Mar 1975	Blue Light.
32	11 May 1975	Blue Light.
44	21 Dec 1975	Blue Light.
45	18 Apr 1976	Light and rose Light.
47	30 May 1976	Red Light, "the other day" for second time.
58	4 May 1977	Blue Light.
63	13 Aug 1977	Light and visions: glimmerings, celestial curtain, the star, the dawning (Light), imagination: carpet full of colours, perfect pattern, stained-glass window, red saint, cloud over a sun.

65	12 Oct 1977	Blue Light.
65	27 Oct 1977	Gold Light, visions: Kandinsky scrivenings (*sic*), floating through patterns towards a sunrise, golden 'cauliflower', gold light with a gold coin of an emperor on it, beautiful Tibetan-like monsters.
70	14 May 1978	Light.
72	11 Jul 1978	Light and surges (healing).
78	18 Oct 1978	Light: blue diamond.
83	13 May 1979	Light.
91	29 Jan 1980	Silver Light, also Fire, also surges (healing).
93	30 Mar 1980	Light, also Fire.
95	2 Jul 1980	Blue Light and vision: elaborate blue light with sparkling 'beads' across it, heavenly vision.
107	10 May 1981	Light.
108	31 May 1981	Golden Light, rose Light, also Fire.
126	25 Aug 1982	Light.
144	31 Dec 1983	Light.
161	7 Aug 1984	Light.
189–190	16 Apr 1985	Light.
200	12 Aug 1985	Light, sleep inspiration: idea for a book showing that the Light makes civilizations grow (reinforcing idea of *The Fire and the Stones*).
260–261	7 Dec 1986	Fire and surges.
264	4 Apr 1987	Fire.
281	11 Dec 1987	Light.
281	13 Dec 1987	Light and Fire.
317	8 Apr 1990	Light.
317	9 Apr 1990	Light.
317	10 Apr 1990	Light.
317	11 Apr 1990	Light (and surge).
331	14 Nov 1990	Light.
334	19 Dec 1990	Light (and surges).
334	24 Dec 1990	Light (and surges).
341	5 Apr 1991	Fire.
341	6 Apr 1991	Light (and surges).
341–342	7 Apr 1991	Light.

343	20 Apr 1991	Light.
346	6 May 1991	Fire (and surges).
351	25 Jun 1991	Light.
367	11 Dec 1991	Light.
373	13 Nov 1991	Light.
375	28 Nov 1991	Light.
383	3 Feb 1992	Light.
394	1 May 1992	Light.
396	9 May 1992	Light.
396	13 May 1992	Light.
397	17 May 1992	Light (healing).
403	21 Jun 1992	Light.
408	20 Jul 1992	Light (and surge).
430	9 Dec 1992	Light.
431	2 Jan 1993	Light.
435	11 Feb 1993	Light.
436	23 Feb 1993	Light.
439	3 Apr 1993	Light.
439	5 Apr 1993	Light.
445	17 Apr 1993	Light.
450	2 May 1993	Light.
455	2 Jun 1993	Light.
463	9 Aug 1993	Light.
467	20 Sep 1993	Light (and surges).
469	8 Oct 1993	Light.
473	2 Nov 1993	Light.
477	4 Dec 1993	Light (and surges).
478	6 Dec 1993	Light.
513	31 Mar 1995	Light.
527	29 Feb 1996	Light.
599	11 Feb 1999	Light (and surges).
692	16 Oct 2003	Light.
742	18 Jan 2007	Light.
804	13 Aug 2009	Light (and surges).
833	11 May 2011	Light.

19 experiences in diaries since 2011

D	12 Sep 2017	Vision: a square screen of quite bright light behind closed eyes, perhaps my soul light-filled.
D	22 Apr 2020	Vision: a large wide oval light, not dazzling, that deepened into a pool with clear transparent water, at the bottom were old statues in stone with semi-Eastern faces, figurines semi-substantial, outlines in light.
D	23 Apr 2020	Vision: the oval again, white and bright, inches above my face with smooth swan's down as large as a double bed, an ethereal light, seemed a faceless angel declaring support for *The Essentials of Universalism* and urging me to continue the project.
D	24 Apr 2020	Vision: another sighting of the oval cloud, which came close, its down transparent, shapes within it, seemed to be a being without a face; wrote 6 'Oval Cloud' sonnets on 25 April 2020.
D	25 Apr 2020	Vision: oval cloud seen faintly, a presence.
D	27 Apr 2020	Vision: oval cloud again, with recumbent (sideways) line-drawn figures within it, images of immortality like the carved knights on tombs and stone sculptures; wrote another 'Oval Cloud' sonnet on 28 April 2020.
D	5 May 2020	Vision: seven sideways profiles, six and then a gap; wrote an 'Oval Cloud' sonnet on 6 May 2020.
D	8 May 2020	Vision: oval cloud again, very white, like a blanket with a pattern coming towards me to be laced on me, wondered if it was my soul, now swan's-down white and full of softness and purity; wrote an 'Oval Cloud' sonnet on 9 May 2020.
D	10 Nov 2020	Light. A dozen pulses of Light in expanding, radiating circles, one at a time, starting from nothing, spreading outwards, expanding circles of Light.
D	25 Mar 2021	Vision: oval cloud, present for half a minute.

D	28 Mar 2021	Vision: oval cloud.
D	5 Apr 2021	Vision: oval cloud for about a minute.
D	6 Apr 2021	Vision: oval cloud for about a minute.
D	9 Apr 2021	Vision: oval cloud like very bright silky lace, with faint, almost transparent silhouettes of beings or people, which slowly came closer and seemed to show the nine Muses, perhaps angels, with fairly equal space between them in two rows, as if embroidered on but seemingly moving, seen through what seemed to be very clear water for at least two minutes.
D	10 Apr 2021	Vision: oval cloud, a bit squashed at the edges and like a rectangular battered package with two silhouettes visible, seen for more than a minute.
D	18 Apr 2021	Vision: oval cloud, very bright, seen for several minutes, came closer behind my closed eyes and turned into a dazzling snowscape like standing on deep fresh snow, many contours under the white, and when I opened my eyes there was a dark black cloud seemingly in the room above my eyes, clouding a dim landing night-light through an open door with seemingly black smoke, it was above me wherever I looked, and when I closed my eyes it seemed to turn into the bright oval cloud seen within and I thought of the Cloud of Unknowing and of Dionysus proclaiming that God is Darkness and of Yahweh visiting Moses in a cloud of smoke, I couldn't get rid of the black cloud, which was continuously clearly visible in the dark – a week previously my optician examined my eyes and said there was absolutely no trace of cataracts.
D	19 Apr 2021	Vision: oval cloud of bright Light, also the external black cloud in the half-light (dimensions about 2 feet by 1 foot, 2 feet above my face as yesterday), put my hands up into it, it was round

my hands and I could barely see them, thought of Yahweh and recalled that on Mount Sinai Moses approached "the thick darkness where God was" (*Exodus* 20.21) and that according to Solomon "The LORD said that he would dwell in the thick darkness" of a dark cloud (*1 Kings* 8.12), and pondered the paradox that the Light seems to dwell in thick darkness, and that this thick darkness is seen within the soul as bright Light (the Inner Light); and that the Light + thick Darkness = the Absolute, the One, just as +A + −A = 0 reflects the Absolute's reconciliation of all contradictions and differences within itself and the unity of the One.

D   23 Apr 2021   Vision: oval cloud, bright, no trace of the external black cloud, it was as if having revealed itself and now I have grasped that the Light + thick Darkness = the Absolute it's no longer necessary for the black cloud to appear, reflected that in this phase of my life the white oval cloud is always potentially there before I sleep, behind my closed eyes.

D   24 Apr 2021   Vision: oval cloud, very bright, and the black cloud again, so thick that when lying on my back and I put my hands up into it in the half-dark to offer a bruise on my arm for healing I couldn't see my hands or half-arm, I now seem to have a permanent +A + −A = 0 (the internal oval cloud of Light + the external thick Dark cloud = the Absolute) and the black cloud seems permanently near me, it is only externally there before my open eyes sometimes after I have seen the white oval cloud within (not always after I have seen it), and when it is there it is always there for several minutes, it is never present at any other time.

Sleep inspiration

33 Experiences of Sleep Inspiration

20 experiences of sleep inspiration extracted from Light appendices of *My Double Life 1* and *2*, 1 experience extracted from *Selected Letters (SL)* and 12 experiences since 2011 extracted from diaries (D), which show Nicholas Hagger received some of his most fundamental ideas (asterisked) in sleep

3 experiences in *My Double Life 1: This Dark Wood*

60	Jun 1954	Sleep inspiration: in a dream 'saw' the 'O' level Greek set book exam paper with four passages to translate.
142	18 Jan 1962	Inspiration: received 'Life Cycle' on a plane above Ur while sitting with eyes closed, anticipated life cycle of 25 civilisations and universal pattern of life.
185	13 Sep 1965	Sleep inspiration: centre-shift – in a dream 'saw' an earthquake, falling masonry, ruins, corpses dancing.

17 experiences in *My Double Life 2: A Rainbow over the Hills*

30	2 Mar 1975	Sleep inspiration: vision of ecumenical unity, union of sects and religions, religious Universalism.
86	24 Aug 1979	Sleep inspiration: idea of *The Fire and the Stones*, civilizations as 'Light-bearers', first metaphysical, then secular. *
112	21 Aug 1981	Sleep inspiration: two images, crab-pots and lighthouse.
136	6 Aug 1983	Sleep inspiration: poem, 12 stanzas of 'Night Visions in Charlestown'.
138	11 Aug 1983	Sleep inspiration: poem, 'Crab-Fishing on a Boundless Deep'.
200	12 Aug 1985	Light, sleep inspiration: idea for a book showing that the Light makes civilizations grow (reinforcing idea of *The Fire and the Stones*). *
277	28 Feb 1988	Sleep inspiration: problem of Israelite civilization's

expansion solved in sleep.

297	29 Apr 1989	Sleep inspiration: beginning of 'Introduction to the New Universalism', and therefore Universalism, received in sleep. *
363	2 Sep 1991	Sleep inspiration: dream showing 20–30 lines of 'Reflection and Reality: Peak Experiences and Tidal Consciousness', Shadow on the clouds.
368	26 Sep 1991	Sleep inspiration: dream, large face of Orpheus, tall as orchard trees, with dozens of green apples in front of it (perhaps symbolising poems). *
386–387	7 Apr 1992	Sleep inspiration: idea that the Light is a fifth, expanding force and responsible for early inflation.
387	25 Jan 1992	Sleep inspiration: received date of UK general election, 9 April 1992, while observing British Prime Minister John Major by a computer showing growth. Prophesies Major's 1992 election victory.
435	9 Feb 1993	Sleep inspiration: idea that Hitler was an Illuminatist.
460	11 Jul 1993	Sleep inspiration: two American Liberty Quintets, 'New York' and 'Boston'.
712	24 Jan 2005	Sleep inspiration: title of *Summoned by Truth*.
806	3 Dec 2009	Sleep inspiration: structure of *The Secret American Dream* to be similar to the structure of *The Secret Founding of America*.
845	17 Mar 2014	Sleep inspiration: specific details within the Table of Contents in *My Double Life 1* and 2 that needed amending, e.g. order of entries.

1 experience in *Selected Letters* in 2007

404 *SL*	28 Feb 2007	Sleep inspiration: title of *The New Philosophy of Universalism*, part of title received in sleep. *

12 experiences in diaries since 2011

D	20 Aug 2011	Sleep inspiration: beginning of *My Double Life 1: This Dark Wood*, opening paragraphs received in sleep.

D	17 Jun 2013	Sleep inspiration: theme of the Epilogue for *My Double Life 2: A Rainbow over the Hills*.
D	8 Sep 2014	Sleep inspiration: title for a new work, *The Order in the Universe*, which became *The Secret American Destiny: The Hidden Order of the Universe and the even Disciplines of World Culture*.
D	25 Dec 2019	Sleep inspiration: the theme of *A Baroque Vision*, certain knowledge that my Baroque vision became Universalism.
D	13 Mar 2020	Sleep inspiration: the structure of *The Promised Land* received in sleep, woke at 3am and scribbled the structure down by 3.30am.
D	17 Apr 2020	Sleep inspiration: amendment to the back cover of *A Baroque Vision*.
D	5 Jun 2020	Sleep inspiration: a line for the front cover of *The Essentials of Universalism*, 75 prose selections from 25 works.
D	24 Jul 2020	Sleep inspiration: amendment to *Selected Letters* p.600, letter to Bronwyn Astor, received in sleep: a lady said I was 30 years ahead of my time, not 20.
D	17 Aug 2020	Sleep inspiration: amendments to the Plan for *The Promised Land* received in sleep: 10 Universalist commandments, Shelley's "Poets are the unacknowledged legislators of the world".
D	10 Nov 2020	Sleep inspiration: woken from deep sleep abruptly with knowledge of all my encounters with the heroic line from the ages of 14 to 19 in Chaucer, Shakespeare, Homer, Euripides and Milton.
D	11 Feb 2021	Sleep inspiration: the title of *The Fall of the West*.
D	28 Mar 2021	Sleep inspiration: the title of *The Algorithm of Creation*.

Oneness

6 Experiences of Oneness

6 experiences of Oneness extracted from Light appendices of *My Double Life 1* and 2, which highlight Nicholas Hagger's early awareness of the One

5 experiences in *My Double Life 1: This Dark Wood*

60–61	Jul/Aug 1954	Experiences the Oneness of the universe on Merrow golf course.
92	Mar 1959	Experiences the Oneness of the universe by Worcester College lake.
160–161	13 Nov 1963	Experiences the Oneness of the universe by Strawberry Hill pond.
177	5–6 Jan 1965	Experience of the Oneness of the universe at Kyoto's Ryoanji Stone Garden.
184	11–12 Aug 1965	Second experience of the Oneness of the universe at Kyoto's Ryoanji Stone Garden.

1 experience in *My Double Life 2: A Rainbow over the Hills*

21	4 Aug 1974	Experiences the Oneness of the universe in the fusion of clouds and ground in Earl's Path pond on Strawberry Hill.

Index

A Baroque Vision xiii, 40, 48, 60, 65, 71, 122, 165, 197, 218

A Mystic Way 61, 116, 189

A New Philosophy of Literature 63, 64, 71, 86, 89, 90, 153, 195

A Smell of Leaves and Summer 61, 190

A Spade Fresh with Mud 61, 190

A View of Epping Forest 63, 104, 120, 195

A White Radiance 61, 69, 189

Aaron 10

Addison, William 120

    Addison's Bookshop 120

Arab Revolt 55, 56, 57, 58, 77, 79

    Sharif Hussein bin Ali 79

Armageddon 63, 71, 116, 117, 122, 147, 194

Athenian Empire 33, 130, 158

Awakening to the Light 61, 189, 190

Baghdad 1, 2, 3, 11, 28, 34, 35, 36, 51, 68, 73, 106, 147, 149, 182, 201

    University of 1, 2, 28, 36, 51, 106, 182

    also see Iraq

Baroque Age 40, 47, 60, 152

Baroque vision 21, 40, 50, 60, 61, 66, 71, 148, 156, 165, 218

    A Baroque Vision xiii, 40, 48, 60, 65, 71, 122, 165, 197, 218

    and Universalism xiii, 21, 40, 50, 60, 61, 65, 66, 71

        'Night Visions in Charlestown' (Hagger) 60, 70, 165, 216

Bate, Jonathan 107

Biggs-Davison MP, John 112, 113, 163, 181, 186, 188

Blake, Maurice 137, 139

    'A Temple-Dancer's Temple-Sleep' (Hagger) 139

    regression 138, 139, 143

Blunden, Edmund 107, 122, 151, 182

Brexit 65, 124, 156, 157, 159

    leaving the EU 157

    referendum 65, 124

Briggs, Asa 61, 116, 148, 151, 186, 188

British Empire 33, 105, 154, 155, 156, 161, 164,

Burford, Earl of (Charles Beauclerk) 65, 115, 190, 192, 196

burning bush xii, 7, 8, 9, 10, 80

    Chapel of the Burning Bush 8, 9

Canterbury Cathedral 125, 196

    Prince Charles' 70th birthday 125, 196

Churchill, Winston xv, 70, 103, 105, 114, 146, 157, 163, 181

Classical Odes 17, 62, 70, 71, 116, 120, 153, 189, 190, 193

Collected Poems 1958–1993 45, 61, 69, 71, 189

Collected Poems 1958–2005 62, 69, 71, 130, 193

Collected Prefaces 65, 133, 197

Collected Stories 62, 69, 193

Collected Verse Plays 62, 69, 193

College of Arms 118, 124, 131, 196

coat of arms 118, 124, 131, 196
Woodcock, Thomas 131
Cornwall 2, 113, 121, 149, 184, 192
Charlestown 113
Covid/coronavirus vii, xiii, xiv, 3, 58,
59, 101, 132, 134, 154, 156, 157, 159,
160, 166, 169, 172, 177, 179, 197
bio-weapon xiv, 133
Covid deaths xiv
Covid vaccine 157
Wuhan xiv, 171
Institute of Virology xiv
Dark Night of the Soul, see Mystic
Way
Dark Night of the Spirit, see Mystic
Way
Dead Sea vii, xi, 1, 3, 6, 7, 16, 17, 18,
21, 22, 26, 178, 179, 201, 208
swimming in 21, 22
Donne, John 74
Egypt vii, xiii, 2, 6, 7, 8, 10, 11, 12, 13,
39, 42, 43, 45, 53, 54, 55, 73, 74, 79,
80, 101, 102, 110, 120, 134, 136, 137,
139, 140, 141, 142, 143, 144, 145, 152,
159, 163, 164, 169, 183, 193, 197, 202,
206
Abu Simbel 142, 144, 145
Cairo xiii, 3, 56, 135, 139, 144, 163,
202, 206, 208
Colossi of Memnon 101, 142
Colossus 141
Eastern Desert 6, 101
Egyptian Museum of Antiquities
136, 139, 144
mummy of Ramesses II 138,
139, 140

statue of Khufu 144
El Alamein 42,70, 110, 114, 183,
202
SAM-3s 42, 110, 183
Karnak 102, 137, 206, 208
Temple of 102, 137
Khafra 102, 135, 136, 144
Khufu 135, 136, 144
Luxor xiii, 2, 3, 42, 43, 101, 141,
142, 202, 206, 208
Pyramids 42, 43, 54, 102, 120, 135,
136, 202, 206
Great (Khufu) 43, 54, 102, 135,
136
of Mycerinus 135
of Khafra 102, 135, 136, 144
'The Great Pyramid as a
House of Eternity' (Hagger)
102, 136, 202
'The Meaning and Purpose of
the Great Pyramid' (Hagger)
102, 136
'The Riddle of the Great
Pyramid' (Hagger) 102, 136
Ra 12, 54, 73, 136
River Nile xi, 7, 42, 101, 112, 135,
138, 139, 141
Sharm El Sheikh 8, 79, 80, 206
Sphinx 135, 136, 144
Valley of the Kings 101, 208
Amenhotep III 101
Carter, Howard 43, 120
Colossi of Memnon 101, 142
Land of the Dead 43
Queen Hatshepsut's tomb 101
Ramesses II, see under

Ramesses II
Ramesses III 101
Ramesses IV 101
Tutankhamun 43, 101, 120,
136
tomb of 43, 101, 120
Eliot, T.S. 32, 36, 44, 45, 105, 107, 121,
122, 147, 188
'The Waste Land' 44, 45
Epping Forest 3, 37, 63, 104, 116, 120,
195, 196
European civilisation vi, 28, 70, 72,
81, 82, 83, 135, 152, 153, 154, 155,
156, 157, 158
central idea of 81, 82, 152, 153,
155, 160
European Union exodus 154
Exodus, the xi, 7, 10, 11, 12, 13, 14,
19, 80, 137, 141, 145, 215
route of 12, 13
Ezard, John 146, 164, 195
Fire 8, 26, 32, 38, 46, 61, 81, 82, 87, 91,
127, 156, 209, 210, 211, 212
Fools' Gold 60, 65, 120, 124, 148, 149,
197
Fools' Paradise 60, 65, 124, 147, 148,
196
Form from Movement Theory
(Hagger) 83, 85, 114, 153, 189
Foundation of the Light 113, 189
Metaphysical Centre 113, 189
mystery school 113, 189
FREE 112, 186, 187
'The European Resurgence'
(Hagger) 111, 185
Gaddafi 42, 44, 59, 110, 113, 117, 148,

150, 164, 183, 187, 195
Gascoyne, David 61, 113, 148, 151,
186, 188
Golden Age 163, 172, 175, 176
new 175, 176
of Universalism 176
golden phoenix, see under Russia
Great Plague 156
Great War 159
Gusi Peace Prize for Literature 64,
117, 124, 196
Hagger, Nicholas vi, 15, 21, 49, 51,
55, 65, 67, 103, 106, 108, 109, 112,
126, 131, 135, 154, 155, 181, 201, 216,
219
coat of arms 118, 124, 131, 132,
196
diaries 39, 47, 61, 70, 71, 100, 119,
209, 213, 216, 217
exhibition at the Albert Sloman
Library 117, 118, 124, 130, 131,
197
experiences of the Light, see Light
formative years, 1960–1980 21, 33,
45, 48, 49, 50, 165
future direction 119–123, 161
Mediterranean cruise 2, 124, 129
Delos 129, 130, 207
pattern in episodes 64, 123–133
Providential direction of life and
destiny 102, 146–151
Providential life 132, 135, 150,
151, 152
regression, see Blake, Maurice
remarkable life 101–119
stag 100, 121, 131

unofficial Ambassador to Edward
Heath 45, 111, 148, 151, 184
view of European civilisation
152–154
view on UK's place in the world
157–158
view on Western civilisation
158–161
wilderness years, 1980–2020 51,
59, 66, 77, 91, 165
works from Providential life 148,
149, 150, 151–152, 153, 154, 161,
165, 197
people, appearing at the right
time 151
56 covers 67
80th birthday 2, 118, 124, 125,
129, 130, 131, 132, 197
family gathering for 124, 132,
197
also see Cornwall
Hemingway, Ernest 106, 121
Horace 105, 166, 201, 205
Bandusian spring 105, 166
'Ode: Spring' (Hagger) 166
illumination 36, 38, 45, 46, 47, 48, 68,
73, 91, 121, 134, 148, 149, 151, 160,
166, 184
Illuminationism 36
'In Defence of the Sequence of
Images' (Hagger) 36, 44
Infinite 62, 80, 81, 84, 85, 86, 87, 88,
89
intelligence work 47, 59, 64, 68, 106,
140, 148, 150
British Intelligence 42, 45, 110,

150
British intelligence agent 45, 111,
128, 134, 148, 151
Secret Intelligence Service (MI6)
148
Hughes, Ted 114, 151
Iran 36, 58, 71, 75, 116, 117, 174, 193,
206
Hidden Imam 117
Natanz 116, 206
Iraq 1, 2, 3, 11, 34, 35, 36, 41, 58, 59,
68, 69, 71, 72, 75, 106, 107, 121, 147,
149, 150, 152, 182, 201
also see Baghdad
Israel xii, xiii, 2, 3, 7, 10, 11, 12, 14,
17, 19, 22, 23, 24, 53, 59, 72, 113, 134,
159, 163, 165, 170, 174, 178, 216
Mount of Olives 1, 16, 17, 201
Sea of Galilee xii, 17, 179
Japan 26, 32, 34, 36, 37, 38, 39, 40, 41,
44, 45, 47, 59, 68, 69, 70, 72, 73, 75,
107, 108, 109, 121, 122, 147, 149, 150,
152, 159, 182, 202
Nishiwaki, Junzaburo 32, 107,
122, 147, 182
$+A + -A = 0$ 32, 63, 77, 85, 90,
108, 122, 147, 157, 182, 215
Prince and Princess Hitachi 37,
59, 72, 75, 107, 108, 109, 147, 182
State visit to the UK 108
Prince Hitachi's birthday 75
'Epistle to His Imperial
Highness, on His Birthday'
(Hagger) 75
Ryoanji Temple, Kyoto 150, 182,
219

stone garden 150, 182, 219

'The Decline of the West' (lectures by Hagger) 34, 37, 72, 122, 159, 160

tsunami 109

urn for ashes 109

Vice-Governor of the Bank of Japan 38, 107

John the Baptist 22, 23, 24, 25, 26, 52, 74, 124, 152

cave of 22, 23, 24, 52, 74

right hand of 24, 25, 26, 124

Jordan vii, xi, xiii, 1, 2, 3, 4, 6, 7, 16, 17, 18, 22, 23, 24, 26, 31, 40, 48, 53, 54, 77, 93, 149, 152, 159, 197, 201, 208

Amman 1, 2, 3, 18, 73, 179, 201, 208

Aqaba xiii, 1, 14, 58, 59, 79, 208

Gulf of 8, 53, 79

Bethany 1, 22, 152, 201

Bethany-beyond-the Jordan 22, 26, 208

Place of Baptism 22, 23,

Dushara 51, 54, 55

and Ra 54

Hejaz railway 6, 55

Jerash (formerly Antioch) 4, 5, 104, 167, 170, 208

Hadrian's Arch 5

six-petalled flower 5

Hadrian's Gate 167

Kerak Castle 26, 27

Khazali canyon 56

Little Petra 28, 51, 208

Madaba 6

Eastern-Byzantine Empire 6, 7, 26, 66

mosaic map of 6

Petra 2, 3, 51, 53, 54, 130, 208

monastery 53

Nabataean Treasury 51

Petra Museum 54,

Dushara 51, 54, 55

and Ra 54

Qumran 1, 17, 18, 179, 201

River Jordan 2, 7, 16, 18, 22, 23, 74, 201

Wadi Rum 1, 55, 58, 59, 77, 152, 208

Jabal al-Mazmar, "the seven pillars of wisdom" 55, 56, 77

Khazali canyon 56

Awad Zubeidi 56, 57

Siq al-mishran '20 springs' 56

'The Mountain of the Plague' 77

Khafra 102, 135, 136, 144

Khufu 135, 136, 144

King Charles the Wise 65, 124, 125, 196

Lawrence, T.E. 1, 3, 6, 55, 56, 57, 58, 77, 79

and Awad Zubeidi 57

and Hejaz railway 6, 55

and Peter O'Toole 56, 57

Lawrence of Arabia 56, 57

The Seven Pillars of Wisdom 77

Libya 41, 42, 43, 44, 45, 59, 63, 68, 73, 110, 112, 122, 145, 147, 149, 150, 152, 168, 183, 184, 192, 202

coup 42, 110, 183

Gaddafi 42, 44, 59, 110, 112, 113,

117, 150, 164, 183, 187, 195
Gaddafi Revolution 110, 148
Ghadames 43, 166, 183, 202
  Ain el-Faras 43, 46
Leptis Magna 41, 168, 183, 202
Libyan Revolution, The, see *The*
  Libyan Revolution
Libyan Revolutionary Command
  Council 110
Maitland, Donald 111, 184
Sabratha 41, 168, 183, 202, 205
Life Cycle and Other New Poems 2006-
2016 64, 71, 195
  pattern of life 216
Light 8, 26, 32, 36, 39, 45, 47, 49, 61,
  62, 68, 69, 74, 81, 82, 87, 88, 91, 93,
  106, 109, 113, 119, 121, 127, 147, 148,
  151, 152, 153, 156, 160, 161, 189,
  209–217, 219
  Awakening to the Light 61, 189, 190
  Light of the World 160
  112 experiences of the 47, 119,
    147, 209–215
Little, Tony 115, 192
Maugham, Somerset vii, 158
Metaphysical Revolution 49, 50, 61,
  68, 77, 85, 90
Montenegro 24, 25, 129, 208
  Kotor 24, 25, 26, 124, 129, 130, 208
  Cetinje monastery 24, 25
Montgomery 70, 104, 114, 146, 181,
  194
Moses vi, xi, xii, xiii, xv, 7, 8, 10, 11,
  12, 13, 14, 15, 16, 17, 18, 19, 74, 79,
  80, 91, 93, 103, 134, 137, 140, 141,
  145, 147, 161, 171, 176, 177, 179, 214,

215
  also see burning bush
Mount Nebo 7, 13, 15, 17, 18, 134,
  171, 176, 177
  and Moses 7, 13, 15, 18, 19, 134,
    171, 176, 177
Mount Sinai xii, 8, 9, 11, 12, 13, 14,
  79, 80, 91, 215
  St Catherine's monastery xii, 8, 9,
    74, 80, 91, 152, 206
  Catherine's wrist bone 8
MS Serenissima 58, 59, 79, 92, 93, 123,
  159
Muses 18, 79, 93, 94, 95, 97, 98, 99,
  100, 102, 119, 127, 132, 133, 134, 146,
  148, 151, 159, 165, 201, 214, 216, 217,
  219
  'Secret of the Muse' (Hagger) 96
  slave of the 133, 134
  ten Muses 93, 99
My Double Life 1: This Dark Wood 38,
  42, 44, 45, 49, 57, 64, 105, 108, 110,
  116, 123, 186, 195, 209, 216, 219
My Double Life 2: A Rainbow over the
Hills 47, 48, 49, 57, 64, 106, 113, 116,
  119, 123, 138, 164, 195, 210, 216, 218,
  219
Mystic Way 21, 34, 39, 42, 47, 48, 49,
  50, 61, 64, 68, 73, 91, 94, 109, 114,
  116, 122, 147, 148, 149, 152, 160, 161,
  165, 189
  awakening 38, 61, 68, 73, 91, 189,
    190
  Dark Night of the Soul 42, 49, 68,
    73, 182
  Dark Night of the Spirit 47, 49,

68, 73, 184, 186

illumination 36, 38, 45, 46, 47, 48, 68, 73, 91, 121, 134, 148, 149, 151, 160, 166, 184

purgation 38, 42, 68, 73, 91

unitive vision 47, 51, 69, 73, 75, 91, 92, 93, 109, 114, 149, 161, 165, 166, 177

nationalism and populism 59

Nature 84, 85, 86, 87, 120, 150, 160, 189

Nishiwaki, Junzaburo 32, 107, 122, 147, 182

+A + −A = 0 32, 63, 77, 85, 90, 108, 122, 147, 156–157, 182, 215

Oak-Tree Group of Schools 116, 148, 190, 192, 195

Braeside School 114, 132, 196, 197

Coopersale Hall School 113, 188, 194, 195

Normanhurst School 114, 190, 191, 192, 193

Oaklands School 48, 104, 112, 115, 120, 148, 150, 181, 185, 186

Oneness 104, 181, 219

experiences of 104, 181, 219

Osymandias/Ozymandias 112, 140, 141, 143

Otley Hall 70, 71, 73, 114, 115, 116, 191, 192, 193, 195

Gosnold, Bartholomew 71, 114, 116, 191, 193

Jamestown 71, 73, 114, 116, 192, 193, 205

Kelso, Bill 116, 193

voyage to 73, 114

knot-garden 71, 115

Landsberg, Sylvia 71, 115

2 libraries on Shakespeare 115–116

Ottoman Empire 4, 55, 58

Overlord 17, 44, 61, 62, 63, 70, 75, 103, 104, 114, 116, 122, 130, 146, 170, 189, 190, 193, 194

Oxford 1, 57, 68, 74, 105, 106, 113, 117, 121, 146, 147, 149, 161, 181, 193, 194, 195

Worcester College 57, 105, 106, 113, 117, 149, 150, 181, 219

'Passage through Antiquity' 2

Pax Romana vii, 4, 158, 166, 167, 168, 169, 170, 171, 179

flower of the *Pax Romana* 166, 168, 170

Peace for our Time 64, 117, 118, 124, 149, 196

Penrose, Roger 92, 114

Philby, Kim 111, 128

Pound, Ezra 17, 44, 70, 111, 122, 151, 184

Rapallo 44, 111, 184, 202

Preface xi–xv, 48, 49, 50, 60, 61, 65, 66, 77, 165, 197

Prince Hitachi, see under Japan

Promised Land, The, see *The Promised Land*

Promised Land, the vii, xi, xii, xiii, xv, 1, 15, 16, 17, 18, 19, 65, 66, 91, 93, 99, 122, 133, 134, 145, 148, 160, 163, 164, 165, 170, 172, 177, 178, 179, 181, 197, 201

Biblical xi, 1, 2, 3, 12, 14, 36, 107

view of 16, 17, 18, 91, 93, 99, 134,
163, 179
Providence 119, 120, 133, 149
also see under Hagger, Nicholas
Raine, Kathleen 61, 113, 148, 151,
186, 188, 189
Ramesses II xiii, 12, 13, 102, 112, 136,
137, 138, 139, 140, 141, 142, 143, 144,
145, 177
as Ozymandias 112, 140, 141, 143
cartouche 141, 142
mummy 137, 138, 139, 140
Ramesseum 140, 141, 142, 143, 145
Reality 32, 61, 81, 82, 87, 88, 89, 121,
217
Red Sea xi, 11, 27, 79, 163
referendum, see under Brexit
Ricks, Christopher 98, 105, 121, 147,
149, 151, 186, 189, 193, 194, 195
Roman Empire 72, 118, 126, 158, 159,
164, 171
also see *Pax Romana*
Russia 26, 30, 38, 42, 45, 69, 110, 111,
118, 125, 126, 127, 128, 129, 134, 158,
184, 190, 197, 205, 207
Moscow 69, 118, 207, 108, 111,
118, 124, 125, 126, 128, 129, 170,
202, 205, 207
BRICS, silver medal 118, 119,
124, 127, 197
Cathedral of the Archangel
38, 69, 75, 108, 129
'Archangel' (Hagger) 37,
38, 69, 129, 183
Mayan Year of the Phoenix
118, 125

Order of the Golden Phoenix
118, 125, 127
Russian Ecological Foundation
118, 125, 127, 197
Union of Russian Writers 128
Selected Letters vi, 65, 71, 86, 98, 119,
126, 131, 133, 148, 150, 165, 196, 216,
217, 218
*Selected Poems: A Metaphysical's Way of
Fire* 49, 60, 61, 69, 71, 77, 113, 188
Selected Poems: Quest for the One 64,
195
*Selected Stories: Follies and Vices of the
Modern Elizabethan Age* 64, 195
seven disciplines 33, 50, 64, 66, 68,
99, 100, 121, 127, 131, 149, 161
Shakespearean Authorship Trust 115,
191, 193
Shelley, Percy Bysshe 33, 40, 100,
107, 112, 140, 141, 143, 147, 193, 218
'A Defence of Poetry' 100
Osymandias/Ozymandias 112,
140, 141, 143
sleep inspiration 159, 161, 164, 165,
166, 211, 216–218
33 experiences of 216–218
Sphinx 135, 136, 144
stag, see under Hagger, Nicholas
Stalin, Svetlana 114, 190
Suez xiii, 13, 80, 93, 103, 105, 110,
119, 132, 133, 134, 135, 145, 146, 152,
158, 161, 163, 164, 181, 208
also see Biggs-Davison MP, John
Canal xiii, 145, 146, 158, 161, 163,
164, 208
Crisis 110, 163, 164

debate 105, 163, 181

Gulf of 13, 80, 93, 103, 119, 152

Nasser, Col. 110, 163, 164

Syria 4, 72, 118, 145, 149, 174, 196

Eldebs, Issam 118, 196

15-point Peace Plan 118, 149, 196

Ten Commandments xii, 11, 12, 14, 79, 80, 91, 92, 145, 161, 165

Moses xii, 11, 12, 14, 79, 80, 91, 145

ten commandments of Universalism (Hagger) 92, 145, 161, 165

Tennyson, Alfred Lord xv, 44, 48, 98, 99, 105, 111, 121, 147, 148, 194

and World State 99

as tenth Muse 98, 99, 100

Farringford 98, 99, 194, 206

Idylls of the King 44

'Locksley Hall' xv

Thatcher, Margaret 111, 112, 185

The Coronation of King Charles 37, 65, 119, 122, 124, 125, 197

The Dream of Europa 64, 124, 153, 195

The Essentials of Universalism xiii, xv, 31, 65, 77, 126, 133, 197, 218

The Fall of the West 122, 159, 197, 218

The Fire and the Stones vi, 34, 37, 49, 60, 61, 62, 69, 72, 74, 77, 113, 114, 123, 152, 153, 154, 156, 165, 186, 187, 188, 211, 216

chart of 25 civilisations 154, 155

The First Dazzling Chill of Winter 64, 195

The Last Tourist in Iran 62, 76, 122, 193

The Libyan Revolution 41, 63, 68, 110, 117, 122, 148, 194

The Light of Civilization 62, 69, 72, 74, 153, 193

The New Philosophy of Universalism 62, 63, 75, 76, 80, 84, 85, 86, 128, 153, 165, 194, 195, 217

the surfer 62, 86

The One and the Many vi, 61, 69, 75, 80, 191

Theory of Everything 86

The Promised Land 122, 133, 148, 164, 165, 197, 201, 218

structure, received in sleep 165, 197, 218

The Rise and Fall of Civilizations 34, 62, 69, 72, 74, 114, 153, 154, 193

The Secret American Destiny 64, 76, 124, 154, 196, 218

The Secret American Dream 63, 117, 147, 165, 195, 217

The Secret Founding of America 62, 193, 217

The Secret History of the West 62, 72, 191, 193

'The Silence' (Hagger) 37, 38, 39, 40, 41, 44, 47, 60, 61, 68, 69, 107, 108, 122, 150, 153, 182

The Syndicate 62, 72, 75, 193

The Tragedy of Prince Tudor 61, 191

The Universe and the Light 49, 61, 62, 75, 153, 179, 189

The Warlords 61, 70, 103, 104, 146, 190, 191, 194

The Warm Glow of the Monastery

Courtyard 61, 191
The World Government 63, 76, 117,
   118, 119, 133, 153, 178, 195
timeline 181–197
Tomlin, E.W.F. 36, 44, 74, 122, 147,
   151, 187, 188
Trump, Donald 154, 159
Tuohy, Frank 37, 111, 122, 147, 151,
   182, 186, 189
Turkey vii, xiii, xiv, 5, 164, 166, 168,
   169, 171, 190, 197, 202, 204, 208
   Alanya 169, 170, 208
   Antalya 164, 166, 168, 169, 170,
      208
   Aspendos vii, 5, 165, 168, 169, 208
      flower of the *Pax Romana* vii,
         166, 168, 169, 170
      Roman theatre vii, xiv, 3, 5,
         168, 169
   Istanbul xiii, 56, 169, 170, 171,
      172, 202, 204, 208
      Bosphorus 170, 171, 172, 176,
         177, 179
         Bosphorus Bridge 170, 171
         Lord Byron 171
   Perge 165, 166, 167, 208
      Hadrian's Gate 167
      six-petalled flower vii, 167
unitive vision, see Mystic Way
Universalism xi, xii, xiii, xv, 18, 28,
   31, 32, 33, 34, 36, 37, 38, 40, 41, 42,
   45, 47, 49, 50, 51, 55, 58, 59, 60, 61,
   62, 63, 64, 65, 66, 67, 68, 69, 70, 71,
   72, 73, 74, 75, 76, 77, 79, 80, 81, 82,
   83, 84, 85, 86, 87, 89, 90, 91, 92, 99,
   100, 102, 103, 123, 124, 126, 128, 133,
140, 146, 149, 150, 152, 156, 164, 165,
   172, 175, 176, 177, 189, 190, 194, 195,
   197, 216, 217, 218
   and nationalism 42, 75, 91, 124,
      128, 140, 150, 164, 177
   and seven disciplines, see seven
      disciplines
   and the oneness of the universe
      and humankind 31, 33–34, 153
   as Theory of Everything 86
   autobiographical 63
   cultural 41, 64, 66, 68, 70, 76, 77,
      88, 92, 124, 154
   developing xiii, 61
   evolution of 66, 86
   Essentials of Universalism, The, see
      The Essentials of Universalism
   Golden Age of 176
   historical 28, 33, 37, 38, 40, 41, 58,
      61, 62, 63, 64, 66, 68, 70, 72, 73,
      91, 99
   intuitional 84, 85, 89, 91, 190
   literary 37, 41, 61, 62, 63, 64, 65,
      66, 68, 69, 70, 71, 86, 87, 88, 89,
      90, 91, 99, 100
      fundamental theme of
   mystical 36, 38, 39, 40, 41, 47, 61,
      62, 66, 68, 91, 154
   philosophical 31, 32, 36, 40, 41,
      60, 61, 62, 63, 66, 68, 74, 75, 76,
      80, 83, 84, 90, 91, 99, 117
   political xii, xiii, 38, 40, 41, 63, 64,
      65, 66, 68, 75, 76, 92, 124, 126,
      153, 176
   principles of xiii, xv, 66, 79, 80,
      83, 90, 92, 99, 103, 165, 172

religious 36, 41, 55, 62, 66, 68, 73, 74, 91, 153, 156, 176, 216

Ten Commandments of 79, 92, 93, 145, 161, 165

5 Universalist reconciliations of contradictory literary traditions 89

10 innovations in stating the fundamental literary theme 89

10 primary aspects of 86

10 principles of xii, 80, 90, 91, 92, 165

10 Universalist commandments xii, 218

12 beliefs of the Universalist Revolution 80

12 characteristics of literary Universalism 86, 87

15 tenets of reunification 84

16 goals of Universalist philosophy 84

Universalist Age 60

Universalist Group of Philosophers 75, 189

Universalist Revolution 80, 82

universe 31, 32, 33, 37, 39, 41, 47, 49, 61, 62, 63, 64, 65, 69, 74, 75, 81, 83, 84, 85, 86, 87, 88, 91, 92, 93, 97, 104, 114, 120, 127, 139, 146, 153, 156, 160, 179, 181, 189, 218, 219

Oneness of, see Oneness

shuttlecock-shaped 62

structure of 81, 84

unity of 31, 32, 37, 47, 63, 65, 69, 75, 91, 92, 153

University of Essex

exhibition 117, 118, 124, 130, 131, 197

Special Collection, Albert Sloman Library 117, 118, 124, 130, 131, 197

Visions of England 65, 71, 124, 196

visits 201–208

West vi, 32, 34, 37, 40, 42, 68, 72, 75, 122, 154, 158, 159, 160, 161, 170

see Japan, 'The Decline of the West'

Wheeling Bats and a Harvest Moon 61, 191

wilderness vi, xii, 10, 11, 12, 13, 14, 15, 24, 34, 41, 44, 56, 59, 66, 68, 74, 77, 80, 91, 93, 145, 147, 149, 151, 152, 161, 165, 166, 177

way out of 177

7 Universalisms 77

wilderness years, 1980–2020, see under Hagger, Nicholas

Wilson, Colin 47, 106, 121, 146, 151, 166, 181, 182, 184, 185, 186, 189

World Intellectual Forum 117, 126, 129, 196

World Philosophical Forum 117

Chairman of the Supreme Council of Humanity 117, 196

Constitutional Convention 117, 176, 196

Kondrashin, Igor 126, 129

Universal State of the Earth 117, 124, 196

World Constitution 92, 119, 124, 133, 176, 197

World Constitution 65, 76, 99, 118,

119, 121, 124, 128, 129, 130, 131, 133,
153, 177, 178, 196
World State xi, xii, xiv, xv, 18, 19, 31,
32, 37, 38, 63, 65, 66, 69, 73, 75, 76,
88, 91, 92, 93, 99, 108, 117, 118, 124,
125, 126, 127, 129, 130, 133, 146, 148,
150, 151, 153, 154, 156, 160, 161, 163,
165, 170, 171, 172, 173, 175, 176, 178,
179, 226
  and 10th Universalist
    commandment 132, 172
  life in regions and nation-states

173
World State xv, 65, 76, 93, 99, 118,
119, 124, 125, 128, 129, 130, 133, 153,
172, 173, 175, 177, 178, 196
  federal World State 93, 154, 156,
    160, 161, 172
      partly-federal World State 178
  7 goals of 172, 175, 176, 178
  7 goals fulfilled 172
Yahweh 7, 8, 10, 11, 12, 19, 79, 80,
140, 145, 177, 214

O-BOOKS

SPIRITUALITY

O is a symbol of the world, of oneness and unity; this eye represents knowledge and insight. We publish titles on general spirituality and living a spiritual life. We aim to inform and help you on your own journey in this life.

If you have enjoyed this book, why not tell other readers by posting a review on your preferred book site?